GEORGE LOCKHART OF CARNWATH, 1681–1731

GEORGE LOCKHART
OF CARNWATH, 1681–1731

A Study in Jacobitism

D. SZECHI

TUCKWELL PRESS

First published in Great Britain in 2002 by
Tuckwell Press
The Mill House
Phantassie
East Linton
East Lothian
Scotland

Copyright © D. Szechi, 2002

ISBN 1 86232 132 9

British Library Cataloguing-in-Publication Data
A catalogue record for this book is available
on request from the British Library

The right of D. Szechi to be identified as the author of this book has
been asserted by him in accordance with the Copyright, Design and
Patent Act 1988

Typeset by Carnegie Publishing Ltd, Lancaster
Printed and bound in Great Britain by
Bookcraft, Midsomer Norton

Table of Contents

Preface

This book first began to take shape in the early 1980s while I was fortunate enough to be spending three formative, happy years as a Research Fellow at the University of Sheffield. With typical postdoctoral overconfidence I insouciantly thought at the time that I could quickly write Lockhart up and move on to other, doubtless more important, things. Even in the first flush of my arrogance, however, the sources soon brought me to earth. After a couple of visits to the archives I soon realised that I could not do Lockhart, or the cultural milieu he represented, justice without going a great deal deeper into the *mentalité* of Jacobitism than I had at first envisaged. It was a much bigger, and far more complex, project than I had imagined, and so the book's progress was buffeted by a series of stops and starts imposed by the exigencies of constructing a career, starting a family and writing and editing other works.

Lockhart only again became the subject of my undivided attention in the mid-1990s, by which time I was living and teaching in Auburn, Alabama, alongside friends and colleagues second to none, but a very great distance from the archives where my sources were housed. At that stage, I might regretfully have had to drop the whole idea, had it not been for the way in which my department supported my research by allowing me extended periods of study-leave in Britain. Indeed, my colleagues' selflessness even extended to voting unanimously to mortgage our entire departmental library budget to buy what was, for me, a single, crucial microfilm collection. Their sacrifices would still not have sufficed to carry the project through to completion in a timely fashion though, had it not been for the generosity of a number of public funding bodies. Auburn University, and especially the Auburn Humanities Foundation, enjoy pride of place among these. Over the years the grants I was awarded made the travel and research necessary to complete this book possible without leaving me with a burden of debt I could not in conscience have imposed upon my family. They provided the backbone of my finances as I toiled away in the archives in Edinburgh, Oxford, Cambridge and London. I would still have been left facing a crippling financial burden, however, but for the support I received at other times from the American Philosophical Society, the British Academy and the Scouloudi Foundation. Transatlantic historical scholarship does not come cheap, and I humbly thank them all, and wish to acknowledge here their part in making this book possible. In much the same vein, I owe a considerable debt to the Institute for Advanced Studies in the Humanities in Edinburgh for the support I received as a visiting Fellow in the summer of 1997, and to the Institute for

Advanced Study at Princeton, which generously domiciled me and paid for a term's leave in the winter of 1998 so that I could put the final touches to my manuscript. Research funding is a vital part of modern scholarship, but without the precious gift of time to write it up, *'oleum et operam perdidi'*.

I am also indebted to Her Majesty the Queen for permission to cite from the microfilm of the Stuart Papers held at Ralph Brown Draughon library in Auburn; to Sir John Clerk of Penicuik for the use of the Clerk of Penicuik MSS held at the Scottish Record Office (SRO, now the National Archives of Scotland), the Earl of Dalhousie for permission to use the Dalhousie Papers also held at the SRO; and to the Keeper of the Records of Scotland for permission to see the Eglinton and Montrose Papers. As well, I am grateful to Cambridge University Press for permission to reuse material from my article: 'Constructing a Jacobite: the Social and Intellectual Origins of George Lockhart of Carnwath', which appeared in the *Historical Journal*, 40 (1997) 977–996.

In addition, in the course of my research I have received the unstintingly generous help of a great many of the staff at the SRO, the National Library of Scotland and many other archives. I am grateful to all who have helped me in finishing the research for this book, but particularly to Christine Johnson of the Scottish Catholic Archives, whose meticulously kept archive is a positive treasure trove and whose kindness is a tonic to the weary researcher; to Tristram Clarke of the SRO, whose Ph.D. thesis was an invaluable guide to the confusing theological politics of the episcopal church and whose knowledge of the legal sources helped me unearth material I would certainly otherwise have missed; and to John Stuart Shaw, also of the SRO, who pointed out to me other sources I had managed to overlook that significantly adjusted my understanding of Lockhart's career.

Scottish history is far from being an overpopulated field, but it has its significant tensions, entrenched positions and an (undeserved) reputation for being especially factious. Yet in researching and writing this book, on a subject many if not most Scottish historians have shied away from, I have encountered nothing but lively interest and a willingness to go out of one's way to help a fellow scholar. Chris Whatley subjected an early draught to some highly cogent criticism that dramatically reshaped the final product. John Robertson has had to endure more of my half-formed ideas and theories than any other human being. Alex Murdoch, Bob Harris and Harry Dickinson (the last two primarily British, rather than Scottish, historians) have not only listened to my ideas as I stumbled around trying to make sense of my material, thereby helping me avoid more than one academic pitfall, but spent a great deal of their leisure time making my long stays in Edinburgh not only supportable but positively enjoyable. All modern scholarship is in some sense a collaborative effort; and it is only just that I acknowledge the hidden help I have received from all those I have already named and two more, to whom I owe a particular intellectual debt: Bruce

Lenman of the University of St Andrews and Paul Monod of Middlebury College (who also read an early draught of the manuscript). Without their perceptive, pathbreaking work on the ideological and cultural world of the Jacobites, this book would still be in gestation and might well have been still-born. Their work constituted the starting point for my interpretation of Lockhart; they pointed the way, I have followed it.

Finally, my patient, beloved spouse Jan deserves an answer. Years ago she expressed the hope that when I finished this book, I would be done with, 'that damned man' (Lockhart), and the whole subject of Jacobitism. And so I can think of nowhere better shamefacedly to confess: I'm even more hooked than when I started.

Abbreviations

APS   *Acts of the Parliaments of Scotland* (11 vols, 1832)

BL   British Library

CJ   *Journals of the House of Commons*

DNB *Dictionary of National Biography* (22 vols, Oxford, repr. 1937–38)

GL   George Lockhart of Carnwath

HMC Historical Manuscripts Commission

LEP   National Library of Scotland, Lockhart of Lee and Carnwath Estate Papers [1]

LL   D. Szechi (ed.), *Letters of George Lockhart of Carnwath 1698–1732* (Edinburgh, Scottish History Society, 5th Ser., 1989)

LP   A. Aufrere (ed.), *The Lockhart Papers* (2 vols, 1817)

NLS   National Library of Scotland

ns   New style date (the British Isles remained on the Julian calendar until 1751, which put Britain's calendar 10 days behind Continental Europe in the seventeenth century and 11 days in the eighteenth. Unless otherwise noted, all dates are given in the old style, Julian Calendar, though it is assumed that each new year began on 1 January rather than 25 March. Where new style, Gregorian Calendar, dates are cited they are denoted by an 'ns' following the date in question).

PRO Public Record Office, Kew

SR   D. Szechi (ed.), *'Scotland's Ruine'. Lockhart of Carnwath's Memoirs of the Union* (*Association for Scottish Literary Studies*, Aberdeen, 1995)

SRO Scottish Record Office, Register House

Stuart Stuart Papers microfilm, Ralph Brown Draughon Library, Auburn University, Alabama

The place of publication of all works cited in the endnotes and bibliography is London unless otherwise stated.

The spelling and punctuation of all quotations has been modernised wherever this helps elucidate the meaning of the text. Commonplace contractions and abbreviations have all been silently expanded.

---

1 The Lockhart estate papers are currently (1998) in the process of a somewhat delayed transition to regular National Library of Scotland accession numbers. Unfortunately, at the time of writing several files were still unfoliated and one had apparently been misplaced. I was thus unable exactly to correlate the old designation with the new. For the sake of consistency I have therefore cited the old estate paper numbers throughout.

Introduction

George Lockhart of Carnwath (1681?–1731) is not one of the 'great men' of Scottish history. He won no battles, did not die gloriously in any cause and did not pen such good prose, or think so perceptively, as to inspire later generations with admiration for his genius. He was briefly notorious in 1706, 1714 and 1727, but otherwise lived a life of quiet, wealthy obscurity. So why write a biography of such an apparently ordinary Scottish laird? Biography is for many historians a flawed form of historical analysis, and writing up the petty deeds of a minor landowner in a poor, backwater region of the early eighteenth-century British polity smacks of nothing so much as scholarly redundancy. My approach and my subject thus require some explanation.

Writing history through biography is definitely problematic. Although it has recently begun to show signs of greater acceptability, over the past three decades the biographic approach to history has tended to be shunned by professional historians. The reason may easily be seen in any bookshop, where accessible, but often superficial, and almost always transient, biographies of the famous (living and dead) abound. Historians look askance at these popular biographies because they know from experience that the vast majority easily slip into hagiography or denunciation and almost all of them inflate the importance of their particular individual in the historical process. Indeed, such a magnification of the role of the individual in history is commonly cited as the besetting curse of biography as a methodology.

Yet every technique in historical writing has an attendant train of philosophical assumptions and methodological problems. The biographical approach to historical analysis also has some obvious advantages, the ones most usually cited being natural limits on the scope of the study and easy accessibility for the general reader. Regardless, advantages like these would normally be insufficient to offset the disadvantages and problems outlined above. The case is altered, however, if the subject of the biography is in effect accorded a passive role vis-a-vis the writer, so that he or she becomes the object of study rather than the events in which that person participated occupying centre stage.

Such an approach offers potential insights of far wider significance than the tale of one human being's doings. By treating the subject of the biography as an aspect of the mental world he or she inhabited we can gain a real insight into *why* events turned out as they did, rather than *how*. When studying the pre-modern era a biography that takes this approach not only offers us the opportunity to enter the foreign country our forbears inhabited, it is more in

keeping with the spirit of the sources. Early-modern sources, especially the letters
and memoirs that are the keystone of early-modern political history, are almost
all individually generated and unabashedly idiosyncratic. To use them as sources
of information about events requires a close critical involvement and interpretation on the part of the author. If, however, the sources are treated not as clues
about events but as products of a particular view of the world, we can treat
them more holistically. Contradictions, lies and misunderstandings cease to be
methodological difficulties and become evidence using this approach. Ultimately,
all sources subtly impose their perception of events on the reader; using them
to recover the mentality from which they arose turns that to advantage.

This book is, then, an essay in the retrieval of a lost mentality couched in
the form of a biography. Given that our understanding of the past is ultimately
no more than an imaginative hypothesis based on the few artefacts and statements
that survive, all history is to some extent the reflection of a mentality: usually
(according to the post-Modernists) our own. For nothing is harder for us to grasp
than the mental world of our ancestors – as the exasperated expostulation: 'the
guy must have been a nut!' that is not infrequently heard among groups of
consenting historians discussing their subjects eloquently attests. Yet we can only
reconstruct our ancestors' worlds and comprehend the internal dynamics of their
behaviour when we have large numbers of personal accounts of their vision of
reality. Even then, uneven survival of the evidence necessarily biases our conclusions towards the perception bequeathed by some social groups rather than
others. Manual labourers and underground organisations do not tend to leave
much evidence of their world-view.

Such gaps in our understanding are always frustrating and necessarily make
the history of mentalities a piecemeal, bitty area to work in. And when the
inevitable lacunae in our sources and historical comprehension relate to a sizeable
politically and/or socially significant element in the societies we are studying the
problem necessarily becomes a lowering presence for the historian working in
the field. For unless such a gap is bridged, our understanding of the actors and
the events that shaped that society is crippled and distorted.

All of which makes it appropriate at this point to consider the Jacobite problem.
For the mind of Jacobitism presents just such a lacuna in our understanding.
Notwithstanding the prodigious output of the Bonnie Prince Charlie industry,
our understanding of Jacobite thought and perception is broken and incomplete,
leaving us in the dark about the nature and motivation of a subversive community
whose importance for the development of state and society in the British Isles –
and Scotland in particular – in the eighteenth century was immense.[1]

---

1 L. Colley, *Britons. Forging the Nation 1707–1837* (1992), pp. 43–54, 364–75; J. C. D. Clark,
  English Society 1688–1832. Ideology, Social Structure and Political Practice During the Ancien Regime
  (1985), pp. 141–98; J. Brewer, *The Sinews of Power. War, Money and the English State, 1688–1783*
  (1989), pp. 250–1.

Part of the problem lies in the inevitable destruction of material wherein the Jacobites revealed their innermost thoughts, fears and dreams. The natural exigencies of participation in eighteenth-century conspiracy and rebellion necessarily militated against record-keeping and memoirs. Most of our sources for the inner history of the Jacobites and their cause thus derive from the records of the Stuart court in exile or the depositions of witnesses, spies and informers of all kinds that pepper the official papers of the British, French and other governments who had to deal with them.[2] Sensible Jacobites still resident in Britain generally tried to keep their business oral, and burnt their correspondence whenever they feared the government of the day was about to embark on a Jacobite hunt.[3] In consequence we have scant resources with which to construct a history of the Jacobite mind.[4] In turn this has meant that until very recently virtually nothing had been written on the subject. Bruce Lenman's insightful and pioneering analysis of the role of the episcopalian Church of Scotland in sustaining Scottish Jacobitism through education and ideology finally broke the ice. Within little over a decade it was followed by Edward Gregg's exploration of the role played by paranoia in Jacobite politics, the present author's re-evaluation of the Jacobite scaffold-speech phenomenon, Frank McLynn's psychological appraisal of the career of Charles Edward Stuart, Murray Pittock's reappraisal of the significance of Jacobite poetry and literature and Paul Monod's pathbreaking work on popular Jacobitism in England.[5] All of these works have offered rich and stimulating new insights into particular aspects of Jacobite psychology, but none of them addressed the mainsprings of Scottish Jacobite commitment and motivation in general.

The upshot of which is that George Lockhart of Carnwath's half a million or so words of autobiography, correspondence and political polemic are of the first importance.[6] For a start, this mass of material is one of a mere handful of

2 There are, moreover, considerable methodological problems in working with sources such as these: L. Colley, *In Defiance of Oligarchy. The Tory Party 1714–60* (1982), pp. 29, 32, 33; P. Langford, *A Polite and Commercial People. England 1727–1783* (Oxford, 1992), p. 200; E. P. Thompson, *The Making of the English Working Class* (repr. 1981), pp. 532–7.

3 See for example, SRO GD 45/14/352/19(5) (Dalhousie Papers): Lord Balmerino to Harry Maule of Kellie [London], 2 June 1713.

4 Of the handful of other sources that lend themselves to the analysis of the Jacobite mind, probably the best is Lord Elcho's unpublished journal, of which a long extract can be found in: E. Charteris (ed.), *A Short Account of the Affairs of Scotland in the Years 1744, 1745, 1746. By David Lord Elcho* (Edinburgh, 1907).

5 B. Lenman, 'The Scottish Episcopal Clergy and the Ideology of Jacobitism', in E. Cruickshanks (ed.), *Ideology and Conspiracy. Aspects of Jacobitism, 1689–1759* (Edinburgh, 1982), pp. 36–48; E. Gregg, 'The Politics of Paranoia', in E. Cruickshanks and J. Black (eds), *The Jacobite Challenge* (Edinburgh, 1988), pp. 42–56; D. Szechi, 'The Jacobite Theatre of Death', in *The Jacobite Challenge*, pp. 57–73; F. McLynn, *Charles Edward Stuart. A Tragedy in Many Acts* (1988); M. Pittock, *Poetry and Jacobite Politics in Eighteenth-Century Britain and Ireland* (Cambridge, 1994); P. K. Monod, *Jacobitism and the English People, 1688–1788* (1989).

6 A. Aufrere (ed.), *The Lockhart Papers* (2 vols, 1817); D. Szechi (ed.), *Letters of George Lockhart of Carnwath* (Edinburgh, Scottish History Society, 5th Ser., 1989); *Letter to an English Lord*

sources broad enough, in terms of the activities it embraces, deep enough, in terms of its chronological span, and indiscreet enough to allow us the real prospect of an insight into the development and working of a Jacobite mind. In addition, precisely because Lockhart was not one of the movers and shakers, but rather one of the understrappers of the Jacobite movement, his testimony is uniquely valuable. For just as the resilience and military effectiveness of an army is a function of the quality of its subalterns, the heart and stamina of a political organisation derives directly from the zeal and efficiency of its *sous ministres*. Finally, his career in active Jacobite politics runs closely parallel to the late seventeenth/early eighteenth-century crisis of the Scottish polity. It began in the era of despair and futility of the late 1690s, passed through the revitalisation of the Jacobite and national cause as a consequence of the Union of England and Scotland and terminated in a second era of despair and futility in the British-centred politics of the late 1720s.[7] The most favourable configuration for restoring the Stuarts after 1691, and with them an (at least nominally) independent Scotland, fell between 1708 and 1720 – the high point of Lockhart's career.[8] No other leading Jacobite whose papers have survived has this claim to fame, and therefore Lockhart's career offers, too, the beguiling prospect of observing the passage of an epicycle within Jacobitism during the twilight of the Scottish polity.

Lockhart's *oeuvre* has, furthermore, been highly influential – even fundamental – in setting the shape and tone of our perception of early eighteenth-century Scotland and Britain. Since 1714, when his *Memoirs of Scotland* was published in a pirated edition,[9] his revelations about the secret inner politics of the Union have had to be taken into account by every historian writing on Scottish politics between 1702 and 1708. Since 1817, when Lockhart's amended text of the book published in 1714 plus two extensive continuations of his story were published by one of his heirs, historians working on the reign of Queen Anne, the Jacobite rising of 1715 and the history of Jacobitism between the '15 and the '45 have

(Edinburgh, 1702); *A Letter to a Lord of Session* (Edinburgh, 1710); *A Letter from a Scots Gentleman in London to his Friend at Edenburgh* (Edinburgh, 1711); *A Letter from a Scots Gentleman Residing in England to his Friend at Edenburgh* (Edinburgh, 1711); *A Letter from a Gentleman at Edinburgh to his Friend in London, Giving Ane Account of the Present Proceedings Against the Episcopall Clergy in Scotland, for Using the English Liturgy Ther* (1711); *A Letter from a Presbiterian Minister to his Friend at Edinburgh* (Edinburgh, 1714); *A Letter to a Minister in the Country, in Answer to a Circular Letter Sent to the Clergy Perswading them to be Against the Dissolution of the Union* (Edinburgh, 1714); *A Letter to Mr George Crawford, Concerning his Book Intituled, The Peerage of Scotland* (Edinburgh, 1719); *A Letter Concerning the Bishop of Salisbury's History of His Own Time* (Edinburgh, 1724); NLS, Acc. 4322 and 7124 (Lockhart of Lee and Carnwath Estate Papers).

7 D. Szechi, 'The Hanoverians and Scotland', in M. Greengrass (ed.), *Conquest and Coalescence. The Shaping of the State in Early Modern Europe* (1991), pp. 119–24.
8 D. Szechi, *The Jacobites. Britain and Europe 1688–1788* (Manchester, 1994), pp. 41–84, 104–10.
9 *Memoirs Concerning the Affairs of Scotland from Queen Anne's Accession to the Throne to the Commencement of the Union of the two Kingdoms of Scotland and England in May 1707* (1714).

had to take his version of events into account.[10] Moreover, one does not have to look far for the reason he has had such an impact. Lockhart had, for the time, a snappy, arresting style, he showed no compunction about revealing almost everything he knew (which was a great deal) about the dynamics of backbench and Jacobite politics and he peppered his text with deliciously sharp character sketches.[11]

Moreover, contemporary reaction to the *Memoirs*, the only part of his auto-biography to be published during his lifetime, confirms that his account of events and analyses of the actors' characters was sufficiently close to the mark to strike a chord with many, if not most, of those who had shared those encounters and experiences. Robert Patten felt the author was 'a gentleman of deep penetration and singular affection for his native country, else he would not make so free with the characters of a great many noblemen and gentlemen'.[12] Jonathan Swift, though catty about the text's style, was delighted with its indiscretion, and described it enthusiastically to a friend as 'a very extraordinary piece, and worth your while to come up to see it only'.[13] James Keith, when draughting some notes as preparation for writing his own memoirs, observed of Lockhart's char-acter sketch of the Earl of Mar that it 'is so exactly given in Lockhart's Memoirs, that it's useless to speak more of it here'.[14] John, Master of Sinclair, specifically appealed to the *Memoirs* for an endorsement of his own passionate condemnation of Mar's character.[15] And though his political foes accused Lockhart of falsehood and inaccuracy in public,[16] even an old adversary like Baron of the Exchequer Sir John Clerk of Penicuik was grudgingly prepared to admit in private that: 'As

10 See for example, T. C. Smout (ed.), 'Journal of Henry Kalmeter's travels', in *Scottish Industrial History. A Miscellany* (Edinburgh, Scottish History Society, 4th Ser., 1978), p. 9; T. Somerville, *The History of Great Britain During the Reign of Queen Anne* (1798), p. 156; G. Elliot (ed.), *Correspondence of George Baillie of Jerviswood 1702–1708* (Edinburgh, Bannatyne Club, 1842), preface; W. D. Macray (ed.), *Correspondence of Colonel N. Hooke, Agent from the Court of France to the Scottish Jacobites in the Years 1703–1707* (2 vols, Roxburghe Club, 1870), i. viii; D. A. Guthrie and C. L. Grose, 'Forty Years of Jacobite Bibliography', Journal of Modern History, xi. (1939) p. 50; P. W. J. Riley, *The Union of England and Scotland. A Study in Anglo-Scottish Politics in the Eighteenth Century* (Manchester, 1978), pp. 150, 165, 186–8, 258, 281, 285–6; G. Holmes, *British Politics in the Age of Anne* (revised edn, 1987), pp. 94, 140, 338, 339, 343, 394–5; B. Lenman, *The Jacobite Risings in Britain 1689–1746* (1980), pp. 214–15.
11 SR, pp. 3–6, 27–32, 34, 40–5, 209–33.
12 R. Patten, *The History of the Rebellion in the Year 1715. With Original Papers, and the Characters of the Principal Gentlemen Concerned in it* (3rd edn, 1745), p. 41.
13 H. Williams (ed.), *The Correspondence of Jonathan Swift* (5 vols, Oxford, 1963), ii. 58.
14 Thomas Constable (ed.), *A Fragment of a Memoir of Field-Marshall James Keith, Written by Himself. 1714–1734* (Edinburgh, Spalding Club, 1843), p. 4
15 Sir Walter Scott (ed.), *Memoirs of the Insurrection in Scotland in 1715. By John, Master of Sinclair* (Edinburgh, 1858), p. 59.
16 See for example, LP i. 9–19 (Sir David Dalrymple of Hailes's introduction to the pirated edition of the *Memoirs*); J. Oldmixon, *Memoirs of North-Britain; Taken from Authentick Writings, as well Manuscript as Printed* (1715), v.

these memoirs are said to have been written by Mr Lockart [sic] in the heat of party-rage 'tis no extraordinary matter to find them erroneous in several particulars, ... Yet many of the characters are just in so far as the author was acquainted with the persons'.[17] Furthermore, Clerk's annotations on his own copy of the *Memoirs* implicitly verify most of Lockhart's version of events and endorse his sketches of the actors.[18]

Later historians followed where Lockhart's contemporaries had led. And in the context of the reviving debate on the Union generated by the recrudescence of Scottish nationalism since the late 1960s, Lockhart's silent impact, through their work, on our vision of how the constitutional fusion of Scotland and England came about has steadily become more important rather than less. Up until the 1930s many, if not most, writers took the *Memoirs* as the final word on the inside story of the Union and the rest of his published works as one of the best available sources for the history of the Augustan era.[19] Lockhart's character sketches and history were implicitly taken as the benchmark against which other contemporary accounts should be judged.[20] Only at the end of the nineteenth century did any serious criticism of his reliability begin to appear.[21] This culminated in 1950 in G. S. Pryde's dismissal of Lockhart as a 'disgruntled and mischief-making Jacobite', and a lofty declaration that: 'No historian, English or Scottish, Whig or Tory, Unionist or Nationalist, who has examined the records has endorsed

---

17 SRO GD18/6080 (Clerk of Penicuik Papers), ii. Dalrymple, Oldmixon and Clerk's scandalised reaction to the *Memoirs* was probably typical of most Whig responses, but it was not universal. Even party stalwarts such as Duncan Forbes of Culloden, it seems, could secretly find the book deliciously amusing: D. Warrand (ed.), *More Culloden Papers* (3 vols, Inverness, 1925), ii. 44.

18 SRO GD18/6080, *passim*, but see particularly, pp. 30, 44, 48, 61, 65, 68, 72, 98.

19 'Journal of Henry Kalmeter's travels', p. 9; *Gentleman's Magazine*, i. 540; T. Somerville, *The History of Great Britain During the Reign of Queen Anne* (1798), p. 156n; C. S. Terry (ed.), *The Jacobites and the Union. Being a Narrative of the Movements of 1708, 1715, 1719 by Several Contemporary Hands* (Cambridge, 1922), x; W. Partington (ed.), *The Private Letter-Books of Sir Walter Scott. Selections from the Abbotsford Manuscripts. With a Letter to the Reader from Hugh Walpole* (1930), p. 313; Guthrie and Grose, 'Forty Years of Jacobite Bibliography', pp. 49–60, esp. p. 50.

20 P. H. Brown (ed.), *Letters Relating to Scotland in the Reign of Queen Anne By James Ogilvy, First Earl of Seafield and Others* (Edinburgh, Scottish History Society, 2nd Ser., 1915), ix–x, xi, xvii; *The Jacobites and the Union*, x; W. K. Dickson (ed.), *Warrender Letters. Correspondence of Sir George Warrender Bt, Lord Provost of Edinburgh, and Member of Parliament for the City, with Relative Papers, 1715* (Edinburgh, Scottish History Society, 3rd Ser., 1935), xxxix–xl.

21 J. MacKinnon, *The Union of England and Scotland: A Study in International History* (1896), p. 348 (cited in C. Whatley, *'Bought and Sold for English Gold'? Explaining the Union of 1707* (Glasgow, Economic and Social History Society of Scotland, 1994), pp. 16–17). John Oldmixon and Sir George Rose's criticisms were so clearly partisan and ill-informed that they appear to have had no effect on the favourable reception Lockhart otherwise received from historians before the late nineteenth century: Oldmixon, *Memoirs of North-Britain*, pp. v, 1–2, 25, 135, 265; Rose (ed.), *A Selection From the Papers of the Earl of Marchmont* (3 vols, 1831), i. lxxxv–cxxxii. I am grateful to John Shaw of the SRO for reminding me of Rose's critique.

Lockhart's judgment'.[22] This, however, went far beyond most historians' reservations about Lockhart's value as a historical source.[23] For when tested against modern historical scholarship and the multiplicity of new sources uncovered in the last century, Lockhart's account has again and again proved honest (if biased) and largely accurate.[24]

In sum, then, George Lockhart is a very rare bird. His extensive autobiographical writings, correspondence and involvement in Jacobite and non-Jacobite politics have ensured that his *oeuvre* has had a profound influence on historical writing dealing with the period 1702–28. At the same time, the indiscretions, reflections and implicit assumptions embedded in his prose offer the opportunity to recover one man's portion of a lost mentality. The book which follows is a response in part to the first, but mainly to the second of these features of the Lockhart phenomenon.

The analysis that follows correspondingly falls into two parts. Part I, which deals with Lockhart as a historical actor, is in a sense merely an introduction to Part II, which explores his perception of the world, himself and his times, though to view the social, economic and political context in which the mind analysed in Part II developed and operated as optional superstructure would be facile. Lockhart's understanding of the human condition and his interpretation of events were critically shaped by his political and social experiences. He, like every other human being, was always acting in multiple roles at any given time: father, brother, husband, leader, led, intellectual, patriot, and so on. Hence, while the major part of the book is principally concerned with placing Lockhart in time and place in order to explicate the dynamics of his mentality, this is not merely ancillary. Late seventeenth-century/early eighteenth-century Scotland shaped Lockhart; and an appreciation of how this process worked in the life of one man will, it is hoped, illuminate similar processes in the lives of others.

22 George S. Pryde (ed.), *The Treaty of Union of Scotland and England 1707* (1950), pp. 31, 32.
23 See for example, A. Browning (ed.), *English Historical Documents 1660–1714* (1953), p. 597; G. Davies and M. F. Keeler (eds), *Bibliography of British History. Stuart Period, 1603–1714* (2nd edn, Oxford, 1970), p. 535; W. Ferguson, *Scotland. 1689 to the Present* (Edinburgh, repr. 1994), p. 429; Whatley, *Bought and Sold*, pp. 16–17, 23.
24 See for example, SRO GD 18/6080, pp. 224, 279; *Seafield Letters*, p. 182: Earl of Glasgow to Earl Godolphin, Edinburgh, 4 Oct. 1706 (cf. SR, p. 252); *Correspondence of Colonel N. Hooke*, ii. 347–409 (cf. SR, pp. 215–18).

PART I

The Background and Career of George Lockhart of Carnwath

CHAPTER ONE

Family Background

A human being is invariably more than the sum of his or her parts. Yet there can be no doubt that George Lockhart's background and childhood played a decisive role in moulding him. He broke free of his roots in many ways, but the directions in which he did so were eerily responsive to his experiences as a boy.

The Lockharts of Carnwath were a cadet branch of a well-established lairdly dynasty, the Lockharts of Lee. The senior line owned a reasonably extensive, though poor quality, estate in Lanarkshire [1] and claimed descent from a supporter of King Robert the Bruce. Whatever the truth of their origins, they remained an obscure gentry family up until the early seventeenth century, only occasionally glimpsed in official records through their involvement in the violent politics of the late medieval lowlands and borders. [2]

In the early seventeenth century, however, the family's fortunes began to improve. James Lockhart X of Lee was indicted for his involvement in the murder of Darnley and was an active participant in the private wars of the borders throughout his long life. His son, also named James, was likewise involved in various border feuds up until the 1610s, and was warded in Edinburgh castle as late as 1626, but nonetheless inaugurated the transition to respectability via service to the state that was to rescue the Lockharts from genteel poverty and obscurity. By the end of his life he had been knighted and appointed J.P. for Lanark, acted as Commissioner for Lanarkshire in the Parliament of 1607, and served as a Commissioner for the Surrender of Teinds, the investigation of witchcraft and the surveying of the laws. [3]

The old borderer's grandson, also named James, was a professional servant of the Stuart state. By 1633 he had already accumulated a knighthood, been appointed a Gentleman of Charles I's Privy Chamber, was in receipt of a royal pension and was serving his master as a Lord of the Articles in the Scottish Parliament. His career underwent a brief eclipse after he subscribed the National Covenant, but he was apparently forgiven and officially appointed a Commissioner of the Exchequer in 1645 and a Lord of Session in 1646. In 1648, as a prominent Engager, he was given command of one of the regiments of the Scots army that went down to disaster at the battle of Preston. Escaping home after

1 S. Macdonald Lockhart, *Seven Centuries. The History of the Lockharts of Lee and Carnwath* (Carnwath, 1976), p. 10.
2 *Ibid.*, pp. 16–17, 19–22.
3 M. D. Young (ed.), *The Parliaments of Scotland. Burgh and Shire Commissioners* (2 vols, Edinburgh, 1992–93), ii. 434–5.

the battle, Sir James eventually worked his passage back into the Covenanting camp and was soon prominently involved in organising the defence of Scotland in the face of the English invasion of 1650.[4] After he was captured in 1651 he correspondingly spent a brief spell in the Tower, and then lived in retirement until the Restoration. At that point his career took flight. In 1660 he was reappointed a Lord of Session. In 1661 he was made a Privy Councillor, reappointed to the Lords of the Articles and became a Lord of Exchequer. Finally, in 1671, he was appointed Lord Justice Clerk and granted a pension of £400 sterling (£4800 Scots) a year.[5]

Meanwhile his eldest son, William, who had spent his early years as a mercenary in France, returned to England at the behest of his friend Lord William Hamilton in 1643, was appointed a Colonel in the Royalist horse and was subsequently knighted in 1646. Despite these tokens of royal favour he defected to the Commonwealth in 1651 (allegedly because he had been insulted by Charles II), assented to, and was one of the Scots negotiators for, a Union with England, served the Commonwealth and Protectorate as a Commissioner of Justice and was deemed sufficiently reliable by the Army grandees to be one of only five Scots nominated to sit in Barebones Parliament. Under the Protectorate he was appointed a Judge of Exchequer and one of the Council for Scotland as well as Keeper of the Signet. In addition, after marrying Cromwell's niece, he was raised to the Protectorate's Other House, negotiated the Protectorate's alliance with France in 1657 and was given command of the expeditionary force to Flanders that was largely responsible for winning the battle of the Dunes in 1658. For his services there he received the governorship of Dunkirk, which neatly enabled him to work his passage back into the good graces of Charles II in 1660 by ensuring the garrison did not resist the Restoration. By 1672 he had been so far forgiven as to be appointed a Lord of the Articles, and was sufficiently trusted to be despatched as Ambassador to France the following year. Sir William rounded out his career by succeeding his father as Lord Justice Clerk in 1673.[6]

Nor were Sir William Lockhart's younger siblings any less assiduous in the service of the powers that were. John began his career serving the Protectorate as a Commissioner for the Cess and trying attempts on the life of the Protector, and sat in two Protectorate Parliaments. After the Restoration he was knighted and made a Lord of Session in 1665 and appointed a Lord of Justiciary in 1671.[7] George, the father of the subject of this book, was also an assenter to negotiations for a Union in 1652, rode Sir William's coat-tails into the office of Advocate

4 Macdonald Lockhart, *Seven Centuries*, pp. 34–5.
5 *Ibid.*, ii. 435–6; Sir Robert Douglas of Glenbervie, *The Baronage of Scotland; Containing an Historical and Genealogical Account of the Gentry of that Kingdom* (Edinburgh, 1798), p. 326.
6 *Parliaments of Scotland*, ii. 436; *Baronage of Scotland*, pp. 326–7.
7 *Parliaments of Scotland*, ii. 433–4

General in 1658 and sat for Lanark in Richard Cromwell's Parliament. This put him in a bit of an embarrassing situation in 1660, but a humble apology, service as a Commissioner for the Cess and family influence soon produced a royal pardon and a knighthood.[8]

Sir George was a highly talented lawyer and soon established a flourishing practice while he waited for a suitably lucrative opening in Scotland's bureaucracy to arise. Reflecting in later years on his own career, Sir George's great rival, Mackenzie of Rosehaugh, recalled Sir George's abilities with more than grudging admiration:

> Lockhart might be called another Corpus Juris and a second Cicero. It was his peculiarity that he could arrange his arguments so that they supported one another like the stones in an arch; and even when pleading without preparation he pointed out what occurred to him with prompt shrewdness and brought it forward in due order. No point in jurisprudence was too deep for him, and as soon as a client had informed him of his case, he at once saw the arguments that might be used on either side, and laid hold of the real gist of the matter.[9]

Consequently, despite the fact that he attached himself to the wrong patron in the 1660s – William Douglas, 3rd Duke of Hamilton – and ended up getting disbarred in 1674 when he tried to appeal a case from the Court of Session to Parliament in furtherance of a sequence of intrigues by Hamilton designed to bring about the fall of the Duke of Lauderdale,[10] Sir George was soon able to make a comeback. Though he remained officially disbarred until January 1678, his ability had so impressed another politician then under something of a cloud, James, Duke of York (the future James II and VII), that in May 1677 he appointed Sir George Advocate-General to the High Court of Admiralty and his personal legal representative in Scotland.[11]

In 1679 he delivered an appropriate return for York's support and patronage by pronouncing in favour of his catholic master's not having to abide by the terms of the Scottish Test Act on the grounds that James was personally exempt from its provisions because his warrant to act in Scotland stipulated that he represented the King in person.[12] In 1680 he signalled his renunciation of any

---

8 *Ibid.*, ii. 433; G. V. Irving and A. Murray, *The Upper Ward of Lanarkshire Described and Delineated* (3 vols, 1864), ii. 518.

9 Irving and Murray, *Upper Ward of Lanarkshire*, ii. 518.

10 G. Burnet, *Bishop Burnet's History of His Own Time, From the Restoration of King Charles the Second to the Treaty of Peace at Utrecht, in the Reign of Queen Anne* (2 vols, 1857), i. 240. For an explanation of what Hamilton was about, see J. Patrick, 'The Origins of the Opposition to Lauderdale in the Scottish Parliament of 1673', *Scottish Historical Review*, liii (1974), 1–21.

11 Irving and Murray, *Upper Ward of Lanarkshire*, ii. 519; LEP, Personal Documents 33: Commission as York's Advocate-General, 26 May 1677.

12 Irving and Murray, *Upper Ward of Lanarkshire*, ii. 520.

remaining links with the political opposition in Scotland by meekly submitting
to Court pressure not to defend the Marquess of Argyll when Argyll was about
to be hounded into exile as a punishment for his association with the Exclusionists,
and subsequently acting as co-prosecutor (with Mackenzie) at the trial of George
Baillie of Jerviswood in 1683. As a reward for these services, and the part he
played as one of the Lords of the Articles in orchestrating the chorus of docility
that emanated from the first session of James II and VII's one and only Scots
Parliament,[13] he was promoted at the end of 1685 to the post of Lord President
of the Court of Session with a pension of £500 (£6000 Scots) *per annum*.[14]

Post-Revolution apologists for the Lockharts have claimed that Sir George
opposed the catholicising tendencies of the Jacobite regime in Scotland,[15] but
there is little evidence that he in fact did so. Rather the contrary. As well as his
other offices, Sir George acted as a Lord of the Articles in the Scots Parliament
of 1685 – a post he would not have attained if his obedience had been in any
doubt. Likewise his appointment as President of the Court of Session. That he
was given the office of Royal Advocate in Scotland after Mackenzie's dismissal
from it for being uncooperative suggests even more strongly that the government
was assured of his untrammeled obedience. As Sir George's commission put it:
'it is most necessary for us to have one to take speciall care of our royall
prerogative and concernes, whose great experience and faithfulnesse to us may
secure it against any incroachment that might be designed upon our royal rights
and prerogatives'.[16] A £700 sterling (£8400 Scots) addition to his already hefty
royal pension in May 1687 and the grant of the estate of Sir William Nicolson
(escheated to the crown by virtue of Nicolson's dying a bankrupt) suggests that
he continued to be considered a vital pillar of the Jacobite regime even as it
entered its most frenetic catholicising phase.[17] Neither of the Drummond
brothers, the Earls of Perth and Melfort, who had eased themselves into Lauderdale's old role as joint satraps by 1687, seem to have found him particularly
obstructive, and he continued to attend to his duties in the winter of 1688–89

13 Irving and Murray, *Upper Ward of Lanarkshire*, ii. 520; F. C. Turner, *James II* (repr. 1950),
    p. 368.
14 LEP, Personal Documents 33 (Charters and Commissions): warrant for a pension for Sir
    George Lockhart of Carnwath, 23 Dec. 1685.
15 T. B. Macaulay, *History of England*, ed. Sir Charles Firth (6 vols, repr. 1968), ii. 774–6.
16 LEP, Personal Documents 33 (Charters and Commissions): commission appointing Sir
    George Lockhart of Carnwath Royal Advocate of Scotland, 24 May 1686.
17 LEP, Personal Documents 33 (Charters and Commissions): warrant for a pension in
    favour of Sir George Lockhart of Carnwath, 22 May 1687; Folder 2, Estate and Legal
    Correspondence: decree of James VII granting estate of Sir William Nicolson to Sir
    George Lockhart of Carnwath and his heirs, 10 Nov. 1687; J. Miller, *James II. A Study in
    Kingship* (Hove, 1978), pp. 174–87; M. Glozier, 'The Earl of Melfort, the Court Catholic
    Party and the Foundation of the Order of the Thistle, 1687', *Scottish Historical Review*, lxxix
    (2000) 233–8.

even as the regime collapsed around him and the vast majority of his colleagues fled abroad or rushed southwards to make their court to William of Orange.[18]

Given that his career up to 1688 smacked of nothing so much as cool opportunism, it seems highly unlikely that Sir George would have fallen with his master. He was still in office in March 1689 on the eve of the (illegal) political Convention called to settle on a government for Scotland in the wake of the disintegration of the old order, and there is no evidence that he intended to surrender his power and position to follow loyalists like Viscount Dundee into the political wilderness of armed rebellion.[19] The historian is ultimately reduced to nothing more than speculation on this point, however, because on Sunday 31 March 1689 Sir George was shot in the back with a pistol at point-blank range by John Chiesley of Dalry as he left Greyfriars Kirk in the heart of Edinburgh. Sir George died almost immediately and Chiesley was arrested on the spot. Even under judicial torture in the form of the dreaded 'boot', which was still legal in Scotland in 1689, Chiesley denied that he had any accomplices or any political motive. Though he came from a south-western Covenanting and nonconformist family, he appears to have murdered Sir George out of pique at a decision Sir George had made in favour of Chiesley's much-abused wife in a civil action against her husband over payment of her jointure.[20]

The murder seems to have genuinely shocked the Scottish political nation. Chiesley was forthwith condemned to be gibbeted between Edinburgh and Leith, with the murder weapon around his neck and his right hand severed and affixed over the West Port (gate) of Edinburgh. The city council not only sat as a court for the first time to sentence Chiesley to death, but also granted the Lockharts of Carnwath the right to bury Sir George in the main body of Greyfriars Kirk, and be buried there themselves in perpetuity.[21] The Duke of Gordon, under siege in Edinburgh castle where he was still holding out for James II and VII, gladly agreed to the Convention's request for a ceasefire while the funeral took place.[22] Years later Lockhart was most easily identified at the outset of his own political career by the simple reference: 'Sir George's son',[23] and one of Chiesley's children, unluckily for her married to James Erskine, Lord Grange of the Court

18 H. Paton (ed.), *The Register of the Privy Council of Scotland* (3rd Ser., Edinburgh, 1932), xiii. 329–30, 343: Glasgow, 15 Oct. and 7 Nov. 1688; P. W. J. Riley, *King William and the Scottish Politicians* (Edinburgh, 1979), p. 11.

19 *Pace* his son's efforts to turn his father into a diehard loyalist: SR, p. 283.

20 Macdonald Lockhart, *Seven Centuries*, pp. 65–8.

21 Scottish Catholic Archives, Blairs Letters 1/128/3: Mr Andrew (?) to Alexander Whyteford, Edinburgh, 3 Apr. 1689; M. Wood and H. Arnet (eds), *Extracts from the Records of the Burgh of Edinburgh, 1681 to 1689* (Edinburgh, 1954), pp. 271, 281–2; H. Paton (ed.), *Register of the Interments in the Greyfriars Burying-Ground, Edinburgh* (Edinburgh, Scottish Record Society, 1902), p. 394.

22 R. Bell (ed.), *Siege of the Castle of Edinburgh* (Edinburgh, Bannatyne Club, 1828), p. 47.

23 Blairs Letters 2/83/2: James Carnegy to Thomas Innes [Edinburgh], 8 June 1703.

of Session, felt the legend of Chiesley's deed was still powerful enough to threaten him with a reminder that she was Chiesley's daughter.[24]

The effect of the murder on the eight-year-old Lockhart is more difficult to ascertain. We do not know if George and his mother were in Edinburgh, or even in Scotland, at the time, though one account of the murder has Lady Lockhart rushing to her dying husband from her sickbed.[25] Certainly, none of the accounts of the murder mentions George as being present. Later in life he hardly ever referred to the incident, and when he did he was surprisingly ignorant about the details, for example denying that Chiesley was ever tortured to reveal his putative co-conspirators.[26] What he made of it as an eight-year-old boy can only be surmised, but it seems reasonable to assume something so traumatic cannot have failed to have had an impact. It is possible, then, that Lockhart's strong sense of family ties and filial obligation stemmed from the sudden loss of his father.[27] It is certain that the murder catapulted him into a politically volatile and dangerous adult world at a very young age.

Moreover, the young George Lockhart had to experience that volatility first hand. This stemmed initially from the intervention of his mother's relations. Sir George Lockhart married his second wife, Philadelphia Wharton, in 1679, and over the next decade she presented him with at least two children: George (in 1681) and Philip (in 1689).[28] Just as importantly for an up-and-coming lairdly dynasty, Philadelphia provided a family connection that elevated the social status of the Lockharts of Carnwath, for she was the daughter of Philip, 4th Baron Wharton in the English peerage. At the point when Sir George married her the political fortunes of the Whartons were under something of a cloud owing to

24 *DNB*, xvii. 413–14; Macdonald Lockhart, *Seven Centuries*, p. 68.

25 Macdonald Lockhart, *Seven Centuries*, p. 66.

26 LP i. 31. Cf. E. W. M. Balfour-Melville (ed.), *An Account of the Proceedings of the Estates in Scotland, 1689–1690* (2 vols, Edinburgh, Scottish History Society, 3rd Ser., 1954), i. 23: Edinburgh, 1 Apr. 1689.

27 See below, pp. 23–5.

28 *Parliaments of Scotland*, ii. 433, states (after *DNB* xxxiv. 44–5) that Philadelphia bore three children: George jr, Philip and an unnamed daughter. Since, however, the birth of the unnamed daughter (actually Barbara Lockhart) is recorded in Sir James Balfour Paul (ed.), *The Scots Peerage. Founded on Wood's Edition of Sir Robert Douglas's Peerage of Scotland. Containing an Historical and Genealogical Account of the Nobility of That Kingdom* (Edinburgh, 9 vols, 1904), iv. 592, as having occurred in 1677 – two years before Sir George and Philadelphia were married, it seems unlikely that Barbara was a child of Sir George's second marriage, but rather the issue of his first, to Barbara Gilmour. There is also a problem with the date of birth of Philip Lockhart, in that the only record that survives of it is an assertion by George that Philip was aged 25 in December 1715 (LP i. 497). This would indicate that he was born at some time in 1690, by which time his father had been dead for at least nine months. It would, therefore, seem probable that George got his brother's age wrong and that Philip was born at some time in late 1688 or (more likely) in 1689. This in turn may explain why Philadelphia is recorded as having been sick at home in bed instead of at church with Sir George at the time of his assassination.

Lord Wharton's dogged commitment to presbyterianism and his alignment with Shaftesbury and Holles in opposition to the Court.[29] Hence although it represented a social step up for the Lockharts, it was also in a sense a bargain-basement association with the aristocracy. The value of the Wharton connection was, however, transformed by the Revolution of 1688–89, in which Philadelphia's brother Thomas and her father played a very active part.[30] The new order correspondingly favoured the family, and as 'Honest Tom' Wharton moved steadily higher in the inner councils of the Whig party, the connection assumed greater and greater value. Philadelphia made no apparent effort to resist her father and brother's attempts to influence the conduct of affairs of their relations, the Lockharts of Carnwath, at first, perhaps, due to grief and shock and later almost certainly because she was preoccupied with her own problems.

Thus although Lockhart's first guardian ('tutor' in Scottish legal parlance), appointed by the Court of Session, was Sir John Lockhart of Castlehill, a kinsman from the Lee branch of the family and a Lord of Session, it was his grandfather Lord Wharton (and possibly his mother, Philadelphia) whom Lockhart subsequently blamed for most of the upheavals in his life following his father's murder. The first of several interventions seems to have been a successful petition to the Scottish Privy Council to have the boys' tutor (i.e. teacher), John Gillane, who was a strong episcopalian, removed.[31] Next came the packing off of George and his brother Philip to live with the now ostentatiously presbyterian ducal family of Argyll.[32] The final straw seems to have been the marrying-off of George's widowed half-sister Barbara to the solidly presbyterian Daniel Carmichael of Maudsley, a younger son of the Earl of Hyndford.[33]

Lockhart was reticent about his childhood in all his written works, but some of the impact of these interventions can nonetheless be discerned in his asides and silences. It is significant that John Gillane subsequently became George's chaplain and that over thirty years later he used all his influence to have Gillane raised to the rank of bishop in the episcopalian church.[34] Likewise, while George valued the friendship he struck up with the future 2nd Duke of Argyll and his brother Lord Archibald Campbell (Earl of Islay and 3rd Duke) during his enforced stay in the ducal household, he seems to have developed a deep aversion to

29 G. F. Trevallyn Jones, *Saw-Pit Wharton. The Political Career From 1640 to 1691 of Philip, Fourth Lord Wharton* (Sydney, 1967), pp. 225–51.
30 *Ibid.*, pp. 258–9; R. Beddard, 'The Guildhall Declaration of 11 December 1688 and the Counter-Revolution of the Loyalists', *Historical Journal*, xi (1968), 403–20; J. Childs, *The Army, James II, and the Glorious Revolution* (Manchester, 1980), pp. 149–50, 155; J. Carswell, *The Old Cause. Three Biographical Studies in Whiggism* (1954), pp. 65–82.
31 LP i. 571.
32 LP i. 394.
33 *Scots Peerage*, iv. 592. Her first marriage was to James Lockhart of Castlehill.
34 Stuart 125/41: John Carnegy of Boysack to Inverness [Paris], 15 Feb. 1729 ns. See below, p. 145.

presbyterianism and his playmates' father, the 1st Duke, while he was there.[35] Most poignantly of all, though the evidence derives entirely from silence, it is striking that despite his strong sense of family Lockhart never once in all his letters and published writings refers to his half-sister Barbara or his six nieces and nephews by her marriage to Carmichael of Maudsley. It is as though she had never existed.

Almost as absent are any details of George's education. The only record we have of the kind of reading material his curators and his tutor thought appropriate dates from 1696 and includes a history of recent events in France (*The Turkish Spy*), a treatise on geography, a set of observations on Caesar's Commentaries and a learned polemic asserting Scotland's independence of England.[36] Going by this reading list and the adult Lockhart, George's education seems to have been thoroughly conventional. His prose is convoluted and Latinate, and throughout his writings he shows a fondness for snatches of the classics (particularly Ovid and Livy) commonly studied by his peers.[37] His stilted attempts at verse are also full of commonplace allusions and tropes.[38] Like most well-brought-up gentlemen of his era he had at least a reading knowledge of French, and the fact that he was able to communicate with a captive Spanish officer in Edinburgh in 1719 and had no trouble getting around in the Low Countries in 1727–28 indicates he could probably speak it as well.[39] Judging by his ability as an adult accurately to cite statutes in Parliamentary debates, Lockhart also seems to have acquired a reasonably good grounding in Scots law.[40] George's knowledge of recent scholarship on Scotland and history in general, however, does seem to have been more profound than was customary amongst his social equals.[41] He also understood the distinction authors aspiring to contemporary relevance needed to make between ancient and recent exemplars. Thus by the time he came to write the first volume of his memoirs (about 1708) it is clear that he was very familiar with Sir George Mackenzie's, *A Defence of the Antiquity of the Royal Line of Scotland*, whose scholarship and arguments underpinned his conclusions.[42] He was also able to cite an aspect of early Tudor foreign policy as proof of Scotland's former greatness and make knowledgable use of the Bishop of Ross's successful rebuttal of a charge of treason levelled against him by the English authorities

35 SR, p. 32; LP i. 526–7.
36 Macdonald Lockhart, *Seven Centuries*, p. 84.
37 See, for example, SR, pp. 160, 170, 212, 239.
38 LP i. 284, 501, 508, 589–96.
39 LP ii. 23, 275; SRO SRO GD 1/1155/78/5 (Small Collections): GL to John Chancellor of Shieldhill, Rotterdam, 9 Jan. 1728 ns.
40 LP i. 572. See also, LP i. 599–600.
41 LP i. 597–603; ii. 415, 419.
42 Cf. Sir George Mackenzie, *A Defence of the Antiquity of the Royal Line of Scotland: With a True Account When the Scots were Govern'd by Kings in the Isle of Britain, in Answer to the Bishop of St Asaph* (1685), pp. 182–5; and SR, pp. 239–44.

(on the grounds that he was the ambassador of a sovereign, albeit deposed, prince) to further an argument against the legitimacy of Mary Queen of Scots's execution.[43] Yet his prose then and later was refreshingly free of the ponderous allusions to Republican Roman history that bedevil most amateur authors' political analyses at this time. The only discernible lacuna in his education, relative to what was customary among the social elite, seems to have been that he did not do the Grand Tour – indeed he appears never willingly to have gone further afield than England. This was probably a consequence of his early marriage. The upshot of all of which was that the adult Lockhart was conventionally literate, even well-read, but somewhat narrow in his understanding of the world. Other factors, however, combined to produce an independent and assertive cast of mind.

It seems reasonable to surmise that by the age of fourteen George was kicking at the traces of his tutelage. When his principal tutor, Lord Castlehill, died in 1693 he was replaced by James Lockhart of Cleghorn who, as was all too common at the time, seems to have begun embezzling what he could from his ward's estate. Lockhart reacted to this by asserting his right at age fourteen to choose his own curators,[44] and by January 1695 had secured the appointment of a more congenial set of guardians headed by the episcopalian Sir James Scougall, Lord Whitehill of the Court of Session.[45] Around the same time Lockhart and/or his curators appointed Martin Martin, subsequently the author of *A Description of the Western Islands of Scotland*, as his 'governour.'[46] By March 1695 George was suing Lockhart of Cleghorn for misappropriating part of the revenue of the estate.[47] His new curators seem to have allowed him a much greater degree of independence, and from 1695 he was not only directly involved in the management of his estates, but also arranging his own marriage.

In April 1697 he married Lady Euphemia Montgomery, a younger daughter of the 9th Earl of Eglinton by his first marriage.[48] To say the least, this was an odd match. The Montgomeries were an old aristocratic house, but they were

43 SR, p. 246; LP ii. 418–19. See also his use of the contrast between the policies of Charles II and David II to make a point about the need to reward suffering loyalists after a restoration (LP ii. 420–4).

44 Sir George Mackenzie, *The Institutions of the Law of Scotland* (1684), pp. 58, 60–1.

45 The others were Richard Lockhart of Lee and William Montgomery of Mcbiehill (the Earl of Arran – subsequently 4th Duke of Hamilton – appears to have declined to serve): SRO SRO GD 406/1/4053 (Hamilton Muniments): Lockhart to Arran, Edinburgh, 31 Jan. 1695 and 406/1/4054: Lockhart's declaration of curators, n.d. [1695].

46 NLS, MS 1307 f. 121: receipt from Sir Donald Macdonald of Sleat to Martin Martin, 15 Jan. 1695. I am indebted to Dr Domnhall Uilleam Stiubhart of Edinburgh university for this reference, and the more so because it revealed Lockhart's connection with Martin, of which I was previously unaware.

47 LEP, Folder 44: Instruments, Lockhart of Cleghorn versus George Lockhart, 1 and 5 Mar. 1695.

48 *Scots Peerage*, iii. 457.

far from the forefront of Scottish politics. The 9th Earl was a dogged episcopalian, but that seems to have been the only fixed principle in his politics. Otherwise he was a common-or-garden placeman; in effect, a supporter of the government of the day whatever its political complexion.[49] It is probably safe to say that George's family connections, especially his association with the Whartons, and his inherited wealth, could have secured him a far better match.

In addition to these incongruities, the bride and bridegroom's ages were highly unusual for their age and social class. George was sixteen at the time of his marriage, Euphemia was nineteen. In general this period was characterised by late marriage.[50] Most couples, and certainly elite couples, did not marry until their mid- to late twenties. Lockhart's marriage is thus strikingly untypical on grounds of age alone. Then there is the apparent oddness of the marriage arrangements. Lockhart committed his family to a relatively small jointure of £6000 Scots (*c.* £500 sterling) despite Euphemia bringing a substantial dowry of 27000 marks (*c.* £1500 sterling) to the marriage. In addition, neither George's mother nor Euphemia's father was present at the signing of the marriage agreement, if the list of witnesses is anything to go by.[51] And yet there is every indication that Lockhart and his father-in-law got on very well in later years.[52] Altogether, these hint at a marriage of which George's family profoundly disapproved.

Equally noteworthy is the character of the Lockharts' relationship. George had a certain (well deserved) reputation for high-handedness and pride; Euphemia's reputation paralleled his.[53] Contemporaries regarded her as prone to 'froward imperious behaviour', as difficult to handle, 'considering the change-ableness of her temper', and used terms such as 'imprudent' and 'passionate',

---

49 Riley, *King William and the Scottish Politicians*, p. 166. There is some evidence, however, that Eglinton was inclined towards Jacobitism (LL, p. 142), though ultimately he was too cautious to risk his neck: R. Wodrow, *Analecta: Or, Materials for a History of Remarkable Providences; Mostly Relating to Scotch Ministers and Christians* (4 vols, Maitland Club, Edinburgh, 1862), ii. 359: 6 Feb. 1722.

50 Though their work is focussed on England, the paradigm put forward by Peter Laslett, *The World We Have Lost – Further Explored* (3rd edn, 1983), pp. 81–4 and David Cressy, *Birth, Marriage and Death. Ritual, Religion, and the Life-Cycle in Tudor and Stuart England* (Oxford, 1997), p. 312, almost certainly applies to Lowland Scotland too.

51 SRO SRO GD 3/2/76/14 (Eglinton Papers): marriage contract between GL and Lady Euphemia Montgomery, 1697. This was nearly three times the dowry that would usually have been given with a laird's daughter in the 1720s (E. Burt, *Burt's Letters From the North of Scotland. With Facsimiles of the Original Engravings*, intro. by R. Jamieson (2 vols, Edinburgh, repr. 1974), i. 254), and represented a substantial financial coup for the Lockharts.

52 LL, p. 97: GL to Maule, London, 13 Apr. 1714; SRO SRO GD 220/5/331/7 (Montrose Papers): Adam Cockburn of Ormiston (Lord Justice Clerk) to Montrose, Edinburgh, 11 Nov. 1714; SRO GD 3/5/965: GL to Eglinton, Brussels, 10 June 1727 ns.

53 SRO GD 18/2092/2: Sir John Clerk of Penicuik's spiritual journal for 1699–1709, 18 Feb. 1702; SRO GD 1/1155/78/5: GL to John Chancellor of Shieldhill, Rotterdam, 9 Jan. 1728 ns.

in their descriptions of her.[54] Nonetheless, the two of them seem to have enjoyed a thoroughly affective relationship. Only one formal, semi-legal letter between George and Euphemia survives, but the balance of the other evidence is clear.[55] Between 1698 and 1718 George and Euphemia had fifteen children, of whom ten survived infancy. Fecundity does not necessarily imply affection, though the fact that there is no evidence of George having had any extra-marital relationships at a time when it was not uncommon for the patriarchs of elite families to do so does suggest it. Likewise Lockhart's somewhat crass attempts to pressure the Old Pretender to 'have a mirry meeting' (i.e. resume conjugal relations) with his estranged wife Clementina, after he had experienced about three months' separation from Euphemia, may suggest their relationship remained intimate long after she had her last child.[56]

Stronger evidence that George and Euphemia enjoyed an affective relationship comes from his formal commitment to a more generous jointure in 1708, after he formally came of age (though the impending Jacobite invasion may have had something to do with this too) and a sneering aside by the Duke of Hamilton, to the effect that George could not be trusted because he discussed everything he learned with his wife.[57] Euphemia also chose to join him both in Edinburgh castle when he was imprisoned there for the first time in 1715, and in Brussels when he was in exile in 1727.[58] Equally suggestive is the agitation and anxiety he displayed when she fell ill. In a letter in 1701 apologising to his virtual next-door neighbour, Sir John Clerk of Penicuik, for his failure to attend the funeral of Sir John Clerk's daughter-in-law, Lady Margaret Stewart, who was also a relation of Lockhart's by marriage and attendance at whose funeral was therefore socially *de rigueur*, he forthrightly stated that Euphemia was ill and that 'I cannot by any means leave her in this condition'.[59] Likewise in 1712 he rushed back from London when he heard that Euphemia, at that time pregnant with her twelfth child, had fallen ill.[60] Euphemia was also fully cognisant of, and personally participated in, George's engagement with active Jacobitism after 1714, as may be seen from her involvement as a messenger in his plotting for a Jacobite

54 SRO GD 18/5246/1/46: Earl of Galloway to Sir John Clerk of Penicuik, Glasertoun, 30 Mar. 1713; SRO GD 18/2092/7: Sir John's spiritual journal for 1720–21, 24 Sept. 1721; SRO GD 220/5/461/12: James Lindsay to the Earl of Hyndford, Edinburgh, 23 [Aug.] 1715.

55 LP ii. 433–5.

56 LL, pp. 305, 314–15, 324, 325: 6 [May], 11 Sept., 18 Nov. and 6 Dec. 1727 ns.

57 LEP, Personal Documents Box 2: jointure agreement, 20 Mar. 1708; Blairs Letters 2/159/13: Carnegy to the Scots College, Edinburgh, 11 Mar. 1710.

58 SRO GD 220/5/461/12: James Lindsay to the Earl of Hyndford, Edinburgh, 23 [Aug.] 1715; SRO GD 3/5/965: GL to Eglinton, Brussels, 10 June 1727 ns.

59 *Burt's Letters*, i. 230, 234; LL, p. 2: GL to Sir John Clerk of Penicuik, Dryden, 23 Dec. 1701.

60 LL, pp. 63–4: GL to the Earl of Oxford, London, 27 Dec. 1712.

rising in Midlothian in 1715 and his transmission of a personal message from her to the Earl of Mar in 1718.[61]

Lockhart's likely warmth towards Euphemia stands in stark contrast to his apparently frigid relationship with his mother and stepfather(s). Soon after Sir George's death Philadelphia was, it appears, swept off her feet by an ex-army Captain named John Mair. Mair was associated with the Jacobite intriguer Henry Neville Payne and may have been involved in Jacobite plotting in Scotland in the early 1690s.[62] In any event, he was living with Philadelphia Lockhart, apparently without benefit of clergy, by 1690.[63] She subsequently claimed that he had in fact married her and that they kept it a secret because Mair was 'in ill circumstances with the government', so that they feared the loss of her jointure if he was convicted, and that 'it was the less inclynatione to own the marriage because he had no estate suitable to the ladie's'. Other than the fact that they were living together, 'sharing bed and board', however, the only real evidence for there ever having been a formal marriage is Philadelphia's determination to get a legal decree of divorce in 1696. In 1693, after she had become pregnant, she and Mair consulted with Payne, and Phildelphia then hid in England at the house of a friend of his until she gave birth to a son, whom she christened Henry after the imprisoned Jacobite. Soon thereafter she learned that Mair was already married to (and had had a child by) a Londoner named Jean Askay and, according to her account and that of Payne (in whom she seems to have confided), threw him out.[64] Inexplicably, however, if in fact she had ever officially married Mair, she made no attempt to seek a legal divorce until 1696, after she had apparently already married another army officer named John Ramsay. Mair obligingly failed to turn up before the Court of Session to present his version of events, and she could certainly prove that if he had ever married her he was a bigamist, so the divorce was granted.

Philadelphia's new husband, Ramsay, was the son of the former Bishop of Ross and a serving officer in the army. Judging by the debts he had racked up by the early 1700s, he seems to have had something of a problem with hanging onto his money (and indeed, anyone else's entrusted to his care), and from at least 1695 to 1698 he sought to squeeze George's inheritance for some extra cash to help keep himself in the manner to which he wished to become

61 LL, p. 135: GL to Mar [Dryden?], 28 Mar. 1718; LP ii. 433.
62 P. Hopkins, *Glencoe and the End of the Highland War* (Edinburgh, 1986), pp. 208, 221, 372–3.
63 SRO CC8/5/1 (Commissariot of Edinburgh, Consistorial Decreets), pp. 274–81. I am indebted to Dr Gordon Debrisay of Saskatchewan University for pointing out to me a printed record of the divorce (F. J. Grant (ed.), *The Commissariot of Edinburgh, Consistorial Processes and Decreets, 1658–1800* (Scottish Record Society, Edinburgh, 1909), p. 6), which put me on the track of the divorce process.
64 CC8/6/3: inventory of the process of divorce, 1698. Henry may possibly be the child whose burial is recorded simply as 'Sir George, a child', under 'Lockhart', in, *Register of the Interments in the Greyfriars Burying-Ground*, p. 394: 16 Jan. 1700.

accustomed. According to his own calculations, Ramsay had got through £37000 Scots (approximately £3083 sterling) out of the estate by June 1695, of which only £7000 Scots had been paid to George and his curators.[65] Doubtless due to the Wharton connection, Ramsay still contrived to get himself promoted to Lieutenant-Colonel by 1703 when Lockhart settled his debts for the last time just prior to his departure on active service in the War of the Spanish Succession.[66] Philadelphia was not much better as a financial manager, and periodically landed George with debts he preferred to meet rather than have his mother arrested for non-payment.[67] Worse still, she peddled her putative political influence over her brother Thomas (by then Earl Wharton) while he was Lord-Lieutenant of Ireland in 1708–10, acutely embarrassing both Lockhart and his uncle when the Commission of Accounts (of which George was a member) uncovered the whole seamy business in 1713.[68] All in all, it is not perhaps surprising that Lockhart mentions her only once in all his writings and letters.[69]

George's relationship with his other relatives seems to have been warm. He recalled years later that he 'lived in good terms, notwithstanding our being of different principles,'[70] with his uncle Thomas, and he often visited him when he was in England.[71] Wharton in turn did what he could to advance his nephew's career, and it was only due to his influence that George received the few crumbs of official patronage he did: Scottish Privy Councillor 1703–4 and Commissioner for the Union in 1703 and 1705–6. In the same vein, Lockhart was prepared to put himself out to help his kinsfolk even when they were of a different political persuasion. In 1704, for example, he tried to persuade Hamilton to back John Lockhart of Lee as Parliamentary candidate for Clydesdale even though he knew Lee was basically pro-Court and correspondingly unreliable from Hamilton's point of view, and in 1717 he paid off mortgages on lands owned by the Lockharts of Lee rather than see them pass out of the family.[72]

65 LEP, Folder 1: Miscellaneous Correspondence: Ramsay to GL and his curators, 'Whythill', 5 June 1695; Folder 44: Accounts: registered discharge of debts, note of 'some' of Ramsay's creditors and discharge of arrestments, Edinburgh, 17 Feb. 1703 and 1704; Ramsay's statement of monies owed him by GL for maintenance of GL, Philip and Barbara Lockhart, from 1692–8, n.d.
66 LEP, Estate and Legal Correspondence, Folder 2: Grant of Authority to Philadelphia Ramsay to Act in his Absence, Captain John Ramsay, 4 Feb. [n.b. endorsement says 2 Oct.], 1704.
67 LEP, Accounts: Folder 44: Instrument of Intimation, Edinburgh, 1 Aug. 1709.
68 CJ, xvii. 356: 16 May 1713. It is interesting to note in this context that though Wharton apparently agreed to let Philadelphia (wrongly referred to as Charlotte) keep the money, he required that the bribe be deposited with a goldsmith rather than given directly to her.
69 LL, p. 125: GL to Simon Fraser [Edinburgh?], 20 July 1717.
70 LP i. 295.
71 LL, p. 267: GL to the Old Pretender [Dryden?], 12 Mar. 1726.
72 LL, pp. 7–9: GL to Hamilton, Dryden, 14 Dec. 1704; LEP, Folder 2: Estate and Legal Correspondence: Acts of Redemption, 11 and 17 Jan. 1717.

But nowhere was George's sense of family and filial obligation better revealed than in his relationship with his children. He was always a very protective, even doting, father (though this was not a trait he respected in others[73]). Hence in 1723 when he by chance discovered that his brother-in-law, the Earl of Galloway, was mocking George Lockhart junior for allegedly having backed out of a duel, Lockhart exploded with fury and himself took up the matter in a scorching letter to Galloway:

> My Lord, So soon as I knew by a very great accident your Lordship's desire of intelligence concerning the cause of my eldest son's late illness, I resolved to satisfy your very extraordinary curiosity. The learned are of opinion that the cheange of air, or of cloaths, or walking on a wet street may chance to give the cold more radyly then strugling with a more mettled younge fellow, and your Lordship's supposition of catching it by danceing is not perhaps fare wronge. However, he got free of it without being oblidged to undergoe a courss of mercury, which your Lordship knows is not the good luck of all who catch accidentall colds. The tender concern which you are pleased to express for my son might have been reserved for some other of your good friends for he stands in noe need therof either on account of his falling into so many inconveniances (the perticulars wherof I imagine are best if not altogether known in Galloway) or often makeing a bad retreat.[74]

Not surprisingly, Galloway and he were never on speaking terms again.[75] Lockhart was also very concerned to secure the welfare and amity of his children after his own death, and in a revealing letter addressed to George junior Lockhart urged him to:

> ... be courteous, kind and obliging to all your brothers and sisters, willing to assist them on all occasions. Let your house be as ane assembly for them to meet frequently and be merry, and ane asylum in case of distress; and wher it happens by misfortunes and not from causes criminall or blameable in them, do not stand upon that patrimony I have alloted them and you have perhaps have paid, but generouslie and like a true freind enable them to set out again in the world[76]

– before going on carefully to outline how he wants each child taken care of.[77]

73 SRO SRO GD 18/4157 (Clerk of Penicuik Papers): GL to Baron of the Exchequer Sir John Clerk of Penicuik, Dryden, 27 May 1729.

74 SRO GD 18/5246/1/134: Katherine, Countess of Galloway, to Baron of the Exchequer Sir John Clerk of Penicuik, 8 Apr. 1723.

75 SRO GD 18/5246/1/190: Katherine Galloway to Baron Sir John Clerk, Glasertoun, 4 Jan. 1729; LP ii. 431–3.

76 LP ii. 428.

77 LP ii. 428–30. See also the supplementary testament in LEP, Personal Documents 33: Charters and Commissions: 14 Dec. 1731.

And it is in the case of his 'problem' children that we can see his affection for them all most clearly displayed. 'Sussie', for whom 'no hopes can be formed of her ever being in a condition to appear in the world', is to be 'put in a way of living privately and comfortably'.[78] James, who 'hath been ane undutifull child', is still 'young and not to be dispaird of' (he was nineteen at the time), and indeed, apparently when he was close to death, George accordingly forgave James his youthful indiscretions.[79] Philip, who was 'a child I love tenderlie, because he evidences a spirit capable of great things', was to be educated as a lawyer or clergyman, as circumstances permitted.[80]

So what kind of character emerged from this, somewhat troubled, childhood? First and foremost, Lockhart was self-assertive and independent. Thus although he was conforming, at least outwardly, to the Kirk at the time he and Euphemia moved into Dryden (1698), it did not last.[81] By 1703 at the latest he had cast off the presbyterianism so painfully inculcated at his grandfather's behest and openly adhered to the Kirk's episcopalian rival.[82] He also showed little compunction about attacking anyone who attempted to exploit his vulnerability as a child. By the age of fourteen he was already suing one of his tutors, and a willingness to fight to the last legal ditch any encroachment on what he considered to be his rights was a running theme throughout his life. Thus, for example, he fought a lengthy legal battle with his neighbour, Sir John Clerk of Penicuik, over his right to the patron's seat in Lasswade Kirk. Despite the fact that by 1720 Lockhart, an episcopalian, never graced the Kirk with his presence, he declared: '... I will in no event part with it ... My right thereto is undisputable and Sir John has no manner of right to it whatsoever, but what he has assumed to himself. If Sir John expects I'le part with my seat in lieu of the bit of ground he's to sell me, I will not do it, for I will not buy gold too dear'.[83] And in the same vein, in 1729 he demanded his share of the seating in Liberton Kirk by virtue of his status as a major landowner in the parish.[84] Just as importantly, he emerged putting a high value on strong, affectionate family bonds. Though his relations with his half-sister and his mother and John Ramsay (it is not clear if he ever met John Mair) were cool, his attitude toward them was not typical of his attitude towards his immediate family, kinfolk and friends in general. In spite of the Wharton clan's disruption of his childhood he grew up to like his uncle Tom

78 *Ibid.*, ii. 428–9.
79 *Ibid.*, ii. 429, 430.
80 LP ii. 429.
81 SRO SRO GD 18/1671/3 (Clerk of Penicuik Papers): statement of his grievances against GL by Sir John Clerk of Penicuik, Aug. 1701.
82 Blairs Letters 2/83/2: James Carnegy to Thomas Innes [Edinburgh], 8 June 1703.
83 LEP, Folder 1: Miscellaneous Correspondence: GL to Robert Wallace of Holmston, 'Friday 14 Febry' [1720?].
84 SRO GD 1/1155/78/8: GL to the minister and elders of Liberton Kirk (copy), 22 Nov. 1729.

and took a great interest in the career of his cousin Thomas jr (the future Duke of Wharton).[85] He likewise described the staunchly Whig Sir Robert Pollock of Pollock as his 'personall friend', saved the son of 'my worthy good friend', Sir James Baird of Saughtonhall, from condign punishment for his activities as a 'Mohock' (a violent gang of elite young Whig thugs active in London in the winter of 1711–12) and remained close friends with the Campbell brothers for the rest of his life.[86] His marriage to Euphemia Montgomery may well have been a love-match, and she certainly acted as his helpmeet and confidante throughout their lives together. Moreover, he played the role of the stern, but fond, patriarch with conviction with regard to his children and younger kin. In sum, for reasons beyond his control George Lockhart was forced to mature early, and quite possibly as a consequence of that experience he sought to create a highly traditional, conservative family environment for his own children to grow up in. It also seems likely that the disorder of his childhood years created in him the desire for order in the world at large that was to manifest itself repeatedly throughout his political career.

85 LL, p. 121: Major Simon Fraser to the Earl of Mar, Verdun, 10 Apr. 1717 ns; p. 125: GL to Fraser [Edinburgh?], 20 July 1717; pp. 211–15: GL to the Old Pretender [Dryden?], 28 Nov. 1724.
86 LP i. 364–5, 463; ii. 10, 332, 393.

CHAPTER TWO

The Economic Context

It was common practice in late seventeenth-century Scotland for successful cadets of established elite dynasties to return to the land later in their careers. Whether they made their fortunes through mercenary service overseas, legal practice or trade, it was not at all unusual to find such men investing their profits in landed estates and hence establishing branch dynasties of their own.[1] Indeed there were very few other ways to secure a family's fortunes. Thus Sir George Lockhart's entry into the land market in the 1680s was a natural corollary of his successful legal career. What was unusual about it was its shrewdness and success.

The foundation of the dynastic fortunes of the Lockharts of Carnwath was laid by the purchase in 1681 of the estate of Carnwath from the heavily indebted earl of that name.[2] Despite its bleak and windswept appearance, Carnwath was, and is, very good arable land, and it was to prove the mainstay of the family's income for the next 150 years.[3] Other purchases and awards of land closer to Edinburgh, in particular a house and lands at Dryden and parts of the baronies of Biggar, Lasswade and Roslin, added substantially to the family's holdings, and by the time of Sir George's death in 1689 the rental income of his lands was in the region of £20000 Scots (c. £1667 sterling) a year.[4] In addition, doubtless greatly aided by the £1200 sterling a year he was receiving for his services as Lord President and Royal Advocate of Scotland, Sir George had loaned money out to various aristocrats and the city of Edinburgh.[5] The suddenness of his demise left his business affairs in some confusion, and his son was correspondingly obliged to fight several lengthy legal battles brought on by challenges to his full

---

1 T. C. Smout, *A History of the Scottish People 1560–1830* (6th impression, 1985), pp. 263–4; R. H. Campbell, *Scotland Since 1707. The Rise of an Industrial Society* (revised 2nd edn, Edinburgh, 1992), p. 10; I. D. Whyte, *Scotland Before the Industrial Revolution. An Economic and Social History* (1995), p. 157.
2 Macdonald Lockhart, *Seven Centuries*, p. 63.
3 Macdonald Lockhart, *Seven Centuries*, p. 61; Irving and Murray, *Upper Ward of Lanarkshire*, ii. 473.
4 Macdonald Lockhart, *Seven Centuries*, p. 61; LEP, Folder 2: Estate and Legal Correspondence: Decree of James VII giving Sir George Lockhart the escheated estate of Sir William Nicolson of that ilk, 10 Nov. 1687; Folder 83: Estate Accounts: Accompt of Charge and Discharge, 1707–09.
5 *Extracts from the Records of the Burgh of Edinburgh, 1681 to 1689*, p. 137; H. Arnet (ed.), *Extracts from the Records of the Burgh of Edinburgh, 1689 to 1701* (Edinburgh, 1962), p. 207; SRO, SRO GD 135/2297/1–60 (Stair Papers); BL, Add. MSS 36147, ff. 312–15: Commission for Forfeited Estates case against GL's claims against the estate of the Earl of Southesk, 6 Feb. 1725.

rights of ownership of various properties and annuities purchased by his father, but there can be no doubt that with even halfway competent management Sir George's land purchases and other investments had left the Lockharts of Carnwath extremely well placed financially.[6]

Embezzlement by Lockhart of Cleghorn while acting as George's tutor, and subsequently by John Ramsay, followed by the harvest failures of the mid- to late 1690s, however, seem to have put a blight on further expansion for some time.[7] George was also caught up in the national frenzy of speculative investment in the Darien colony, personally ventured £1000 sterling (£12000 Scots) in 1696[8] and ultimately made a net loss of £425 sterling (£5100 Scots) on its collapse.[9] Consequently he did not feel confident enough of his financial situation to register a more generous jointure agreement for Euphemia until 1708, and he made no further land purchases until 1711 when he bought a house and lands at Walston. By 1713 this had boosted his rental income in Scotland by a further £7000 Scots, bringing it to a total of about £31000 Scots (*c.* £2583 sterling).[10] Of the profits from his Scottish estates, approximately £4000 Scots (*c.* £333 sterling) came from George's coalpits.[11] These were all located on the family's lands in Midlothian and though at first sight it would appear the profits from them only constituted about 13% of the family's revenue, they were in fact far more important than that. Quite possibly as much as two thirds of Lockhart's rents and dues were

6 SRO GD 135/2297/1–60: legal documents concerning pension payable by the house of Stair; LEP, Folder 2: Estate and Legal Correspondence: Minute of [Dean of Guild] James Nicolson of Trabroun vs GL, 8 July 1718; Legal decision by the Court of Session, Edinburgh, 3 Jan. 1721.

7 LEP, Folder 1: Miscellaneous Correspondence: Jo[hn] Ramsay to GL's curators, Whythill, 5 June 1695; Folder 44: Accounts, 1624–1856: Instrument, Lockhart of Cleghorn vs GL and his curators, 1 and 5 Mar. 1695; Folder(s) 96: Estate Papers 1672–1927: Declaration of the Condition of Carnwath's Tenants, Carstairs, Pettimain, Carmichell, Dunsyre, Bigger, 17, 18, 19 and 28 Jan. 1698; Whyte, *Scotland Before the Industrial Revolution*, p. 124.

8 NLS, Adv. MS. 83.1.1.: Darien Co. subscription book, p. 44: 31 Mar. 1696. N.b. the subscription is in GL's own hand and on his own behalf; there is no mention of an agent or curator.

9 Adv. MS. 83.1.6.: Darien Co. entrybook of instalments paid by shareholders, p. 20.

10 LEP, Folders(s) 97: Estate Papers: Account of Walston [1711?]; Walston Accounts, 1711/12 and 1713/14. Lockhart may also have owned some land in England at least until 1708 (I have been unable to locate where or how much), and though his estate there is not likely to have been extensive, we must therefore take the profits of his total landholdings cited here as the minimum amounts the family was taking in annually (SRO GD 18/2092/2: Sir John Clerk's spiritual journal, 9 Feb. 1708). In this context it is also worth noting that the French agent Colonel Nathaniel Hooke estimated GL's income at more than 100000 livres (£6222 sterling) a year in 1707, based on other Jacobites' reports of it (*Correspondence of Colonel N. Hooke*, ii. 369–70). I take this, however, to be more an indication of GL's reputation for great wealth than an accurate statement of his annual revenue.

11 LEP, Folder 2: Estate and Legal Correspondence: Minute of [Dean of Guild] James Nicolson of Trabroun vs GL, 8 July 1718; BL Add. MSS. 22229 (Strafford Papers), f. 7: 'The State of Mr Lockart's [George jnr's] Affairs' [1725?].

paid in kind.[12] Hence the £333 the family received from its collieries in reality made up some 37% of its Scottish cash income. In addition, the profits from coalmining were to some extent insulated from the vagaries of the weather and the harvest – a major consideration when so much of a landlord's rent was received in kind and at a time when Scottish agriculture was struggling to recover from the disasters of the 1690s.[13] Another problem associated with agriculturally based income was that arrears of rent tended to accumulate on even the most efficiently managed estates at this time because eviction *de facto* entailed the landlord writing off the arrears of those he evicted. In any case there was little guarantee that new tenants would be any better than their predecessors in paying their rent. Most landlords accordingly tried to bear with defaulting tenants for quite some time, with the result that large arrears of rent built up and were carried over from year to year. This was exactly Lockhart's case, and by 1712 the arrears were running at £23500 Scots (*c.* £1958 sterling).[14] The only extra financial input the family receieved while Lockhart was at its head came in 1706, when he received £500 (£6000 Scots) for his service as a Commissioner for the Union and between 1711 and 1713 when he was in receipt of an annual salary of £500 sterling as a Commissioner of Accounts.

Because Lockhart was arrested before he could take part in the Jacobite rebellion of 1715 the family's estates fortuitously escaped the swingeing penalties that hit many Jacobite landowners hard in the aftermath of its failure. Theoretically any property owned by Philip Lockhart, who was living with his brother in 1715 and was executed for his part in the rebellion, should have been confiscated, but as far as can be ascertained from the scanty evidence surviving from that period in the family's history, George was able to confound the Commission for Forfeited Estates' efforts to do so.[15] Nevertheless, he seems to have learned from the travails of the forfeited landowners, and before he embarked on his career as the Old Pretender's agent in Scotland he entailed his entire estate on his oldest son.[16] Such canny legal reinsurance was of a piece with Lockhart's increasingly well developed understanding of contemporary finance and associated commercial opportunities, which in part stemmed from the knowledge he gained as a Parliamentary Commissioner of Accounts from 1711 to 1713.[17] The losses he sustained by investing in the Royal Company of Scotland

12 Macdonald Lockhart, *Seven Centuries*, p. 89.
13 C. A. Whatley, *The Scottish Salt Industry 1570–1850. An Economic and Social History* (Aberdeen, 1987), pp. 73–4.
14 LEP, Folder 83: Estate Accounts: Accompts of Rents Owing, 1712.
15 LEP, Folder 2: Estate and Legal Correspondence: Account of Expenses, by John Loch W. S., Edinburgh, 20 May 1718.
16 LEP, Folders(s) 97: Estate Papers: Biggarshiels Petition of Sir Alexander Macdonald Lockhart, 18 Feb. 1807.
17 LL, p. 107: GL to Harry Maule [London], 24 June [1714]; p. 340: GL to Andrew Fletcher, Lord Milton, Dryden, 2 Nov. 1730

were never to be repeated. Thus in 1713 he (correctly) perceived that a reduction in Treasury interest rates would be bound to raise the price of land,[18] and in 1720 confided to a friend that his experience on the Commission had convinced him that a stock-market crash was 'all alongst unavoidable', and that as a consequence 'I keept myself free'.[19] Indeed, he saw to the heart of the basic economic fallacy underpinning the South Sea Company stock boom, when he described it as

> ... like a meditation on eternity, that appears the more incomprehensible the more narrowly it is canvassed. One thing is plain, the Company has no fund to pay at the rate of half a crown interest on the 100 pounds, as the stock is now sold at, nor is there, I beleive, as much species in Europe as what the stock is now screwed up to.[20]

He also percipiently predicted before the crash (when 'he was reckond more than [a] simpleton and worse than an infidell that talkd and belived after that manner'[21]): 'I doe conclude this stupendous structure will terminate in some very extraordinary event, which at present noe man can foretell, only in so far that it may come to have quite a contrary effect from what is designed by it'.[22] Thus the Lockhart of Carnwath estates once more emerged unharmed from an economic crisis that ruined or crippled the finances of many landowning families for over a generation (particularly among the Scots Whig elite) when the speculative bubble burst.[23] The upshot of which was that by the mid-1720s further judicious land purchases and improvements in their estates had raised the family's annual revenue to something in the region of £3750 sterling (£45000 Scots).[24] This was an extraordinary achievement. Many English, and many if not most Scottish, aristocrats' annual income from all sources was far less.[25] As one contemporary observed of his estate, it was, 'one of the best, perhaps, in Scotland possessed by a private gentleman'.[26] By any standard it raised the Lockharts of Carnwath to a place among the wealthiest landowners in Scotland, and indeed the British Isles.

In large part this steady improvement in the family fortunes was owing to close involvement in his estate's management by Lockhart himself. Like many

---

18 LL, p. 105: GL to Harry Maule [London], 19 June 1714.
19 LL, p. 153: GL to James Murray [Dryden?], 22 Dec. 1720.
20 LL, p. 148: GL to James Murray [Dryden?], 2 August 1720.
21 LL, p. 153: GL to James Murray [Dryden?], 22 Dec. 1720.
22 LL, p. 149.
23 J. Carswell, *The South Sea Bubble* (1961), pp. 195–9.
24 Add. MSS 22229, f. 7: 'the State of Mr Lockarts affairs' [1725].
25 G. Holmes, *The Making of a Great Power. Late Stuart and Early Georgian England 1660–1722* (1993), p. 410; D. Szechi, 'Some Insights on the Scottish M.P.s and Peers Returned in the 1710 Election', *Scottish Historical Review*, lx (1981), 62–3.
26 Patten, *History of the Rebellion*, p. 41.

of his peers among Scotland's early eighteenth-century landed elite, George took an almost professional attitude towards the management of his estates, with a view to maximising their profitability.[27] The estate's account books are accordingly full of marginalia written in his distinctive hand, which show he kept a very careful eye on the day-to-day operations of his estate steward.[28] In addition, he sought to hold his stewards to the highest possible professional standard. His first steward, William Montgomery of Mcbiehill, was one of the curators chosen by Lockhart himself in 1695, and if there was a formal contract between them it has not survived. But when Montgomery retired in 1712, George certainly imposed a written contract on his new steward, George Morison. The contract empowered Morison to act on his behalf in all the usual forms, but also required him to present legally verified accounts annually and to make up any shortfalls out of his own salary.[29] Such a clause was unusual at this time and tells us a good deal about the economic approach favoured by Lockhart. It was clearly centred on accountability and results.

He also closely supervised the operations of his colliery.[30] So much so, indeed, that in 1710, when a fire in a seam spread from a neighbour's pit to one of George's own, he personally directed efforts to put it out, and was reported to have been killed in the process.[31] His correspondence with his neighbours, the Clerks of Penicuik, is also peppered with references to plans for more efficient exploitation of the coal reserves found on his lands. In 1703 he sponsored legislation in the Scottish Parliament consolidating and extending the rights of colliery owners.[32] In 1709 he shored up old mineworkings on Clerk's lands the better to keep his own mines working close to Bilston Burn. In 1719 he established a 'horse gang' to pump the water from new pits he was developing. And in 1730, with a view to tapping his neighbour for a contribution to pumping operations that incidentally favoured him, George proposed a profit-sharing scheme with regard to certain of Baron Sir John Clerk's collieries.[33] In the larger perspective George's management style and thoroughly commercial attitude towards his estates evoke comparison with the stereotypical tough, capitalist businessmen who were to be the cutting edge of the industrial revolution.

Lockhart displayed his hard-nosed approach to the running of the family estates from the outset of his involvement in their management. Soon after he

27 Campbell, *Scotland Since 1707*, p. 33.
28 LEP, Folder 83: Estate Accounts: passim.
29 LEP, Folder(s) 96: Estate Papers 1672–1927: George Morison's Contract, 1712.
30 SRO GD 18/1671/5: GL to Sir John Clerk, Edinburgh, 17 Nov. 1709
31 SRO GD 18/2092/3: Sir John Clerk's spiritual journal for 1710-Apr. 1712, 27, 28 and 30 Mar. 1710.
32 SRO GD 18/1018: Baron John Clerk to Sir John Clerk, Edinburgh, 7 July 1703.
33 SRO GD 18/1031: GL to Sir John Clerk, Dryden, 15 July 1709; SRO GD 18/1388: GL to Baron Sir John Clerk, Dryden, 6 June 1719; SRO GD 18/1058: draught letter, Clerk to Lord Garlies, 12 Mar. 1730.

and Euphemia took up residence at Dryden the Clerks of Penicuik were not amused to find Lockhart's colliers dumping spoil in their temporarily abandoned workings, storing coal on Clerk lands, using their coal roads to transport Lockhart coal without permission (and indeed in the face of Sir John Clerk's express refusal of it) and working coal on land whose mineral rights were owned by the Nicolson family.[34] In addition, despite having signed a solemn obligement that he would not detain colliers loaned to him by the Clerks if they requested their return, Lockhart in 1701 tried to hang onto mineworkers whom Sir John had asked be returned to work for him, claimed his grieves had only made verbal agreements that did not bind him, and threatened to sue if Sir John did not release the workers.[35] The Clerks were so incensed they not only took George to court, but contemplated securing an act of the Scottish Parliament to prevent the like sharp practice in the future.[36] The President of the Court of Session eventually found in the Clerks' favour, but Lockhart continued to refuse to admit any responsibility – instead casting any blame on his servants – and they were still waiting for him to pay the cost of cleaning up their coalpits seventeen years later.[37] In another indicative incident, in 1704 George absolutely refused to be browbeaten by the Duke of Montrose over a prize coach-horse Montrose had asked to purchase. Lockhart wanted a minimum of thirty guineas and demanded the horse back if Montrose continued to quibble over the price.[38] By 1709 George's neighbours had learned to keep a close eye on his mineworkings and other activities, and were responding immediately to the slightest hint of encroachment on their property rights.[39]

Nor was he any gentler with his own people. The period 1696–98 in Scotland was characterised by dearth and famine. Over ten per cent of Scotland's population are estimated to have emigrated or died as a result of successive bad harvests.[40] And George's tenants in Lanarkshire did not escape unscathed. In 1698 the ministers of the Presbyteries of Lanark and Biggar petitioned on behalf of his tenants for a reduction in rent payments.[41] Lockhart was willing to acquiesce in this, but his reasoning is revealing:

---

34 SRO GD 18/1671/3): statement of grievances against GL by Sir John Clerk, Aug. 1701.
35 SRO GD 18/1013: Obligement by GL to Sir John Clerk, Dryden, 7 Nov. 1700; SRO GD 18/1014/1–4: Sir John Clerk to John Clerk, Penicuik, 8 Nov. 1701.
36 SRO GD 18/1018: draught bill to be introduced by Baron John Clerk governing coalmines, 1703 and same to Sir John Clerk, Edinburgh, 7 July 1703.
37 SRO GD 18/1671/4: GL to Sir John, Dryden, 28 Jan. 1708; SRO GD 18/1671/8: Sir John's Claim versus GL, Court of Session, 8 Aug. 1718.
38 LL, pp. 4–5: GL to Mungo Graham of Gorthie, Dryden, 13, 14 and 15 Sept. 1704.
39 SRO GD 18/1671/5: GL to Sir John, Edinburgh, 17 Nov. 1709.
40 M. Flinn (ed.), *Scottish Population History from the 17th century to the 1930s* (Cambridge, 1977), pp. 13, 58, 242; Whyte, *Scotland Before the Industrial Revolution*, pp. 124–5.
41 LEP, Folder(s) 96: Estate Papers 1672–1927: Declaration of the Condition of Carnwath's Tenants, Carstairs, Pettimain, Carmichell, Dunsyre, Bigger, 17, 18, 19 and 28 Jan. 1698.

I realise the truth of their complaint and that the state of my tenants is such that without an abatement most of them will not be able to continue their holdings, and so will embezzle everything they can lay hands on which should go towards the payment of their rent, for they will be without any hope of ever getting it all paid off. Whereby I shall be a far greater loser than I would be if I gave them sufficient abatement to encourage them to set to work again with some hope that they'll be able to live under me on their holdings. Besides, it may be that the law would allow them more than I propose to give them. Therefore I desire the consent of your Lordship and of Mr Montgomery to grant to my tenants an abatement of half their rent for the year 1696, as others have done before me, seeing its against all equity that when the ground fails to produce its increase some consideration should not be given to those who work it. When they have got this abatement they will still be losers, but all their losses can be made up.[42]

Such an unsentimental, and distinctly unpaternalistic, approach to his 'people' was to be characteristic of George's dealings with them throughout his life. Thus he was, for example, quite ruthless in prosecuting his rights as a landowner and coalmaster. Until 1799 possibly as many as half the coalminers in Scotland were technically enserfed, in that they were legally bound to work for the colliery owner in whose pit they first accepted employment.[43] Nonetheless, because coal-mining was so profitable, and skilled miners in such short supply, more than one colliery owner was willing to wink at runaways moving into his workforce and offer lucrative fringe benefits calculated to attract and keep them there.[44] As the Clerks discovered, George was not averse to poaching other mineowners' workers himself. With regard to his own workforce, however, Lockhart took a very different attitude. His coalpits were deep and even George was prepared to admit that work in them was 'severe' compared with conditions in neighbouring collieries. In 1723 when one of his coalbearers, whom he had graciously allowed to work in Baron Sir John Clerk's pits because she was 'young and weak', got close to establishing her right to work for the Clerks instead, he peremptorily demanded her return and was incensed by the refusal of the Clerks' overseers to cooperate.[45] Likewise when his colliers sought to escape his juris-diction by flight Lockhart was quite prepared to go to the trouble and expense of advertising in the newspapers and offering rewards for their apprehension. Nor did he shrink from threatening legal action against any of his neighbours

42 LL, pp. 1–2: GL to Sir James Scougall, Lord Whitehill of the Court of Session, Edinburgh, Feb. 1698.

43 I am grateful to Chris Whatley for this information.

44 C. Whatley, '"The Fettering Bonds of Brotherhood": Combination and Labour Relations in the Scottish Coal-Mining Industry c. 1690–1775', *Social History*, 12 (1987), pp. 139–54.

45 LL, pp. 191–2: GL to Baron Sir John Clerk, Dryden, 13 May 1723.

who sheltered them and pursuing them at law as far away as Ayrshire.[46] In the same vein, George believed in extracting every last ounce of his due as a landowner. In 1723, for example, he showed no compunction about working up a petition from the local colliery owners to the Midlothian Commission of the Peace to get the local highways repaired under recent legislation that required his tenants to work without pay on such public works projects for six days a year 'for indeed if the highwayes be not repaird you and I need expect few carts next winter at our coall hills'.[47]

George was also a classic example of the improving landlord. As with many of his peers his first essay in this direction seems to have been the modernisation and emparking of his main residence.[48] Dryden was virtually rebuilt in the style of Hamilton Palace and Melville House by James Smith,[49] one of the foremost (and most expensive) architects of his day and by the time it was completed required the services of a well-paid full-time gardener and – if the numbers employed in the late eighteenth century are a good guide – an army of at least 43 servants.[50] Either the expense or the experience of remodeling his home and its immediate environs then seem to have encouraged Lockhart to undertake a more general programme of agricultural improvement. Either George or his curators had been sufficiently interested in the prospect of enhancing his revenues to secure a charter in 1695 for a fair to be held twice yearly at Carnwath (which kept going until at least the 1720s), but there matters remained for over a decade.[51] From 1706, however, when he secured an Act of Parliament giving him permission to move a public highway that would obstruct his enclosure of Anston, the process of improvement took flight, and by the 1720s he was seeking to enclose any property in which he held an interest – even where doing so violated other people's property rights.[52] Lockhart's approach was thorough

46 Edinburgh City Library, YAN E23 EC, *Edinburgh Evening Courant*, Number 93: 14 July–16 July, 1719, p. 458 and Number 94: 16–20 July, 1719: p. 564; C. A. Whatley, 'The Finest Place for a Lasting Colliery. Coal Mining Enterprise in Ayrshire c. 1600–1840', *Ayrshire Collections*, xiv (1983) 83.

47 LL, p. 185: GL to Baron Sir John Clerk, Dryden, 18 Feb. 1723. See also, SRO GD 18/1389: same to same, Dryden, 31 Oct. 1726.

48 LL, p. 53: GL to Sir John Clerk, Essex House, 6 Dec. 1711.

49 J. Macauley, *The Classical Country House in Scotland* (1787), p. 53. I am indebted to Howard Colvin of St John's College, Oxford, for this reference and his invaluable help in tracking down the details of Dryden's design and construction.

50 Macdonald Lockhart, *Seven Centuries*, p. 95; LEP, Folder(s) 96: Estate Papers 1672–1927: list of servants and their wages, late eighteenth century.

51 LEP, Personal Documents 33: Charters and Commissions: charter for a twice-yearly fair at Carnwath, Edinburgh, 17 July 1695; LL, p. 161: GL to Harry Maule, Carnwath, 17 May 1721.

52 *APS*, xi. 336: 26 Nov. 1706; SRO GD 18/1363: petition by GL and Baron Sir John Clerk to the Court of Session, 17 Nov. 1721; SRO GD 1/1155/78/4, 6: GL to John Chancellor of Shieldhill, Dryden, 26 Sept. 1726 and 23 Aug. 1729; LEP, Folder 35: Papers Concerning Teinds: Interlocutor's Report, Edinburgh, 16 Dec. 1732.

and unsentimental. He systematically evicted tenants who had run up substantial arrears in order to take their tenancies under his direct control. The vacant tenancies were then combined to create larger farms so as properly to round out the enclosure, dykes and fences were erected, the runrigs erased and the land improved by marling and pasturing cattle on it for a number of years. It was then let out at a substantially higher rent to new, doubtless carefully selected, tenants.[53] In addition, George began planting orchards and afforesting suitable land on his estates and established something of a reputation as a pioneer in new techniques of raising and fattening cattle.[54] The steady rise in the family's rental income and its regular, profitable, involvement in one of post-Union Scotland's more successful industries, the production and export of live cattle to England, clearly underpinned its rising prosperity.[55]

Nor did agricultural innovations exhaust Lockhart's zeal for improvement. Almost inevitably, given his evident interest in improvement of all kinds and his manifest desire to maximise the output of his coalpits, he was one of the first colliery owners in Scotland to introduce a steam engine to pump the water out of his mines. Unfortunately no records of the type, purchase or maintenance of the engine survive, though in all likelihood it was a Newcomen similar to that installed at Stevenston in Ayrshire in 1719 by a consortium which included George's father-in-law Eglinton.[56] In any event, the Swedish agent Henry Kalmeter was highly impressed by the machine, which apparently could draw up water from a depth of 180 feet, and from the early 1720s onwards Lockhart's correspondence on the subject of his coalmines revolves around the establishment of communicating passages and other techniques designed to make best use of his engine.[57]

There was, though, a hidden price to pay for Lockhart's determination to wring the maximum profit out of his estates. His tenants and miners do not seem to have been very happy about his enthusiasm for improvements that cut back on their customary rights, and he faced growing, albeit intermittant, opposition from them, including fence-breaking and attacks on his forests, all of

53 Macdonald Lockhart, *Seven Centuries*, pp. 85–6, 88–9, 91–2, 97.

54 LL, pp. 52–3, 190: GL to Sir John Clerk and Baron Sir John Clerk, 1 Nov. and 6 Dec. 1711 and c. Apr. [1723]; *Miscellany of the Spalding Club, Volume Second* (Aberdeen, 1842): 'Papers From the Charter Chest at Monymusk', p. 99.

55 T. C. Smout, 'Where had the Scottish Economy got to by the Third Quarter of the Eighteenth Century', in I. Hont and M. Ignatieff (eds), *Wealth and Virtue. The Shaping of Political Economy in the Scottish Enlightenment* (1983), pp. 54–5.

56 C. A. Whatley, 'The Introduction of the Newcomen Engine to Ayrshire', *Industrial Archeology Review*, ii (1977), 69–74. I am indebted to Chris Whatley for this reference.

57 'Journal of Henry Kalmeter', p. 48; LL, pp. 189–90: GL to Baron Sir John Clerk, Dryden, 30 Mar. 1723; SRO GD 18/1058: draught letter, Baron Sir John Clerk to Lord Garlies, 12 Mar. 1730.

which he sought to punish severely.[58] For while by strict economic standards Lockhart was a highly successful landowner, socially he was not. He built upon the strong foundations laid by his father to make the Lockharts of Carnwath a very wealthy family. His estates were run according to the most modern precepts of efficiency and were some of the most agriculturally 'improved' in early eighteenth-century Scotland.[59] His coalmines employed the latest technology and techniques. In these areas there can be no doubt that George was ahead of his time. The problem was that almost all his gains were at the expense of the customary relationship between landlord and tenant. He disrupted the moral economy of landlord-tenant relations wherever and whenever he deemed it to his advantage, while simultaneously exploiting all his own legal rights. Here too Lockhart may have been ahead of his time, but the consequences were not so happy. And it is to his social relations and milieu that we must now turn.

58　See for example, LL, pp. 203–5 and 218–19: GL to Baron Sir John Clerk, Dryden, 28 Oct. 1723 and 1724[?]. The Clerks of Penicuik were facing similar problems with their workforce, though probably not to the same extent as the Lockharts, for which see R. Houston, 'Coal, Class and Culture: Labour Relations in a Scottish Mining Community, 1650–1750', *Social History*, viii (1983), pp. 1–17.

59　Campbell, *Scotland Since 1707*, pp. 28–35.

CHAPTER THREE

Social Context

Seventeenth- and early eighteenth-century Lowland Scotland was a society of orders. Contemporary Scots men and women conceived of it as a multi-level pyramid with rigid boundaries between the different levels. Atop the pyramid was the monarch, then came the nobility, and so on down to the humblest landless labourer or vagabond in a fermtoun.[1] It was a model of society that reflected the general belief in the virtues of stasis.

Such was the theory of society. In practice some categories and levels *de facto* merged while others' theoretical placement within the hierarchy bore little relation to their status or the esteem other categories held them in. The difference between farm servants and landless labourers, for example, tended to be temporal rather than permanent because many children of poor families passed through service to 'independence' as cottars and labourers, and the poverty of the 'bonnet' lairds definitely affected the way other elite groups perceived them. The net effect was to create two overarching groups: landowners and non-landowners. The 'heritors' who owned the land enjoyed social authority by dint of the power this gave them over their tenants and their tenants' sub-tenants, cottars, labourers and servants.[2] Within each of these groups there was a certain amount of jockeying for status and position (particularly at the level of the heritors), but by far the most important social dynamic was the relationship between the two groups. This was based to a large extent on a mutual reciprocity. In return for the generic exercise of paternalism on the part of the heritors the tenants *et al* would treat their social superiors with overt deference.[3] Paternalism was construed as covering everything from direct charity to intervention in the market in times of dearth to ensure that the lower orders could afford to buy food. Deference ranged from doffing one's bonnet before a social superior to sending a son to enlist in a heritor's regiment if one's family happened to live on his lands. The relationship was further arbitrated by a moral economy very similar in its operation to that described by E. P. Thompson in England, in which customary prices and customary privileges were usually more important than supply and demand and the law.[4] And if a heritor was felt to be failing in his duty to be paternalistic, or otherwise violating the reciprocity of relations between

1 Smout, *History of the Scottish People*, pp. 123–43, 148, 262–4, 282–7; C. Larner, *Enemies of God. The Witch-hunt in Scotland* (Oxford, 1981), pp. 42–51.
2 Larner, *Enemies of God*, pp. 44–5; Whyte, *Scotland Before the Industrial Revolution*, pp. 152, 155.
3 Whyte, *Scotland Before the Industrial Revolution*, pp. 153, 161.
4 E. P. Thompson, *Customs in Common* (New York, 1991), pp. 185–258.

landowners and tenants of all kinds, he would become subject to direct action on the part of the non-landowners to assert their 'rights'.

In England direct action often meant riots (though these were normally vituperative rather than violent), fence-breaking or even arson.[5] In Lowland Scotland, where the social dynamics were akin to those prevailing in England, the commons seem to have been somewhat less prone to riot (conversely the Scottish elite may have been more mindful of their social duty[6]), but still willing and able to signal their disapproval of a given heritor's behaviour by covert attacks on his property.[7] The Scottish Gaeltacht, which was still a society organised for war in the period 1680–1730, had its own unique social dynamics which need not concern us here.[8]

In this period, too, the constituent groups composing the heritor category in Scotland were subject to a chronic undertow of tension between themselves. The lairds resented the arrogance of the nobility, the urban merchant elite periodically found themselves in conflict with the rural heritors, and depressed groups among the landowners, such as demobbed army officers and bonnet lairds resented the airs and graces of their more economically fortunate peers.[9] Most of the time these grievances were expressed on an individual, personal basis, but they could on occasion find common public expression by the aggrieved group. Usually, however, the patriarchs of families within the various sub-categories of heritors were principally concerned with dynastic aggrandisement. The pinnacle of heritor social achievement was promotion to (or within) the peerage,[10] and building up the connections and landed base necessary to achieve this – or otherwise enhance the family's power and status relative to its peers – was correspondingly the principal focus for their activities.[11]

Which brings us back to the Lockharts of Carnwath. Lairds who sought to

---

5 J. Stevenson, *Popular Disturbances in England 1700–1832* (2nd edn, 1992), pp. 45–68.

6 W. H. Fraser, 'Patterns of Protest', in, T. M. Devine and R. Mitchison (eds), *People and Society in Scotland I. 1760–1830* (Edinburgh, 1988), pp. 73–7.

7 Whyte, *Scotland Before the Industrial Revolution*, pp. 221–3; C. Whatley, 'An Uninflammable People?', in, I. Donnachie and C. Whatley (eds), *The Manufacture of Scottish History* (Edinburgh, 1992), pp. 55–71.

8 Smout, *History of the Scottish People*, pp. 313–20; A. I. Macinnes, *Clanship, Commerce and the House of Stuart, 1603–1788* (East Linton, 1996), pp. 1–24.

9 SRO GD 18/2092/2: Sir John Clerk's spiritual journal for 1699–1709, 14 Mar. 1704; LP i. 123: clause II of Fletcher of Saltoun's proposed reform of the Scottish constitution; W. Ferguson, *Scotland's Relations with England: a Survey to 1707* (Edinburgh, 1977), p. 221; C. Kidd, *Subverting Scotland's Past. Scottish Whig Historians and the Creation of an Anglo-British Identity, 1689-c. 1830* (Cambridge, 1993), pp. 169–76; Lenman, *Jacobite Risings*, pp. 39–43; Edinburgh City Library, YAN E17, *Edinburgh Eccho/Edinburgh Weekly Journal*, no. LIV. 14 Jan. 1730, p. 2016.

10 Though it should be noted there were exceptions to this such as Sir John Clerk of Penicuik, who refused a peerage in 1703 (SRO GD 18/2092/2: Sir John Clerk's spiritual journal for 1699–1709, 14 Mar. 1704).

11 Smout, *History of the Scottish People*, pp. 264–5.

move into the nobility usually had to pass through a period of purdah and only became fully accepted by their new social peers in the second or third generation after the initial transition.[12] Raising the family's status to the point where it could seek ennoblement was also difficult. The accumulation of a sufficient body of property to support the dignity of the rank was a *sine qua non*, but it was not in itself sufficient to secure elevation to the peerage. The monarchy, in deference to the aristocratic culture of which it was a part, was generally loth to 'cheapen' the value of a peerage and consequently only created new peers in any numbers in response to special circumstances and emergencies. The greatest expansions of the nobility had thus taken place around the turn of the sixteenth century and during the mid-seventeenth century. In the first instance James VI and I was trying to create a pan-British nobility and keep the social elite sweet on both sides of the border while the Union of Crowns took root. In the second, Charles I and Charles II were buying support for the royalist cause at a time of crisis. Hence the supply of new admissions to the peerage progressively dried up after 1660.[13] This of course stimulated those desiring ennoblement to strive still harder for the few that could still be coaxed out of the monarchy, principally by competing for royal favour.

In such circumstances there can be no doubt it was a distinct advantage to be a good lawyer. Most of the few promotions of commoners to the peerage that were still occurring were going to successful lawyers with pre-existing aristocratic connections, men like James Ogilvy, 1st Earl of Seafield and Sir John Dalrymple, 1st Earl of Stair.[14] Once he had been received back into royal favour in 1677, therefore, Sir George began to be well placed to attract this final seal of royal approval. His marriage to a woman descended from a long-established English noble family (albeit one that was out of favour) further improved his prospects, and his rise to the Presidency of the Court of Session made them still stronger.[15] All Sir George's efforts to advance the family socially came to naught, however, when James VII and II was overthrown in 1688. He was theoretically still well placed to ingratiate himself with the new order, but of course any hope of exploiting William III's need for support from the servants of the old regime to advance the family was negated by Sir George's murder.

Any further plans to advance the family socially had of necessity to be put on hold until Lockhart came of age, but the groundwork laid by Sir George and the Wharton connection continued to offer the prospect of such advancement in due course. The Wharton connection was doing very well in the politics of post-Revolutionary England, Barbara Lockhart's marriage to a son of Lord

12 Whyte, *Scotland Before the Industrial Revolution*, p. 157.
13 J. Cannon, *Aristocratic Century. The Peerage of Eighteenth-Century England* (1987), pp. 13–14, 20.
14 *DNB*, xiii. 415–20; xlii. 29–31.
15 Cannon, *Aristocratic Century*, p. 30.

Carmichael (the future Earl of Hyndford) established a new connection with a very successful dynasty of post-Revolution Scottish politicians, and Lockhart's own boyhood relationship with the ducal house of Argyll all augured well for the family's future promotion. His marriage to Euphemia also linked the Lock-harts of Carnwath to other noble houses into which her siblings had married (such as the Earls of Galloway), directly connected George to a nobleman who had made himself useful to the controllers of the new order and immediately increased the famiy's social significance amongst the Scottish elite.[16]

When he came of age, in 1702, George was thus quite well placed to resume the social advancement of his family. And, indeed, his connections gave him a flying start. Despite his youth he was elected Commissioner for the premier seat among the estate of barons in the Scottish Parliament (Midlothian) in 1703, and shortly thereafter appointed to the Scottish Privy Council.[17] What-ifs are always dangerous ground for historians to explore, but it does seem likely that if Lockhart had been willing to keep his mouth shut and obediently vote with the Court party in the turbulent years leading up to the Union, he would have stood a very good chance of being taken into government office and eventually receiving a baronetcy or even a peerage.[18] In a letter to Robert Harley in 1711 he certainly claimed that his adherence to Cavalier/Tory principles had 'disso-blidged some of my nearest freinds, who both coud and woud have done for me, woud I have enterd into ther measures'.[19] The fact that he did not compromise his principles on this score offers us a silent, but significant, insight into his character. In dynastic terms, however, his alignment with the opposition to the Court between 1703 and 1707 was a disaster. By committing himself to the political wilderness of Scottish patriotism and Jacobitism George doomed the Lockharts of Carnwath to, at best, maintaining their status rather than advancing it. Hence his oldest son was able to make a good match from a financial point of view by marrying a social equal (Fergusia Wishart, sole heiress of Sir George Wishart of Clifton Hall), but was previously unable successfully to negotiate a match with either Lady Anne Cochrane or a daughter of the Duke of Queensberry.[20] Likewise Lockhart's daughters Grace and Euphemia junior were able to marry into the peerage, to the Earls of Wigton and Aboyne respectively, but only into the impoverished, Jacobite (and in both cases possibly

16 SRO GD 18/2092/2: Sir John Clerk's spiritual journal for 1699–1709, 28 Feb. 1699.
17 *Parliaments of Scotland*, ii. 433.
18 In the dedication to GL that prefaces the patriotic author Patrick Abercromby's, *The Martial Achievements of the Scottish Nation* (2 vols, Edinburgh, 1711/15), Abercromby hints that he had received such offers (ii. v).
19 LL, p. 44: GL to Harley, 6 Jan. 1711.
20 SRO GD 45/14/220/120: Margaret, Countess of Panmure, to the Earl of Panmure, Edinburgh, 27 Feb. 1721; SRO GD 18/5337/4: Earl of Glasgow to Baron Sir John Clerk, Kelburn, 25 Jan. 1724.

crypto-catholic) peerage.[21] It is correspondingly interesting to note that George was nominated for a Jacobite shadow peerage in 1713 and his grandson, James Lockhart, was created a Count of the Holy Roman Empire in 1783 in large part for his long career in Habsburg military service, but also for the 'ancient noble lineage', which qualified him to be an Imperial Chamberlain.[22]

In the day-to-day interplay of social relations between members of the landowning class, Lockhart was nonetheless fairly successful throughout his life. Like Andrew Fletcher of Saltoun and other lairds he was critical of the nobility, but despite this and his tendency to ruthlessness in the conduct of his business affairs, he seems to have had more than sufficient social grace to be able to overcome the ill-will he created by such behaviour and his notorious Jacobitism and get on well with all levels of the social elite.[23] A major component of his social success was undoubtedly his convivial involvement in two activities beloved of the nobility and gentry throughout the British Isles: hunting and horse-racing. George (like his son after him) was a keen hunter who kept his own pack of twenty hounds, and by 1707 he had already converted part of his estate at Carnwath into a racecourse.[24] By the 1720s he was racing his horses against all comers at meetings near Leith, and shortly after his death one of his horses won the annual silver plate race there.[25] Lockhart also seems to have been a master of the little, convivial gesture which was the everyday cement of elite relationships. In 1711, for example, he passed on some appletree saplings he had picked up for a song in England to his much put-upon neighbours the Clerks of Penicuik. In 1723 he made a further gift of several thousand alder saplings.[26] The upshot of these and other courtesies was that even after having had to deal with him for over thirty years Baron Sir John Clerk could observe: '... I shall be glad at all times to accomodate Carnwath in every thing that one good neighbour can expect from another'.[27] Correspondingly, to the very end of his life, Lockhart's friends included catholics, protestants, Whigs, Tories and Jacobites. This was extremely fortunate for him on several occasions, and never more so than when he was in danger of being arrested in 1727. According to Lockhart, Islay (his

21 *Scots Peerage*, i. 103–4; viii. 554; Blairs Letters 2/241/3: Bernard Baillie to William Stuart, Ratisbon, 10 July 1722 ns.

22 Blairs Letters 2/181/16: James Carnegy to Thomas Innes, 'Quelbeuf', 4 Nov. 1713 ns; Macdonald Lockhart, *Seven Centuries*, p. 259.

23 LP i. 298.

24 *Correspondence of Colonel N. Hooke*, ii. 230–1: GL to Patrick Lyon of Auchterhouse, Dryden, 30 Apr. 1707; SRO GD 18/5246/6/2: Lord Garlies to Baron John Clerk, Dryden, 1 Oct. 1718; Macdonald Lockhart, *Seven Centuries*, p. 179.

25 *Eccho/Edinburgh Weekly Journal*, no. II: 17 Jan. 1729, p. 8; no. XXXIV: 'Scoto-Germanicus', 27 Aug. 1729, pp. 127–8; *Caledonian Mercury*, no. 9417: 21 Dec. 1731.

26 LL, p. 52: GL to Sir John Clerk, London, 1 Nov. 1711; p. 190: same to same [Dryden, Apr. 1723].

27 SRO GD 18/1058: draught letter, Baron Sir John Clerk to Lord Garlies, 12 Mar. 1730.

friend from childhood, and by this time virtually Walpole's minister for Scotland)
instructed Andrew Fletcher of Saltoun, Lord Milton of the Court of Session
(Islay's *sous ministre* and nephew of the patriot, with whom Lockhart was also on
good terms), to despatch the King's Messenger designated to seize George's
courier John Corsar first, so that George would thereby receive a timely warning
and get away before a Messenger was despatched to arrest him.[28] The Solicitor-General, Charles Erskine of Tinwald, and James Erskine of Grange, Lord
Justice Clerk, also secretly sent Lockhart notice that he was about to be seized.[29]
Once he had escaped to the Continent, the Campbell brothers and another
friend, Duncan Forbes of Culloden, the Lord Advocate, successfully interceded
on George's behalf to secure him permission to return home.[30]

   In contrast to his social success with his peers (at least with those who were
not his neighbours), Lockhart's relations with his social inferiors were very poor.
Obviously, his 'capitalist' approach to estate management was not calculated to
endear him to his colliers, servants and tenants (though he still expected to
receive their respect and deference[31]), and consequently by 1710 (if not earlier)
he was facing the customary forms of Lowland plebeian resistance. When, in
1710, he used his rights as a prominent heritor of Lasswade parish to arrange
for the call of a new minister to whom the local people were averse, there was
a near-riot as the ordinary parishioners 'evidenced by their exclamations ... and
by their lamentations', against him and his allies; and some threatened to attack
him physically.[32] His colliers, who had valuable skills to trade, could decamp to
better employers, and by 1719 George had been sufficiently vexed by the problem
to go to the expense of advertising threats of punishment in the Edinburgh press
and offering rewards for information to recover one runaway collier and his
family.[33] Lockhart's agricultural tenants could not so easily escape and instead
had recourse to nocturnal raids on his property. His afforestation of large tracts
of land seems to have been particularly resented, and attacks on his plantations,
like the flight of his colliers, exasperated him so much that by 1721 he was
advertising rewards for the apprehension of raiders and threatening collective
punishment of all the local inhabitants if they were not discovered:

   WHEREAS, on Monday the 8th of May at Night, two Men, one whereof with
   a Hat, and without Stockens and Shoes, and the other in a common Country
   Dress, were seen cutting Trees in Mr Lockhart of Carnwath's Woods on the

28 J. S. Shaw, *The Management of Scottish Society 1707–1764. Power, Nobles, Lawyers, Edinburgh Agents
    and English Influences* (Edinburgh, 1983), pp. 86–7, 147–8; LP ii. 332; LL, p. 341: GL to
    Milton, Dryden, 15 May 1731.
29 LL, p. 308: GL to the Old Pretender, Brussels, 20 May 1727 ns.
30 LP ii. 396.
31 LP ii. 434.
32 SRO GD 18/2092/3: Sir John Clerk's spiritual journal for 1710-Apr. 1712, 26 Sept. 1710.
33 Edinburgh City Library, YAN E23 EC: *Edinburgh Courant*, no. 93, 14–16 July 1719, p. 458.

River Esk, in the Parish of Lasswade, and being pursued after having wade the Water, into which one of them fell, and was wet. These are promising a Reward of two Guineas, to any who will discover the said Persons, so as they or any of them may be convicted, and if any one of the said Persons will discover the other, he shall not only have the said Reward, but likewise be pardoned, as to his Part of the Crime; and Notice is hereby given, that unless the said Persons are discovered, Mr Lockhart is resolved to pursue the neighbouring Villages, in the Terms of the late Act of Parliament, which imposes a Fine on such, where Woods are cut; so that all the Neighbourhood are for their own Sakes concerned to endeavour a Discovery of the Authors.[34]

Nor was he making an idle threat. Lockhart's response to another example of such insubordination, a fence-breaking incident in which some confiscated cattle were retrieved by their owners in 1723, well illustrates the distinct tone of class hostility that coloured his relations with his social inferiors:

I have seen so much prevaricating amongst countrie people on the like occasions, that I doubt not but John Hunter has taken such precautions, that he will venture to swear, depending upon some Jesuiticall equivocation or another, but as it's certain some body or other is guilty, by examining the neighbourhead perhaps the sadle may be laid on the right horse. And in order therto I propose to summon all the men in Lonehead and Broughlie, as also in Roslins and my part of Roslin and oblige them to depone if they or any by their directions and councill were concernd in down the said dike and taking out the ox. [I] Suppose I shoud not [i.e. will not] find out the truth, yet such a proceeding will probably scare others from such future practices.[35]

As he observed in other circumstances, George did not 'much care for rables'.[36]

Doubtless most improving landlords in early eighteenth-century Scotland also faced popular disapproval on occasion. What made it such a problem was Lockhart's special need for local support. Lowland Scotland south of the Tay was overwhelmingly presbyterian in the early eighteenth century.[37] Lockhart was a staunch episcopalian from at least 1703. This meant that his household was an episcopalian enclave in a sea of presbyterianism, particularly at Carnwath. Traditionally, the best source of recruits for a rebellion in which a laird participated would have been his tenants. Lockhart's religious persuasion intrinsically militated against such a customary response on their part. Moreover,

34 *Edinburgh Courant*, no. 378: 9–11 May 1721, pp. 3541–2.
35 LL, p. 204: GL to Baron Sir John Clerk, Dryden, 28 Oct. 1723.
36 LL, p. 17: GL to Hamilton, Dryden, 12 Apr. 1705.
37 Ferguson, *Scotland*, p. 103; Lenman, 'Scottish Episcopal Clergy', pp. 39–40.

he deliberately chose not to reside in what should have been the heartland of his power and authority, Carnwath, and made little effort to cultivate his people's goodwill there or anywhere else on his estates.[38] To take one example: despite the fact that Lockhart must have known beforehand that the devout presbyterianism of his tenants at Carnwath and Dunsyre would dispose them to be hostile to any minister of the Kirk willing to take the abjuration oath imposed on all clerics in Scotland in 1712 and to pray for the House of Hanover in the terms laid down by the act, he deliberately chose conformists to serve in both Kirks. At Dunsyre there were active attempts to resist the imposition of the new minister, and in a show of collective defiance at Carnwath Lockhart's tenants walked out of the Kirk and sent a delegation to tell him they would not hear his appointee.[39] The upshot of his poor relations with his tenants was a distinct lack of enthusiasm for the laird's cause amongst the common people on Lockhart's lands. The forces his brother Philip led off to join Kenmuir's rising in the lowlands in 1715 are recorded as being a 'troop' of horse, i.e. theoretically a body of about 43 men.[40] Had he raised forty-three men this would still have been a rather small force for a heritor of George's wealth and power, but in reality the Carnwath troop probably numbered a mere nineteen.[41] Since Lockhart had been preparing for a rising for months, this makes the turn-out amongst his 'people' almost derisory. This impression is further reinforced by the fact that few of the troopers were actually George's tenants; most of them were servants recruited from among the demobilised veterans of the War of the Spanish Succession.[42] Clearly Lockhart did not expect the laird's call to arms to produce any significant response from his own people.[43] Moreover, poor relations between the Lockharts of Carnwath and their tenantry seem to have persisted long after his death. In 1745 not only did George's grandson (another George) have to ride alone to join Charles Edward Stuart's rebellion (though his father may have been present with him at Prestonpans), the family's tenants actively opposed the rising and a mob of them even sought

38 C. A. Malcolm (ed.), *The Minutes of the Justices of the Peace for Lanarkshire, 1707–1723* (Edinburgh, Scottish History Society, 3rd Ser., 1931), p. 131: Lanark Quarter-Session, 7 Aug. 1711.

39 LL, p. 60: GL to the Duke of Hamilton, Dryden, 23 Oct. 1712; T. N. Clarke, 'The Scottish Episcopalians 1688–1720' (unpublished Edinburgh Ph.D thesis, 1987), p. 330. Lockhart had used his influence with the Oxford ministry to persuade them to appoint James Bradfoot at Dunsyre, where the living was in the gift of the crown.

40 LP i. 493; D. Chandler, *The Art of Warfare in the Age of Marlborough* (1976), p. 46.

41 SRO GD 18/2092/4: Sir John Clerk's spiritual journal for Apr. 1712–1715, 13 Oct. 1715. By contrast, according to Sir John (20 Sept. 1715), on 29 August the episcopalian, possibly even crypto-catholic, Earl of Winton was able to proclaim the Old Pretender at the head of 200 of his colliers and tenants.

42 LL, p. 126; Patten, *History of the Rebellion*, p. 41; HMC, *Various Collections*, i (Berwick on Tweed Corporation), p. 21: examination of Alexander Fleming, 28 Jan. 17[16].

43 LP i. 487.

to take the young laird prisoner when he briefly returned to Carnwath after the débâcle at Culloden.[44] The devout presbyterianism of the inhabitants of Carnwath doubtless had much to do with their opposition to Jacobite adventures. Nonetheless, it seems fair to surmise that they would not have been so actively hostile to the Jacobite cause if the laird had been more popular.

44 Macdonald Lockhart, *Seven Centuries*, pp. 225, 230–1.

CHAPTER FOUR

Early Years, 1703–1708

Lockhart's formal political career began in 1702 when he was elected for Midlothian to the first (and only) Parliament of Queen Anne's reign in Scotland while it was still nominally an independent kingdom. Scotland had been joined with England in a Union of Crowns since 1603, when James VI and I inherited the English throne on the death of Elizabeth I. Theoretically both kingdoms remained sovereign states, but in practice English politicians and English measures inevitably dominated the conduct of government throughout the British Isles. In large part this stemmed from the fact that England's population and economy far outweighed those of Scotland and Ireland, yet almost as important was the Anglicisation of the royal house. The Stuarts' Scottishness terminated with James VI and I; all of his successors approached Scotland and its problems from an English perspective. Hence as the seventeenth century went on, Scottish politics and politicians adapted themselves to fit the new reality. Since power in Scotland flowed from favour and influence at Whitehall, the 'great men' and magnates of Scottish politics (such as the Earl of Lauderdale, the Duke of Hamilton, etc) began to beat a path to London on an increasingly regular basis. Once there, they sought allies and patrons among the various factions of English politicians in the hope of manoeuvring themselves into office back in Scotland.[1]

Naturally enough, the most obvious way to please the Anglocentric monarch and his advisers was to offer to run Scotland in accord with their policies. These rarely included a Scottish dimension (or even an awareness of separate Scottish interests). Instead they stressed the need to keep England's sister kingdoms within the British Isles quiet, so that the politicians in London could concentrate on more important things, such as personal and imperial aggrandisement. As a result, by the late 1660s a virtual system of neo-satrapy had established itself. The 'satrap' enjoyed almost complete control over Scotland's government and patronage in return for keeping the kingdom quiet and obediently responsive to the direction of policy at Whitehall. The first and greatest of these viceroys was the Earl (later Duke) of Lauderdale, who was eventually succeeded after his fall in 1681 by the Drummond brothers, the Earls of Perth and Melfort. These three were, however, only the successful hegemons of power in Scotland. Champing at the bit behind them was a crowd of eager place-seekers and frustrated magnates, such as the Earl of Middleton, the Duke of Hamilton and the

---

1 Szechi, 'The Hanoverians and Scotland', pp. 119–20.

Duke of Queensberry, all looking for a good opportunity to discredit those in power and replace them with themselves.[2]

The customary forum for political manoeuvre of the kind required to bring down a dominant magnate like Lauderdale was the royal court. There carefully conducted intrigues could swiftly disgrace one minister and elevate another. Both Lauderdale and the Drummond brothers, however, effectively closed off that means of overthrowing the neo-satrap by assiduous attendance on the monarch and unctuous compliance with his wishes. By careful control of the agenda for debate in the Scots Parliament through the standing committee known as the Lords of the Articles Lauderdale and his heirs could also usually neutralise any attempt by their rivals to discredit them there, so that by the 1680s Scotland's representative assembly had become something of a rubber stamp (though it did get restive when James II and VII's managers tried to repeal the penal laws against catholicism).[3] The net effect of both developments was to create a false calm within Scottish politics. Beyond resorting to arms, it had *de facto* become very difficult to oppose the government and its policies if one lay beyond the charmed circle of the dominant magnate and his cronies.

This artificial peace was, however, permanently destroyed by the Revolution of 1688. The 'outs' amongst the magnates seized the opportunity offered by the downfall of the Jacobite regime to dismantle its control of the Scottish Parliament by abolishing the Lords of the Articles, and then threw themselves into a furious political battle with each other to win the favour of the new order in London. Scottish politics in the 1690s were correspondingly volatile as magnates, factions and religious zealots struggled with each other in two arenas: the Scots Parliament and Whitehall. To be successful one had to control both arenas, but because William III and II was basically uninterested in Scotland and Scottish politics (when he was not exasperated by them) it was hard to retain the untrammeled hold on royal favour (and hence patronage) that was a pre-requisite for control of the Scots Parliament.[4] Moreover the problem for Whitehall was increasingly compounded by the virtual bankruptcy of the Scottish state as a result of the Highland War of 1689–91, which meant that Scotland's military forces needed to be supported by English subsidies.[5] Nevertheless, it was not until the end of the 1690s that William III and II became impatient enough with the turbulence of Scottish politics to revert to the neo-satrap system favoured by his immediate predecessors.[6]

2 J. Buckroyd, *Church and State in Scotland 1660–1681* (Edinburgh, 1980), pp. 39, 50, 107–8, 119–20; Turner, *James II*, pp. 366–73, 376–8.
3 D. Szechi and D. Hayton, 'John Bull's Other Kingdoms: the Government of Scotland and Ireland', in C. Jones (ed.), *Britain in the First Age of Party, 1680–1745. Essays Presented to Geoffrey Holmes* (1987), pp. 245–9.
4 Riley, *King William*, pp. 1–20.
5 Hopkins, *Glencoe*, pp. 180, 191, 267, 359.
6 Riley, *King William*, pp. 148–9.

His choice, the Duke of Queensberry, was a good one, in that Queensberry was a clever and effective politician whose fundamental loyalty to the new order could not be in doubt. The problem was that Queensberry's elevation came too late to put the lid back on Scottish politics. By the time Queensberry was allowed the controlling hand in the direction of Scotland's government Scottish politics had passed beyond such a mode of control. Since 1689 a vital polarity had developed in the Scottish Parliament and Scottish politics in general. At one end of the spectrum lay a 'patriot' or 'Country' position; at the other lay a 'Court' or ministerial position. The Country position was seldom taken up by any politician on a permanent basis, but provided a powerful rhetoric of opposition to the existing establishment for irate magnates doing one of their periodic shuttles between government and opposition. It also increasingly commanded widespread support among the merchants and lairds who made up the vast majority of the electorate: the political nation.[7] The Court position relied primarily on the traditional obligation of Scotland's elite to provide service and loyalty to the reigning monarch to win the hearts of politicians, and deployed the country's meagre resources of patronage to bolster that appeal. In addition, an amorphous religious divide overlay the Court and Country alignments. Those who identified themselves as Episcopalians were opposed to the Presbyterians who had seized control of the Kirk in 1689, but did not necessarily align themselves with the Country axis except for occasional votes on contentious religious issues. Likewise those who identified themselves as Presbyterians usually, but not necessarily, supported the Court as representing the new (presbyterian-dominated) status quo, but could turn against it on patriotic or religious grounds.[8]

These alignments, and particularly the Country axis, became steadily more powerful and charged as the 1690s went on. This was due to a series of governmental failures and scandals. The most important of these were the massacre of the Macdonalds or MacIans of Glencoe after their surrender to the government at the end of the Highland War in 1692 and the Darien fiasco of 1697–1700. The slaughter of men, women and children at Glencoe was investigated by the Scots Parliament in 1695–96, and although the main instigators escaped punishment it permanently tarnished William III and II and the 'Revolution interest' that had controlled Scotland's government since 1689.[9] The Darien fiasco arose from an attempt by the Company of Scotland Trading to the Indies to establish a commercial colony on the isthmus of Darien in Spanish central America between 1698 and 1700. Three expeditions, all outfitted through appeals for 'patriotic' public subscription and sent on their way with fervent

---

7 Szechi and Hayton, 'John Bull's Other Kingdoms', pp. 251–2.
8 Riley, *King William*, pp. 6–7, 134–6.
9 Ferguson, *Scotland 1689 to the Present*, pp. 23–5.

prayers and support from across the whole nation, failed disastrously. In the recriminations that followed, English hostility to the project and William III and II's indifference (he was deeply embarrassed by the whole business, which was directed against the colonial empire of one of England's most important Continental allies) received most of the blame for the disaster. And by implication, so did William's agents in Scotland: his ministers. The net effect of all this was to boost support for, and render 'patriotic', opposition to the ministers of the Revolutionary regime, whatever their political origins.[10] By the end of the 1690s it was all too apparent that the established order in Scotland rested on a narrow basis of support and was increasingly politically beleaguered.[11]

Lockhart thus entered national politics at a time when Scotland was in danger of becoming ungovernable, at least from the point of view of the existing political establishment. The election of 1702 was itself unusual in that it took place in particularly heated circumstances. By the Act of Security of 1696, which was designed to safeguard the Revolutionary regime against a possible Jacobite coup d'état in the immediate aftermath of the monarch's death, the existing Scottish Parliament (elected in 1689) was allowed to continue functioning after the death of the monarch who summoned it.[12] This violation of the constitution had originally been envisaged merely as a temporary expedient, but, sensing the mood of the political nation was actively hostile, Queensberry and the other ministers persuaded Queen Anne and the triumvirate who were managing the English Parliament for her (the Duke of Marlborough, Lord Treasurer Godolphin and Speaker Robert Harley) to recall the Parliament of 1689 for another complete session.[13] Such a gross constitutional enormity immediately produced an outcry in Scotland and culminated in the ostentatious secession of the 4th Duke of Hamilton and the Country opposition closely followed by a declaration from the Faculty of Advocates that the whole proceeding was illegal. This was followed up (in some parts of the country at least) by a refusal to pay taxes.[14]

At that point Queensberry recognised the inevitable, and though the pro-government rump defiantly passed legislation declaring it treason to impugn the continued authority of the Parliament of 1689 and set up a commission to negotiate a union with England, he recommended that Anne call a new Parliament.[15] Recognising, too, that the administration was going to need to conciliate part of the opposition, the Earl of Seafield (the Lord Chancellor) was authorised to make overtures to the nascent 'Cavalier' party within the Country

10 J. Prebble, *The Darien Disaster* (1968), *passim.*
11 Ferguson, *Scotland 1689 to the Present*, pp. 33–5.
12 Riley, *Union*, pp. 32–3.
13 *Ibid.*, pp. 33–4.
14 Ferguson, *Scotland 1689 to the Present*, p. 37; *APS*, xi. 28, appendix 4–7; *Correspondence of George Baillie of Jerviswood*, pp. 8, 9: Johnston to Baillie, 21 Nov. and 22 Dec. 1702.
15 *APS*, xi. 16: 12 June 1702; Riley, *Union*, pp. 36–9, 180–1.

opposition.[16] Significantly, this was an Episcopalian-cum-Jacobite alignment. Hostility to Queensberry, national resentment at English slights and English refusal to aid the Darien venture and plain dislike of the Revolution settlement of Kirk and state constructed since 1689 then duly combined to return a Parliament in which connections (groups of Commissioners and peers loosely organised on a kinship/friendship basis around a particular nobleman) and other groups opposed to the administration outnumbered the government's sure supporters.[17] And the disparity would have been much worse had it not been for a quarrel between Hamilton and the Cavaliers over the appropriate response to Seafield's overtures, to which the Cavaliers wanted to respond positively, as a result of which Hamilton opposed a number of Cavalier candidates.[18] Lockhart was returned for Midlothian as part of what was for the time an anti-court avalanche. The new, heavily, but not entirely, crypto-Jacobite 'Cavalier' alignment, led by the Earl of Home, was about seventy strong in the new Parliament, as against about sixty for the old Country party and approximately ninety for the Court.[19] Though by this time he was an overt episcopalian, George appears to have kept his views on Kirk and state to himself during the election campaign, doubtless for good, tactical political reasons to do with the Midlothian electorate, only declaring that he had 'no designe but to serve my country'.[20] As a consequence he may have initially been thought to be a Courtier (not an unreasonable inference given his background and family connections), and was certainly not seen as a pro-Hamilton candidate.[21]

By the time Lockhart's first session opened on 3 May 1703 Seafield's overtures had been turned into a political alliance between the Cavaliers and the Court despite Hamilton's opposition to any deal that left Queensberry in office.[22] George was at this time identified with the Cavalier party and clearly approved of the pact with the administration, which seemed to offer hope of a legal toleration of episcopacy.[23] His own appointment to the Privy Council early in 1703 was one token of the administration's good faith.[24] When the first session opened, moreover, the Cavaliers delivered the political goods. As agreed before the session, they legitimised the last meeting of William's Parliament in 1702

---

16 SR, p. 19.
17 Ferguson, *Scotland 1689 to the Present*, p. 38.
18 SR, pp. 19–20; SRO GD 45/14/245/2: Lady Margaret Nairn to Margaret, Countess of Panmure, Nairne, 22 Dec. 1702.
19 Riley, *Union*, p. 49.
20 LL, p. 2: GL to Sir John Clerk, Dryden, 28 Sept. 1702. Sir John, at least, was nonetheless fully aware of GL's unsoundness on the religious issue (SRO GD 18/2092/2: Sir John's spiritual journal for 1699–1709, 26 Sept. 1702).
21 HMC *Hamilton* (Supplement), p. 148.
22 Riley, *Union*, pp. 49–50; SR, p. 19.
23 SR, pp. 27–30.
24 SRO PC 1/52: Acta, July 1699-May 1703: p. 505: 24 Feb. 1703.

(thus effectively indemnifying Queensberry and his fellows for their conduct at that time) and recognised the queen's accession.[25] They then prepared to support the passage of a supply bill – at which point the alliance broke down. Faced with the prospect of continued cooperation with the Cavaliers (which was bound to involve the passage of a religious toleration for episcopalians and a purge of officeholders), many of the Presbyterians and long-established officeholders among the Court party grew restive. They finally forced a breach by threatening Queensberry with a mutiny unless legislation confirming the existing power and authority of the (presbyterian) Kirk was passed. Queensberry had little choice but to back down, and allowed Home's motion to grant supply to be tabled, effectively signalling his alliance with the Cavaliers was at an end.[26]

Lockhart and the other Cavaliers registered the shift in the ministry's position when Episcopalian members of the Court party began voting against episcopalian religious toleration.[27] They promptly held a meeting at which it was decided to send a delegation to visit Queensberry to find out what was going on. And one of the delegation was George Lockhart of Carnwath.[28] Since he was a very young and junior Commissioner to Parliament at this point (he was about 22 years old), and as late as 1706 was regarded by a percipient observer as one who 'can neither penetrat into a deep design nor make speeches',[29] it seems likely that George was chosen by his fellow Cavaliers on the basis of his status as a Commissioner for Scotland's premier shire and his seat on the Privy Council. In any event, Queensberry tried to obfuscate and prevaricate his way out of his predicament, but to no avail: the delegation refused to accept his by now suspect assurances of continued friendship. And upon their reporting back to the rest of the Cavaliers, the whole party 'unanimously' resolved to sever its links with the court while simultaneously refusing to ally with the Country party.[30]

These fine commitments soon began to fray in the face of Seafield and Queensberry's efforts to win over individual Cavaliers and the attraction of the thoroughly 'patriotic' measures being pushed by the Country party, and the Cavaliers quickly fragmented.[31] Lockhart, along with the majority of the Cavaliers, increasingly aligned himself with the Country party. He differed with his peers, however, about the position the Cavaliers should take with regard to religious toleration. On purely practical grounds it made sense for the Country-aligned Cavaliers not to oppose measures securing the presbyterian settlement

25 Riley, *Union*, p. 49; SR, pp. 28–9.
26 *APS*, xi. 45: 26 May 1703; SR, pp. 30–2, 32–3. For a slightly different view see: Riley, *Union*, p. 54.
27 SR, pp. 32–3.
28 SR, p. 33.
29 Blairs Letters 2/124/10: James Carnegy to the Scots College [Edinburgh], 16 Mar. 1706.
30 SR, p. 33.
31 Riley, *Union*, p. 55.

of the Kirk, because they would thereby alienate the substantial body of Country party Presbyterians. In addition, the Cavaliers' leaders may have hoped that by not opposing such a bill they could persuade Presbyterian members to vote for episcopalian religious toleration. George flatly refused to compromise on his hostility to the Kirk, though he seems to have been willing to allow positive efforts to secure religious toleration to drop for the time being. Thus when the Earl of Marchmont proposed an act securing the presbyterian settlement of the Kirk, George, in a highly symbolic and widely noticed act, was the first member of Parliament to cast a vote against it.[32]

For Lockhart the rest of the session was dominated by a struggle between the Court and the Cavalier-Country coalition. The Court was determined to secure a vote of supply for the armed forces and was prepared to try and offer some constitutional concessions to achieve this.[33] Some of the more strongly Presbyterian elements of the Court party, led by the Earl of Marchmont, in addition sought an act assigning the succession to the throne after the death of Queen Anne (all of whose 18 children had died by 1700) to the house of Hanover.[34] The Cavalier-Country opposition, which spanned the ideological spectrum, from radical crypto-Republicans like Andrew Fletcher of Saltoun through self-interested magnates like Hamilton, to diehard Jacobites like Home, focused their attention on defeating the Court and passing patriotic measures that would preserve their fragile unity. In the course of the disputes and manoeuvring that characterised this fraught session this impulse ultimately reified itself into two measures: the Act Anent Peace and War and the Act of Security.[35] The Act Anent Peace and War declared that in the future Scotland would no longer be bound by declarations of war by England: the Scottish Parliament would have to be separately consulted. The Act of Security laid down that, pending a satisfactory settlement of Scotland's economic problems with England, no person inheriting the throne of England could inherit the throne of Scotland, and that such a successor would be subject to various new constitutional limitations. Both measures galvanised the opposition and, just as importantly, appealed to some on the Court side. The net effect was that the opposition was able to gain the upper hand and secured the passage of the Act Anent Peace and War, though not of the Act of Security.[36] Lockhart was enthusiastic about both measures, espcially the Act of Security, but his role in these epochal events

32 Blairs Letters 2/83/2: James Carnegy to Thomas Innes [Edinburgh?], 8 June 1703; SR, p. 35; SRO GD 18/2092/2: Sir John Clerk's spiritual journal for 1699–1709, 3 May 1703; NLS Wodrow Letters, Octavo III, ep. 59: George Logane to Robert Wodrow, 12 June 1703.
33 Ferguson, *Scotland's Relations with England*, p. 207.
34 Riley, *Union*, pp. 55–6.
35 Ferguson, *Scotland's Relations with England*, pp. 208–11.
36 Riley, *Union*, pp. 57–8.

(which forced the Scottish political crisis onto the agenda of the ministry in London – a most unwelcome development there) was minor and consequently invisible.[37] By September, though, the Queensberry administration had been reduced to trying to pass an act allowing the importation of French wine so that they could at least raise some revenue to fund the government of Scotland, and at this point Lockhart reappears in the Parliamentary record in such a way as to suggest his political allegiances were shifting. At the beginning of September he had signalled that his Episcopalianism was hardening into outright Jacobitism by advocating, in a tumultuous sitting, that a bill proposed by Marchmont for settling the succession to the Scottish crown on the house of Hanover be burnt.[38] His response to the wine bill, however, indicated he was in other areas moving away from his Cavalier confrères. The bill had acted as an apple of discord for the opposition. A ragbag of different interest groups were inclined to favour the measure even if it meant supporting the ministry. These ranged from various commercial interests to the bulk of the Cavaliers (who hoped it would give them easier access to France and the Stuart court at St Germain en Laye).[39] Lockhart refused to go along with this position, and instead joined the more Whiggish elements of the Country party, led by Tweeddale, Fletcher and Hamilton, in a formal protest on the grounds that the measure 'ought not to pass, as being dishonourable to her Majestie, inconsistent with the grand alliance wherein she is engaged and prejudiciall to the honour, safety, interest and trade of this Kingdom'.[40] From this point on Lockhart, without ever compromising his increasingly hardline Jacobitism, was to move into ever closer engagement with the Country party in general and Hamilton in particular. Shortly afterwards, rather than wait until matters got still more out of hand, Queensberry terminated the session.

In the nine and a half months between sessions of Parliament that followed, the most significant development was a botched attempt by Queensberry to smear selected leaders of the Country opposition by implicating them in a bogus Jacobite conspiracy. As well as the usual suspects such as Sir John Maclean, Simon Fraser (later 11th Lord Lovat) obligingly accused Queensberry's *bêtes noires* the Dukes of Atholl and Hamilton.[41] Atholl promptly went to London to clear his name, and at his request a delegation of other Country party leaders soon followed.[42] Hamilton went through the motions of conferring with the leading

---

37 SR, pp. 37, 39–40.
38 Riley, *Union*, p. 56; J. Hope (ed.), *A Diary of the Proceedings in the Parliament and Privy Council of Scotland. May 21, 1700 – March 7, 1707. By Sir David Hume of Crossrigg, one of the Senators of the College of Justice* (Edinburgh, Bannatyne Club, 1828), pp. 131–2: 6 Sept. 1703.
39 Ferguson, *Scotland's Relations with England*, p. 212.
40 *APS*, xi. 102: 13 Sept. 1703.
41 Riley, *Union*, pp. 62–3.
42 SR, pp. 52, 61–2.

men of both the Cavalier and Country parties who happened to be in Edinburgh at the time, including Lockhart, but then bounced the Cavaliers into agreeing to a delegation entirely drawn from the more radical Whiggish Country party members. Lockhart and the other Cavaliers were not best pleased and clearly viewed the embassy with suspicion from the outset.[43] And indeed when they got to London George Baillie of Jerviswood and the Earls of Rothes and Roxburghe were soon being sounded out on their attitude to the succession by the English ministers, who were transparently interested in finding an alternative to the failing Queensberry.[44] The upshot of their visit to London was that the Tweeddale group were able to negotiate a takeover of the administration in Scotland in anticipation of the coming Parliamentary session. As well as jobs for their friends, the 'New Party' secured various ideological concessions. In particular, they persuaded the Marlborough-Godolphin ministry to agree to the passage of popular patriotic measures such as the Act of Security. The *quid pro quo* was that they would secure supply and Parliamentary confirmation of the Hanoverian succession.[45]

Consequently, when the session opened in July the angry Cavalier-Country alliance, quietly bolstered by Queensberry's connection, almost immediately went on to the offensive in an attempt to discomfit the new ministry. Hamilton proposed a resolution 'that this Parliament will not proceed to the nomination of a successor to the crown until we have had a previous treaty with England in relation to our commerce and other concerns with that nation'.[46] The Court, alerted to their vulnerability when it became clear that Queensberry's connection were aligning themselves with the Cavalier-Country axis, promptly began obfuscating. At first it looked as if a ministerial alternative to Hamilton's resolution might succeed in dissipating the threat, for after a very acrimonious debate the resolution, strengthened and extended by an amendment proposed by Sir James Falconer of Phesdo, seemed to be about to be stalled by their procedural evasions.[47] At which point Lockhart made his only significant recorded intervention for the session[48] when he threw Roxburghe's fighting words from the 1703 debate on the Act of Security (when Roxburghe had threatened to take a vote with his sword in his hand if the appropriate officers did not do it forthwith[49]) back in his teeth, and then declared:

43 SR, p. 62.
44 Ferguson, *Scotland's Relations with England*, p. 216.
45 Ferguson, *Scotland's Relations with England*, pp. 216–17.
46 SR, pp. 68, 72–3.
47 SR, pp. 73–4.
48 I am assuming here, as seems highly probable, that the, 'certain member', referred to by GL (SR, p. 74) was, in fact, GL himself.
49 SR, p. 38. It should be noted, however, that in his marginal notes on GL's *Memoirs* Baron Sir John Clerk denied this incident ever occurred: SRO GD 18/6080: p. 120: 'I remember no such words. I am very sure no member durst have spoken in this style'.

And ... I cannot see but the encroachment upon the liberties of the house is as great now as then. And if such measures were allowable and necessary then, they are certainly so still. To avoid which, and the pushing matters to the last extremity, I move the vote may be stated, 'approve the resolve or not', and if I am seconded in the motion, I will not sit down till the vote be begun.[50]

The Cavaliers 'unanimously' seconded the motion and the Court's resistance finally crumbled. To Lockhart's manifest delight the opposition triumphantly passed the resolution – effectively barring further discussion of the succession pending a suitable treaty settling Scotland's commercial and other grievances with England.[51] For once George even appreciated the cheers and enthusiasm of the common people, who greeted the united opposition's success with 'jollity, mirth, and an universal satisfaction and approbation of what was done'.[52]

Making the best of a bad job, the ministry now turned to securing the supply Scotland's administration and armed forces so desperately needed.[53] An attempt to separate the Cavalier-Country alliance from its erstwhile allies in the Queensberry connection by proposing formal consideration of Queensberry's handling of the Scots Plot failed when Fletcher deflected the debate with a resolution condemning the English House of Lords' presumption in taking up the matter.[54] Hamilton then condescended to support a temporary vote of cess. After some further manoeuvring the Court won over enough of the Cavalier-Country coalition to secure a bill for six months' cess, only to have the opposition counter by a *de facto* linkage of the vote of supply with the Act of Security. Rather than lose the cess, Tweeddale persuaded the reluctant ministry in London to allow him to pass the Act of Security.[55] The session then wound down and was adjourned at the end of August.[56] With it ended the opposition's salad days.[57] In retrospect, Lockhart correctly perceived the far-reaching significance of the Cavalier-Country party's only serious check: their failure to nominate the negotiators ('treaters') who were to sit on a Commission to treat with its English counterpart on terms for a Union. Equally significantly from the vantage point of his study at Dryden in 1708, he ascribed this failure to the 'private animosities and quarrels' of Atholl and Hamilton, who could not

50 SR, p. 74.
51 Riley, *Union*, p. 98.
52 SR, p. 75.
53 Riley, *Union*, p. 98.
54 SR, pp. 75–6.
55 Riley, *Union*, p. 99.
56 Riley, *Union*, pp. 101–2.
57 J. Robertson, 'An Elusive Sovereignty. The Course of the Union Debate in Scotland 1698–1707', in J. Robertson (ed.), *A Union for Empire. Political Thought and the British Union of 1707* (Cambridge, 1995), pp. 203–10.

abide the thought of allowing Seafield and Queensberry an official role in the negotiations.[58]

Such a shrewd analysis came only with hindsight, however, and at the time what probably impressed itself most on George was his gathering importance as a politician. Despite the lack of concrete information about his doings during the session it is clear from his correspondence during the winter of 1704–5 that Lockhart had become closely associated with Hamilton and a significant actor in opposition politics. We do not know at what point he became attached to Hamilton, though it is possible that George's insistence on a vote being taken on Hamilton's resolution on the succession may have rekindled former ties.[59] What is apparent is that by December 1704 he was looked on as the appropriate channel through which the Cavalier leadership should seek to influence the duke.[60] Likewise, the frank admiration he had developed for Fletcher, whom he later characterised as the ideal Scottish patriot and whose ideas profoundly influenced him,[61] made Lockhart the perfect intermediary for reconciling Fletcher and Hamilton after one of their quarrels.[62] In addition, he was known to be well enough connected within the ranks of the opposition ('I drink your Grace's health evry day with Hume and Stormont', he told Hamilton in January 1705) for politicians like Seafield and the Earl of Rothes to make an effort personally to convince him of their *bona fides* and to seek to use him to communicate with the Cavalier-Country alliance.[63] None of his activities are those of a politician of first-rank importance, but George had clearly risen to the level of organiser and understrapper within the opposition in general and the Cavaliers in particular, as may also be seen from the fact that the Tweeddale ministry thought it would serve as a useful warning to others to have him dismissed from the Privy Council.[64]

Regardless of the political situation at the time, this was not entirely surprising. After the first flush of enthusiasm had worn off, Lockhart's attendance at Privy Council meetings had become distinctly sporadic and transparently politically motivated.[65] Overall he attended 36 of the 86 meetings of the Privy Council that took place during his time on it, and was appointed to only two committees: one to deal with matters arising during the vacation (which almost certainly stemmed from the proximity of his main residence to Edinburgh) and the other

58 SR, pp. 78–9.
59 See above, pp. 13, 19 n45; SRO GD 406/1/4053: GL to Hamilton (then Earl of Arran), Edinburgh, 31 Jan. 1695.
60 LL, pp. 12–13: GL to Hamilton, Dryden, 10 Feb. 1705.
61 LP i. 77. For evidence of Fletcher's influence see the notes to part II below.
62 LL, p. 15: GL to Hamilton, [before 26 Mar.] 1705.
63 LL, pp. 10, 17–19: GL to Hamilton, Edinburgh and Dryden, 25 Jan. and 12 Apr. 1705.
64 LL, p. 6: GL to Hamilton, Dryden, 14 Dec. 1704.
65 SRO PC 1/52: Acta, July 1699-May 1703, pp. 505–56; PC 1/53: Acta, June 1703-Apr. 1707, pp. 1–294.

to hear appeals against impressment in the army and navy.[66] His only other appointment was to the moribund, but well-paid, commission established by King William's parliament for negotiating a union with England, and that had ceased to meet before ever he took his seat on the Privy Council.[67] Significantly, of the 36 meetings he did attend, 19 were concerned with investigating the bogus Scots Plot of 1703–4, and he was manifestly only attending those in order to keep the Cavalier-Country leadership appraised of what was afoot in the administration. All in all, George was not much of a loss to the administration of Scotland when he was dropped in November 1704.

Ironically enough, however, he was soon joined in the political wilderness by the men who had put him there. Following the classic pre-Union path to power in Scotland, Argyll (discreetly but warily supported by Queensberry) successfully undermined the Tweeddale ministry in London on the basis of their failures during the 1704 Parliamentary session and after, and by the time the 1705 session was due to open Tweeddale and his group (already beginning to be designated the 'Squadrone', a contraction of *Squadrone Volante*, 'flying squadron') had been dismissed and Queensberry's connection, though not yet the Duke himself, were back in the saddle.[68] Argyll's remit was to bring the Scots Parliament round to the point where it would either accept the Hanoverian succession or establish a (favourable) commission for negotiating a Union with England, and he was backed up by the English Parliament's Alien Act of 1704, which threatened economic sanctions against Scotland if the Scots Parliament refused to comply. Once in Scotland, however, he was persuaded to abandon the idea of getting Parliamentary acceptance of the Hanoverian succession and to concentrate instead on getting an act authorising the appointment of a commission to negotiate a union with England.[69]

For Lockhart and the Cavalier-Country group, however, the session nonetheless opened fairly promisingly. As well as getting a number of minor measures through their initial stages, they were also able, before Queensberry's arrival in Scotland shifted the support of his connection from the opposition to the government, to pass a motion prohibiting legislation to nominate a successor to Queen Anne until a trade treaty with England had been negotiated and sundry constitutional safeguards enacted.[70] Looking back on the session from the bitterness of post-Union Scotland, George felt that this was a golden opportunity

66 SRO PC 1/52: Acta, July 1699–May 1703, p. 529: 9 Mar. 1703.
67 SRO RH 2/4 (copy of Entry Books of Out-Letters, North Britain T. 17 vol. 1, 1707–9), p. 296. N.b. though GL was supposed to receive £500 sterling for his service on the commission I could find no evidence he ever received a penny. I am indebted to John Shaw for pointing out this entry to me.
68 Riley, *Union*, pp. 127–39.
69 Riley, *Union*, pp. 138–40.
70 SR, pp. 90–2, 93–8.

permanently to cripple any chance of an incorporating Union which the Cavaliers
had missed:

> ... for had they immediately called for the Queen's letter (which, and likewise
> the Commissioner's and Chancellor's speeches, chiefly insisted on the necessity
> and advantage of treating with England) in order to return an answer to it,
> the treaty would have naturally fallen under consideration; and then the Duke
> of Queensberry's friends and party not being gone off from them, they might
> easily have either rejected it altogether, or at least framed and clogged it as
> they pleased, and chosen such members as they had a mind to be commis-
> sioners for meeting and treating with the commissioners from England.[71]

Yet for all his retrospective insight the safeguards and limitations on the
commissioners for Union probably seemed more than adequate insurance at the
time, and though the Queensberry connection were about to defect back to the
Court, the ministry could by no means rely on the Squadrone to back its
measures.[72] Hence Hamilton and Atholl were able unconcernedly to enjoy
themselves, wasting further time excoriating Queensberry's conduct in the Scots
Plot affair as 'villanous, dishonourable, false, and scandalous, and not to be
tolerated in a well-governed kingdom', without the ministry daring to try and
move its closure.[73]

The opposition's come-uppance only came very late in the session. A bill
establishing a commission to negotiate a Union with England had been slowly
progressing through Parliament since 20 July.[74] By the end of August the opposition parties 'observing that there was a great inclination in the House to set a
treaty on foot, thought it improper to oppose it any longer in general terms', and
that they needed to adjust their approach accordingly. The Cavalier-Country
alliance duly decided to let the bill progress to the point where the establishment
of the commission was being debated, and there 'clog' it with amendments that
would render it nugatory.[75] The first essay at this, in the shape of a clause proposed
by Hamilton that 'the Union to be treated on should no ways derogate from any
fundamental laws, ancient privileges, offices, rights, liberties and dignities of this
nation', failed by two votes on 31 August.[76] But on 1 September the opposition
did succeed in forcing the Court to accept a resolution that no negotiations take
place until the English Parliament withdrew its threatened trade sanctions.[77]

Earlier the same day Lockhart had been delegated by a meeting of the

---

71 SR, p. 90.
72 Riley, *Union*, pp. 144–5, 147–8.
73 SR, pp. 98–100.
74 *APS*, xi. 216: 20 July 1705.
75 SR, p. 100.
76 *APS*, xi. 236: 31 Aug. 1705; SR, pp. 102–3.
77 SR, pp. 103–4.

Cavaliers to speak to Hamilton with regard to when the opposition should bring in proposals to vote for treaters by estate, which they (correctly) believed to be their best chance of securing a strong presence on the commission – though, since the Court dominated the noble estate, if it passed it would almost certainly extinguish Hamilton's chances of being chosen. Encountering the Duke just outside the chamber, Lockhart asked the question and received the answer: 'it shall not be in this day'.[78] Consequently, 'it being by this time late, and having been a long *sederunt*', when the opposition (including on this occasion the Squadrone[79]) had registered their adherence to a formal protest by Atholl at the danger of not having the opposition clause included in the body of the act establishing the Commission, many opposition members went home. Judging his moment expertly, Hamilton then did a complete *volte face* on the question of who should choose the commissioners for Union and proposed the nomination should be left to the queen. As he was doubtless well aware, this was tantamount to handing over the conduct of the negotiations to the Court.[80]

Lockhart's response to what looks *prima facie* like an attempt by Hamilton to ingratiate himself with the Court is illuminating. While writing his memoirs, George analysed and refuted every one of Hamilton's excuses for this episode, and correctly divined the real reason for the Duke's conduct: 'His Grace had a great mind to be one of the treaters himself' ('This was indeed the Duke's grand motive', observed Baron John Clerk, a well-placed Courtier at the time, in his notes on Lockhart's *Memoirs*).[81] But even so George ultimately shied away from the logical conclusion: that Hamilton, who was manifestly seeking to work his passage into office by making himself useful to the Court at crucial junctures, was fundamentally untrustworthy.[82] Other Scottish politicians, such as the Earls of Home, Erroll and Panmure, perceived the duke's basic unreliability and by the autumn of 1705 were making their plans accordingly.[83] George was, moreover, capable of very cogent analysis of the motives and personalities of peers quite as complex as Hamilton, so why could he not accept the evidence of his own eyes?[84] Ultimately it comes down to a question of loyalty. Once Lockhart had given his allegiance to a man, he found it hard to believe that his trust could be betrayed. If loyalty to a friend can be a character flaw, it reached to the core of George's personality.

The Court was naturally delighted with Hamilton's handing-over of the nomination of the Union commissioners to them, and followed up their

---

78 SR, pp. 106–7.
79 *APS*, xi. 236–7: 1 Sept. 1705.
80 SR, pp. 105–6.
81 SR, pp. 107–9; SRO GD 18/6080, p. 176.
82 SR, *idem*.
83 *Correspondence of Colonel N. Hooke*, i. 373, 380–1, 398–9, 404.
84 SR, pp. 18–19.

unexpected success by rapidly winding up the session.[85] The stage was now set for the negotiation of a treaty of Union. Many Scots had for some time felt the kingdom faced a bleak future if it continued its existing relationship with England, hence Roxburghe's shrewd (and much-quoted) prediction that a Union treaty would pass the Scots Parliament because of 'trade with most, Hanover with some, ease and security with others, together with a general aversion at civill discords, intollerable poverty, and the constant oppression of a bad ministry, from generation to generation, without the least regard to the good of the country'.[86] The key to a successful conclusion was thus terms that would hold a sufficient coalition of interest groups together within the Scots Parliament. For purely practical political reasons this meant the Courtier connections, especially Queensberry's, had to be assured that their offices and influence would survive the Union, the Squadrone had to be conciliated with the hope of future preferment, the presbyterian clergy assured their control of the Kirk would endure and the merchants' and lawyers' fears of eclipse in a pan-British polity soothed.[87] The first stage in the process was the negotiation of a package with enough special deals to have some prospect of achieving all of the above, but not so many as to annoy the English negotiators, whose own agenda was firmly centred on the incorporation (and implicit future domination) of the Scottish polity. And obviously a team of reliable, savvy negotiators was required to achieve that.[88]

Hence it came as a surprise to many contemporary Scots politicians (including himself) to find Lockhart named as one of the Scottish commissioners. Ironically, his appointment was a manifestation of exactly the kind of pernicious, ignorant English interference in Scottish politics that so outraged him in other circumstances, for it stemmed directly from his uncle, Lord Wharton's, influence at Whitehall.[89] Wharton was one of the English commissioners for the Union, and by 1705 one of the acknowledged leaders of the English Whig party. The Marlborough-Godolphin ministry in England was Tory in origin, but by 1705 had become virtually dependent on Whig support for its survival, due to the gathering disenchantment of the backbench Tories with the ministry's lack of Anglican zeal and its determination to fight the War of the Spanish Succession to the bitter end.[90] The Whigs were wholeheartedly committed to the Hanoverian succession and hence – since by 1706 they could see no other way of securing it than by a fusion of the two kingdoms – to union

85 SR, pp. 109–10.
86 *Correspondence of George Baillie of Jerviswood*, p. 68: Roxburghe to Baillie, 28 Nov. 1705, cited in: P. H. Scott, *Andrew Fletcher and the Treaty of Union* (Edinburgh, 1992), p. 165.
87 Szechi, 'The Hanoverians and Scotland', p. 123.
88 Ferguson, *Scotland's Relations with England*, pp. 233–4.
89 LL, p. 28: GL to Hamilton, Dryden, 16 Mar. 1706; SR, i. 82–3, 119.
90 E. Gregg, *Queen Anne* (1980), pp. 199–208.

with Scotland.[91] Sensibly enough in the circumstances, Godolphin therefore *de facto* allowed the Whigs to dominate the English negotiating team.[92] And it appears that Wharton, under the misapprehension that George supported the idea of an incorporating union of the two kingdoms (and possibly recalling his phantom service on the 1702–3 Scottish commission for union), exerted his influence to have him appointed to the Scottish commission, doubtless much to the surprise of the Scottish ministry, who were all too well aware of Lockhart's affiliation with the Cavalier party and his friendship with Hamilton.

By a piece of pure nepotism, then, Lockhart became the only opponent of the Union capable of influencing the final form of the agreement. Despite this dubious honour, his first inclination was to refuse the nomination,

> for if I dissent from them, which is more than probable I will, how shall I behave? If I tautly pass over and be only silent, yea tho I should reason and vote against sevrall points that will be cognosed (such as the succession, incorporating Union, etc), if I do not protest against them or att least desire my dissent may be marked in the minutes, how shall it be known but that I concurrd and went alongst with them, and therby I shall run the hazard of obtaining the same character with the rest, and if I shoud protest I draw the odium of the whole party upon my back, and it will soon render me uncapable to do any service to my freinds by getting into their secrets, which is the reason Mr Fletcher makes use of to perswade me to go up.[93]

In the end he reluctantly agreed to accept the post at the urging of the leaders of the Cavalier party as well as Fletcher of Saltoun.[94] Not that their seal of approval saved George's reputation among his fellow Cavaliers in the medium term. As he bitterly recalled, he became subject to a good deal of abuse from his erstwhile friends, who believed that he had sold out the Cavalier cause, until his conduct in the last session of the Scottish Parliament restored his reputation amongst them.[95]

Lockhart found such criticism particularly hard to bear given the injuries he felt his principles sustained in the course of the Union negotiations. Theoretically, there was one other opponent of a union of the two kingdoms involved in the bargaining: John Sharp, the Tory Archbishop of York. But since Sharp refused to participate in the meetings of the English commission, George was

---

91 Holmes, *British Politics*, pp. 83–5; C. Jones and G. Holmes (eds), *The London Diaries of William Nicolson, Bishop of Carlisle 1702–1718* (Oxford, 1985), pp. 292, 357–8, 392–5, 423; J. Macpherson (ed.), *Original Papers; Containing the Secret History of Great Britain, from the Restoration to the Accession of the House of Hanover* (2 vols, 1775), ii. 68–9: Lord Halifax to the Electress Sophia, 15 Oct. 1706; LP i. 144–6. For a different interpretation of the Whigs' motivation, see: Riley, *Union*, pp. 163–6.

92 Riley, *Union*, p. 166.

93 LL, p. 29: GL to Hamilton, Dryden, 16 Mar. 1706.

94 SR, pp. 119–20; *Correspondence of Colonel N. Hooke*, ii. 53.

95 SR, pp. 120–1.

left virtually isolated for the three months it took to hammer out the treaty of
Union.[96] To make matters worse his fellow Scots Commissioners, with the partial
exception of Sir Hugh Dalrymple of North Berwick, Lord President of the Court
of Session, and William Seton of Pitmedden jr, were suspicious of him and
excluded him from the crucial private meetings.[97] Thus at first he was nonplussed
by what he saw as the English Commissioners' insistence on demands he was
convinced were unacceptable to any Scottish politician who wanted to survive
presenting them to the Scottish Parliament. 'I allwayes was of opinion that a
scheme of Union was concerted and woud be agreed to here, and yet I know
not what to think, now that I see the English so positively insist upon equality
of taxes ...', he confided to Harry Maule of Kellie.[98] Only as the negotiations
continued and the treaty began to take shape did he realise that the formal
sessions he was participating in were a sham and that the main points were
being settled in advance of the Commissions' meetings.[99] Nonetheless the
Scots commission did its job well enough (whether by public or private dealing)
to extract some serious fiscal and institutional concessions from its English
counterpart.[100] Though George claimed to be (and, indeed, may genuinely
have been) scandalised by proposals to pay off himself and his fellow shareholders of the Company of Scotland with the Equivalent payments (which
repatriated that portion of post-Union Scottish taxes which in England went to
service the English national debt) at the expense of the people of Scotland, he
must have known that this 'clear bribe' would greatly appeal to many members
of the Scottish Parliament.[101] Ultimately George's problem was that even such
effective bargaining – albeit selfishly biased towards the Scottish elite – was
pernicious from his point of view, in that these side-agreements steadily built
up the package of special-interest deals and exemptions necessary to get a treaty
for an incorporating Union through the Scots Parliament.[102]

96 SR, p. 119.
97 LL, p. 31: GL to Harry Maule of Kellie [London], 9 May 1706; Riley, *Union*, pp. 184,
    186–7; Ferguson, *Scotland's Relations with England*, p. 234. Baron John Clerk confirmed in
    his notes on the *Memoirs* (SRO GD 18/6080, p. 212) that GL was indeed excluded on
    more than one occasion: 'No paper of this kind [the Scots commissioners' answer to the
    English commissioners position on taxation and representation] was drawn without a
    previous consultation upon the several heads, and the draughts themselves were always
    shouen to the most intelligent amongst the Scots, but were indeed not communicated to
    those who could not make them better and who possibly were suspected as the supposed
    author of these memoirs was in a particular manner. On which account I'll very readily
    agree with him that he saw few of them'.
98 LL, p. 31: [London], 9 May 1706.
99 LL, pp. 32–6: GL to Harry Maule [London], May-June 1706; SR, pp. 131–2.
100 Whatley, *Bought and Sold*, p. 47, and cf. the main points of the Union, summarised in:
    Holmes, *Making of a Great Power*, p. 430.
101 LL, pp. 33, 35: GL to Maule [London], mid-May and 4 June 1706.
102 C. Whatley, 'Economic Causes and Consequences of the Union of 1707: A Survey', *Scottish
    Historical Review*, lxviii (1989) 162–5.

Despite his manifest frustration, Lockhart endured the negotiating process to its conclusion, reporting back regularly to the opposition leadership, before signalling his disapproval by refusing to sign the treaty.[103] As soon as he was back in Scotland, however, he began to disseminate all he knew about the way the treaty had been constructed and was thus probably instrumental in setting in train the tide of popular revulsion against it that followed hard on the heels of the initial, positive reaction to early reports of the treaty's terms.[104] By the time the autumn session of the Scottish Parliament was due to open this reaction threatened to mobilise even groups who had secured very preferential treatment by the terms of the treaty, such as the presbyterian clergy, against the Union.[105]

The Cavalier-Country alliance meantime anxiously counted heads and prepared to try and defeat the Union in Parliament. When all was said and done, favours called in, threats exchanged, bribes distributed and waverers cajoled on both sides, the fate of the Union rested in the hands of one group: the Squadrone.[106] Of the 210 members of the Scottish Parliament present and active in the autumn of 1706, Patrick Riley, one of the foremost authorities on the passage of the Act of Union, categorises 99 as Courtiers, 87 as opposition and 24 as Squadrone.[107] Had the Squadrone decided to oppose it, the treaty would therefore *ipso facto* have been rejected.[108] Once they decided to support it, the Union was bound to pass in Parliament. Hence there is an increasingly despairing quality to the opposition to the Act of Union from 15 October onwards, when the Squadrone signalled that it intended to support the passage of the treaty by voting for immediate consideration of the articles of the proposed Union rather than that Commissioners should forthwith consult their constituents on the subject.[109] Thereafter the Cavaliers and Country party could do little more than play for time in the hope that jealousy and covert unhappiness with the terms

103 SRO GD 45/14/337/4–5: Andrew Fletcher of Saltoun to Harry Maule [Edinburgh?, 1706?], and Saltoun, 21 May 1706.
104 J. M. Grey (ed.), *Memoirs of the Life of Sir John Clerk of Penicuik* (Edinburgh, Scottish History Society, 1st Ser., 1892), pp. 58, 64–5; HMC *Mar and Kellie*, pp. 284–5: Earl of Mar to Sir David Nairne, Edinburgh, 4 Oct. 1706; SR, p. 134.
105 LL, p. 36: GL to Hamilton, [Edinburgh], 1 Aug. 1706; *Letters Relating to … First Earl of Seafield*, pp. 173–4: Viscount Dupplin to Godolphin, Edinburgh, 25 Oct. 1706.
106 Riley, *Union*, pp. 254–9, 260–8; Whatley, *Bought and Sold*, p. 47.
107 Riley, *Union*, p. 328.
108 See Baron Sir John Clerk's observation in SRO GD 18/6080: p. 216: 'I believe indead the gentlemen who composed the party called the Squadrone had not then solidly disgested the measures they were to take. But this must be acknowledged, that what way soever they inclined, their resolutions would have cast the ballance between the contending parties'.
109 *Baillie*, p. 164: Baillie to Johnstone [Edinburgh], 15 Oct. 1706; *Letters Relating to … First Earl of Seafield*, p. 97: Seafield to Godolphin, Edinburgh, 16 Oct. 1706.

of the Union would produce a split on the Court-Squadrone side.[110] Nor was this beyond the bounds of possibility. A number of Courtiers crossed over to the opposition during the Union debates (and a smaller number of the opposition went over to the Court), and other Courtiers and Squadrone members, such as Sir James Stewart, the Lord Advocate, and Sir John Anstruther point blank refused to support the Union and absented themselves.[111] Hence the passage of the Act of Union was punctuated by formal protests over particular violations of Scottish law and custom inherent in an incorporating union, and endless prevarications and time-wasting by the opposition in the hope that something would turn up.[112]

Lockhart is correspondingly listed as adhering to six formal protests and as having presented a further two himself.[113] Likewise he and most of the rest of the opposition are recorded proposing amendment after amendment as each clause of the Union came up for consideration.[114] The opposition also encouraged the political nation to send in addresses against the Union to their representatives, and in a remarkable testimony to the deep unpopularity of the measure outside Parliament a flood of these duly followed.[115] The Court, according to Lockhart 'having resolved to trust to their number of led-horses, and not to trouble themselves with reasoning',[116] responded by effectively refusing to debate the terms of the Union in detail, instead stolidly using its majority to bulldoze the Act through Parliament: 'the Courtiers had ears and would not hear, hearts and would not understand, nay mouths but would not speak. Few or no answers were to be made, but a vote required, whereby the sense of the House was to be known and the matter determined; and thus they drove furiously on ...'[117] Behaviour which, however tactically shrewd, outraged George and many other observers' sense of constitutional propriety, and created in its wake a legacy of bitterness it would take two generations to assuage.[118] By deploying the best efforts of their best orators (amongst whom Lockhart was not numbered [119]) to play the patriot card against the pro-Union

110 SR, pp. 158–9.
111 Riley, *Union*, pp. 329, 335 n. 21.
112 *APS*, xi. 309–405 *passim*; and see for example, LP i. 185, 186–9, 206.
113 *APS*, xi. 309: 25 Oct. 1706; 313: 4 Nov. 1706; 315: 15 Nov. 1706; 328: 18 Nov. 1706; 366: 24 Dec. 1706; 369: 27 Dec. 1706; 386–8: 7 Jan. 1707.
114 See for example, *APS*, xi. 322–4: 14 Nov. 1706; 362–6: 23 Dec. 1706; 383–4: 6 Jan. 1707.
115 SR, pp. 147–50. Even the Union's protagonists did not seriously dispute the fact that the measure was deeply unpopular, for an example of which, see: SRO GD 18/6080: pp. 224, 338.
116 SR, p. 143.
117 SR, p. 168, but cf. Baron Sir John Clerk's marginal comment in SRO GD 18/6080: p. 265.
118 B. Lenman, 'A Client Society: Scotland between the '15 and the '45', in J. Black (ed.), *Britain in the Age of Walpole* (1984), pp. 69–94; Szechi, 'Hanoverians and Scotland', pp. 122–6.
119 Blairs Letters 2/124/10: James Carnegy to the Scots College [Edinburgh], 16 Mar. 1706.

side, the opposition did manage briefly to crack the Court's formidable discipline on a couple of occasions, but ultimately they proved unable to divide them or the Squadrone permanently.[120] The opposition, or at least the more aggressive Jacobites among them such as Lockhart, correspondingly began to turn their attention to mobilising forces outside Parliament that might yet intimidate the Courtiers and Squadrone into allowing the Union to fall.

There was widespread public hostility to the Union before the Scots Parliament even met in October, and the opposition would have been fools not to try and exploit it. The question then became, how far should they go? With very little effort on its part the opposition had been able to generate an outpouring of constituency and institutional addresses against the Union which the Court proved completely incapable of matching with counter-petitions in its favour.[121] The problem was that the Court was singularly unabashed by the manifest hostility of the people and institutions of Scotland. Argyll famously described the addresses flooding into Parliament as of no other use 'than to make kites',[122] and the rest of the ministry showed a similarly flinty refusal to be deterred by the public's clear opposition to the Union.[123] The next stage was obviously public demonstrations of some kind. The problem with this was that demonstrations in the early modern era were usually categorised by those in power as minor insurrections or riots, and given the mood of the Scottish public and the nervousness of the authorities, any formal attempt to organise mass protests was liable to degenerate into violence.[124] In any case, by the time the administration had convincingly demonstrated its impeturbability in the face of public addresses from so much of the political nation, there had already been several riots against the Union and its supporters, following which potentially riotous assemblies of all kinds had been banned and troops deployed on the streets of Edinburgh and Glasgow.[125]

If George and those like him had had their way, the next step would have been an armed march on Edinburgh. By November George and several other violent anti-Unionists were already in contact with Major James Cunningham of Eickett, one of the leaders of a militantly anti-Union presbyterian association in the southwest of Scotland. Cunningham was a distinctly dubious character

---

120 SR, pp. 159–60; *APS*, xi. 360–2: 20 Dec. 1706.
121 SR, pp. 146–57; SRO GD 18/6080: p. 230. Cf., too, the Earl of Mar's silence in the face of a suggestion from Sir David Nairne (then in London) that the Court work up some pro-Union addresses: HMC *Mar and Kellie*, p. 320: Whitehall, 14 Nov. 1706.
122 SR, p. 150.
123 SRO GD 18/6080: p. 273.
124 Stevenson, *Popular Disturbances*, pp. 6–11.
125 SR, pp. 143–4, 177; HMC *Portland*, iv. 340–1, 352, 364, 365: Daniel Defoe to Robert Harley, Edinburgh, 24 Oct., 16 Nov. and 7 Dec. 1706; HMC *Mar and Kellie*, pp. 298–9: Mar to Sir David Nairne, Edinburgh, 26 Oct. 1706; *Letters Relating to … First Earl of Seafield*, p. 107: Seafield to Godolphin, Edinburgh, 16 Nov. 1706.

with a long track record of treachery and dissimulation, though at this stage George's belief that he was sincere was apparently well-founded.[126] The association he represented, which apparently contained a good number of Cameronians (who had a well-earned reputation for using physical force against regimes that displeased them), had already briefly seized Dumfries in order to burn the articles of Union at the market cross, and Cunningham now offered to join their forces with the Cavaliers in a general uprising.[127] The plan agreed upon was for a sudden muster at Hamilton followed by a rapid march on Edinburgh to overawe or evict the Parliament. This was to be supported by the Cavaliers throughout the Lowlands and directly aided by the turning out of the clans of Highland opposition magnates such as Atholl.[128] It was a bold, straightforward plan and might have stood some chance of success (at least in the short term) but for the covert opposition it encountered from within the leadership of the anti-Unionist coalition in Parliament.

In the face of the crisis they faced in the autumn of 1706 the various strands of the opposition had come together in a concerted effort to block the Union. Following the death of the Earl of Home shortly before the session opened, leadership of the Cavalier-Country axis had devolved on four men: Hamilton, Atholl, the Marquess of Annandale (a disgruntled Courtier) and Fletcher, with Hamilton the most influential of the group. Together they concerted formal protests, organised votes in Parliament and led the debate for the opposition side.[129] Annandale and Fletcher were both Whigs and there is no indication that they were ever consulted regarding plans for a rising.[130] Hamilton and Atholl, however, were competitors for leadership of the Cavalier element in the opposition.[131] Whichever magnate won them over accrued most political clout. Hamilton was therefore privy to plans to overthrow the Whig regime and systematically used his involvement to sabotage them.

Hamilton had been meeting secretly with government ministers since 1705 and had apparently promised that he would, 'do nothing that might effectively mine [i.e. destroy] the Union'.[132] Going by his behaviour, what he meant by this was that he would not take, or endorse, extra-Parliamentary action against its passage. By the end of November 1706 he was thus caught in a serious political dilemma. In order to cut any figure at all in politics, Hamilton had to be able to command a formidable following. By late November a considerable number of his erstwhile followers, i.e. the Cavaliers, were getting angry and

126 SR, pp. 180–1; SRO GD 18/6080: p. 279.
127 SR, pp. 177–9.
128 SR, pp. 181–3.
129 *APS*, xi. 313, 328, 386, 415; SR, pp. 133–4, 143, 160, 161–3, 188–94.
130 SR, pp. 44–5, 110.
131 SR, p. 135.
132 SRO GD 18/6080: pp. 252, 325, 326.

restless. They wanted direct action to stop the Union, including an uprising if necessary. If he led a rebellion his hopes of working his passage with the Court were at an end; if he refused to lead them, the Cavaliers would abandon him for Atholl (as, indeed, they subsequently did in 1707–8), he would have no significant following and the Court could safely ignore him. Hamilton accordingly seems to have settled for a typically devious compromise: he made sympathetic noises regarding Cavalier (and other groups') plans for demonstrations and uprisings while they were in the planning stage, then sabotaged them just before they were about to take place. Thus when asked if he would support Cunningham's rising he, 'insinuated he would do every thing that an honest man could desire',[133] then obstructed the actual launching of the rebellion (by sending out last-minute orders postponing it) so effectively that the rising never got off the ground, upon which Cunningham lost heart and eventually defected to the ministry.[134] Lockhart and the other militants were to become all too familiar with this pattern of behaviour. On three seperate occasions they found themselves baffled and frustrated by last-minute objections and prevarications stemming from their putative leader.[135]

The final straw came when Hamilton undercut a very shrewd maneuvre of his own in order to avoid irretrievably offending the Court. This came in early January 1707, when he proposed that the opposition introduce a bill placing the succession to the crown of Scotland in the house of Hanover. When the Court and Squadrone majority rejected this the opposition would register a collective formal protest in Parliament, then secede as a body, draw up a national petition against the Union and send it direct to the queen.[136] By dint of great deal of personal lobbying on the part of Hamilton and his close adherents (including George) and after some anguished reflection on the part of the more rigidly Jacobite Cavaliers, the duke finally brought the opposition as a whole round to supporting the plan.[137] It was a good ploy, and probably stood a very real chance of stopping the Union even at that late stage. Contemplating Lockhart's account of it ten or so years later, Baron Sir John Clerk, a solid Courtier Unionist in the autumn of 1706, succinctly noted: 'I belive this methode would have done'.[138]

The whole project came to naught, however, when Hamilton lost his nerve. It is possible that he had not thought through the full consequences of the secession he proposed to lead. In the heated political atmosphere of winter 1706–7 such a secession and national petition (with the ghost of the National Covenant in the wings) could have led to a great deal more than constitutional protest.

133 SR, pp. 181–2.
134 SR, pp. 182–3; *Correspondence of Colonel N. Hooke*, ii. 353, 372–3.
135 SR, pp. 183–96.
136 SR, pp. 188–9.
137 SR, pp. 193–5; LL, p. 37: GL to Harry Maule, [Edinburgh, Dec. 1706].
138 SRO GD 18/6080: p. 294.

Will he, nil he, Hamilton might well have found himself leading a national movement that polarised the country and set it on track for a civil war. Either because of his belated realisation of this, or else due to secret threats from the ministry, the duke tried to weasel out of being the person designated to enter the formal protest against the rejection of the bill on the grounds that he was suffering from toothache. When his supporters finally shamed and bullied him into going to Parliament he obdurately refused to introduce the protest, though he disingenuously offered to be the first adherer to it.[139] Such outrageous pusillanimity finally broke the spirit of the opposition. Angry and frustrated, more and more of them abandoned the hopeless Parliamentary struggle against the Court and returned to their homes. Lockhart too began to make fewer and fewer appearances, despite the fact that his main residence was within easy reach of Edinburgh.[140] And even George, Hamilton's true friend, could not conceal his *schadenfreude* when Hamilton's hopes of being named as one of the first batch of Scottish Representative Peers to be sent up to Westminster were casually thwarted at the last moment by Queensberry.[141]

The failure of their constitutional campaign to block the Union was far from being the end of the struggle as far as Lockhart and many of the Cavaliers were concerned. The next step was obviously armed resistance. Unfortunately for the would-be rebels, by the spring of 1707 Hamilton's double-dealing had produced a bitter split in their ranks. Lockhart, loyal as ever, soon forgave him for his duplicitous conduct, but most of the duke's other contemporaries on the anti-Union side refused to overlook what they (from their point of view, correctly) construed as his treachery.[142] Most of those who were willing to contemplate rebellion accordingly attached themselves to Atholl and sought a French invasion forthwith. A handful, including Lockhart, still adhered to Hamilton and were more dubious about the immediate prospects for success of an insurrection.[143] Correspondingly, though both parties entered into negotiations with the French government via its agent, Colonel Nathaniel Hooke (who arrived in Scotland in May 1707), it was the more militant Atholl faction who made the running as far as the French were concerned.[144] Louis XIV and his ministers were primarily interested in diverting the attention and resources of the British government from the war in Flanders, where, by dint of the brilliant generalship of the Duke of Marlborough, the Grand Alliance was rolling back two generations of French

---

139 SR, pp. 195–6; Ferguson, *Scotland's Relations With England*, p. 264.
140 *APS*, xi. 391 *et seq*; SR, pp. 196–7, 202–3.
141 HMC *Mar and Kellie*, pp. 373–6: Mar to Sir David Nairne, Edinburgh, 13 Feb. 1707; SR, p. 204.
142 SR, pp. 213–14; *Correspondence of Colonel N. Hooke*, ii. 349.
143 SR, pp. 217–18.
144 *Correspondence of Colonel N. Hooke*, ii. 347–410 *passim*.

conquests.[145] Given the demand for men and equipment for existing battlefronts in Flanders, Italy, Spain and the Caribbean, moreover, France had little to spare to support a Scottish rising. Consequently the French government was interested in securing a firm commitment to rebel on the part of the Scots in return for the minimum investment of troops and munitions by themselves. Hooke made this transparently clear in his negotiations.[146] Hence it can only be surmised that when Hamilton demanded an expeditionary force of 10–15000 men, with supplies and money to match, he was once again surreptitiously attempting to sabotage the enterprise.[147] Nonetheless he clearly managed to persuade George and the other Cavaliers who still adhered to him that such demands were pragmatic and sensible.[148] The upshot was that Lockhart *et al* found themselves very much on the fringes of planning and preparation for the putative rising.

George as a result found himself torn between loyalty to his friend and a wish to be in the thick of any rebellion. He resolved his dilemma by loftily criticising the terms agreed between Hooke and the Atholl group as based on a foolishly optimistic assessment of the situation, while making his own preparations for a separate Hamilton group rising.[149] As far as we can tell, Hamilton did not discourage this initiative, which centred on a rising in Lanarkshire, presumably on grounds of reinsurance (if a French landing occurred and the rebellion succeeded he would need to have been involved at some level to retain his political credibility in an independent, Jacobite Scotland).[150] Such a rising would have been made or broken by the attitude of the local, devoutly presbyterian, population, since episcopalians and catholics were tiny minorities in the south-west of Scotland. And certainly, later in the eighteenth century, any plan for a Jacobite rising which assumed presbyterian support would have been seen by contemporaries – and modern historians – as either bogus or insane. In 1707–8, however, there was still a good deal of anger abroad at the way the Union had been foisted on the mass of Scots.[151] Indeed George had a surprising encounter underscoring the depths of popular discontent when, despite his poor relations with his tenants, a delegation from the locality visited him while he was at Carnwath,

145 *Correspondence of Colonel N. Hooke*, ii. 157, 442; D. Chandler, *Marlborough as Military Commander* (2nd edn, 1979), pp. 94–183.
146 *Correspondence of Colonel N. Hooke*, ii. 364–5, 379–80.
147 *Correspondence of Colonel N. Hooke*, ii. 364; 268–9: Hamilton to Louis XIV, 30 May 1707 ns; 291–2: James Carnegy to Hooke, 23 May 1707. Hooke certainly thought so: ii. 354–5, 363–4, 368.
148 *Correspondence of Colonel N. Hooke*, ii. 255–6: Viscount Kilsyth to Hooke, 19 May 1707; SR, p. 218.
149 SR, pp. 216–18.
150 SR, pp. 220–1.
151 HMC *Portland*, iv. 425: Daniel Defoe to Robert Harley, 8 July 1707; SR, pp. 211–12; *Correspondence of Colonel N. Hooke*, ii. 359; 230–1: GL to Patrick Lyon of Auchterhouse, Dryden, 30 Apr. 1707.

telling him they were ordered by a considerable party to enquire of him against what time he thought the king [the Old Pretender] would land; and upon his answering that he wondered how they could ask such a question of him ... they answered ... they doubted not but he knew, and they would be glad to know likewise, that each of them might spare one or two of their best horses from work, and have them in good condition against he landed.[152]

Thus Lockhart's plans may not have been entirely foolhardy.

In any case all the preparations and backbiting eventually proved pointless. The French navy was firmly opposed to the project, which would have committed it to sustaining a French army in Scotland in the face of the overwhelming battlefleet superiority of the Maritime powers (England and the Dutch Republic) in home waters.[153] The French government consequently delayed sending the expedition in the hope that something less hazardous would turn up. In the meantime France's strategic situation improved as a result of victories in Spain and Germany and the defeat of Prince Eugene's invasion of Provence.[154] Hence despite some desperate lobbying by the Scots Jacobites the 1707 campaigning season eventually came to a close without any decision having been taken.[155] Louis XIV was only finally brought round to ordering the expedition in December by the personal intervention of his *dévot* wife, Madame de Maintenon, and the bleak prospect for French arms in the forthcoming year.[156] It finally sailed in March 1708 after still more delays, some legitimate, such as the Old Pretender being struck down by measles as he was about to go aboard, others transparently foot-dragging on the part of the French navy. By dint of some good seamanship the fleet evaded Sir George Byng's squadron hovering off Dunkirk and reached Scotland, but when it became clear to the naval commander, the Comte de Forbin, that, because of the closeness of Byng's pursuit, the only way he could land the soldiers in Scotland would be at the cost of his ships he effectively abandoned the enterprise. Despite the Old Pretender's pleas to be landed alone in a rowing boat if necessary, Forbin adamantly refused to delay and the expedition returned to Dunkirk.[157]

Meanwhile the Scottish Jacobites waited for news of the French landing before they rose. By any criterion the garrison of Scotland had been run down to dangerously low levels and the fabric of its fortresses had been allowed to

---

152　SR, p. 212.
153　*Correspondence of Colonel N. Hooke*, ii. 184–5: Hooke to the Marquis de Torcy and the Marquis de Pontchartrain, 22 Mar. 1707 ns; J. S. Gibson, *Playing the Scottish Card. The Franco-Jacobite Invasion of 1708* (Edinburgh, 1988), pp. 108, 111–12, 118–19.
154　Chandler, *Marlborough*, pp. 184–200.
155　Gibson, *Scottish Card*, pp. 101, 103.
156　Gibson, *Scottish Card*, p. 104.
157　Gibson, *Scottish Card*, pp. 117–31.

deteriorate.[158] In the event of a national uprising in 1708 the loyalty of many of the common soldiers could also not have been guaranteed. Hence Lockhart and his confrères awaited the arrival of the expedition with some anticipation.[159] They were correspondingly utterly downcast when the whole operation fizzled out. Only three Stirlingshire lairds had so jumped the gun as to be indictable for high treason for their behaviour in the day or so when the expedition's landing was imminently expected, but many more had made preparations that were distinctly suspicious, George among them. The government at Westminster and the administration in Scotland had also been badly frightened by the whole episode, and correspondingly turned vindictive when the danger receded. As a result there was a wave of arrests of suspected Jacobites in the aftermath of the fiasco.[160]

Fortunately for him, Lockhart was not one of those detained, at great expense to themselves, in London. Hamilton and quite a number of others were seized and sent there for interrogation and indictment, so this oversight (given George's role in the preparations for a rising by the Hamilton faction) *prima facie* looks very strange.[161] In fact, and not for the last time, Lockhart's friends and family retrieved him from a difficult situation. Wharton's influence enabled him to escape being arrested or even questioned about his role in the conspiracy.[162] Hamilton's cool exploitation of his enforced stay in London to do a deal with the Squadrone and its Whig allies for a political alliance in the 1708 general election in return for the release without trial of the prisoners if anything improved George's future prospects.[163] The duke thereby eclipsed Atholl as the putative leader of the Scottish Tories (as we may now call the former Cavaliers), and those who had stuck by him, such as Lockhart, were consequently well placed to resume their political careers.

The years George had spent as an aspiring politician at the fag-end of the Scottish polity were formative ones. By 1708, when he was about to launch himself into British politics at Westminster, he was already directed and driven by the ideas and connections that would shape the rest of his life. In tangible ideological terms he was firmly identified with the militantly episcopalian, Jacobite end of the Scottish Tory party. Underlying these positions, however, was an incoherent but pervasive belief in Scottish 'patriotic' values that at times is

158 SR, p. 222; HMC *Portland*, iv. 466: Captain John Ogilvie to Robert Harley, 25 Dec. 1707; HMC *Mar and Kellie*, p. 429: James Erskine of Grange to Mar, Edinburgh, 2 Mar. 1708. The estimate of Government forces in Scotland the French seem to have been working from amounted to a mere 1460 men (*Correspondence of Colonel N. Hooke*, ii. 310–11).
159 SR, p. 227.
160 Gibson, *Scottish Card*, pp. 140, 142.
161 SR, pp. 232–3.
162 LP i. 294–5.
163 *Baillie*, pp. 192–3: Earl of Roxburgh to George Baillie, London, 27 Apr. 1708; LP i. 293–4.

redolent of nothing so much as modern nationalism. In a sense George's Jacobitism was already being increasingly powered by his belief that Jacobitism was the best way to serve and defend the Scotland he loved, though he never expressed it in such a formal manner and was perhaps incapable of making the connection. As regards his personal network, Lockhart was by 1708 definitively associated with the Scottish Tories and Hamilton in particular. Only very rarely would he prove able to go against the emotional ties that wedded him to them both. He had also just about reached the limit of his rise as a party man. George was the archetypal zealous understrapper and mid-level organiser, but not one of those destined for greater things. In conventional politics he had risen to the level of henchman or lieutenant; he would go little further. Not until the 1720s would Lockhart carry greater weight among his peers.

CHAPTER FIVE

Parliamentary Jacobitism, 1708–1715

From 1708 to 1714 Lockhart's life was dominated by his involvement in politics at Westminster. It was a strange new world he found himself in. He characterised it years later as a place 'full of confusion and disorder', in which most politicians behaved like 'Bedlamites'.[1] Moreover, despite a superficial similarity in its procedures to those which had operated in the Scots Parliament, the new British Parliament often worked in ways that he was to find mystifying almost to the end of his involvement with it.[2] This stemmed directly from the nature of the Act of Union, which had essentially grafted a Scottish accretion on to an existing legislature. Because of the overwhelming predominance of English M.P.s and peers in the new British Parliament (513 English to 45 Scots in the Commons; 179 English to 16 Scots in the Lords), politics at Westminster were inevitably dominated by English mores and assumptions. Hence the political dynamics of Parliamentary politics prevailing in the English Parliament before 1707 persisted for some considerable time after the Union.

And the engine of Parliamentary politics in 1708 was the bitter division between the Whig and Tory parties. The Whigs traced their origins to the Exclusion Crisis of 1679–83 and presented themselves as the true guardians of the *protestant* cause in the British Isles. This catch-all term subsumed for them a relatively tolerant attitude towards English protestant religious nonconformity and (by the 1700s) a legalistic, constitutional perception of the monarchy. Though they have been characterised as the 'businessman's' party, and certainly enjoyed the support of most of London's post-1688 population of financiers and bankers, they were thoroughly aristocratic in their leadership and social attitudes, even to the extent of shading off into aristocratic republicanism among their more extreme elements.[3]

The Tories, by contrast, traced their origins back to the Cavaliers of the Great Civil War (and often accused the Whigs of being the heirs of the old Roundheads). Their ideology rested in theory on two pillars: loyalism and anglicanism. By the 1700s, as a result of bitter experience at the hands of James II and VII and William III and II, their original quasi-divine-right approach to loyalism had quietly metamorphosed into a more conditional attitude to their obligation to support the monarchy. The key condition was that the

---

1 LP i. 351
2 LL, pp.74–5: GL to [Harry Maule?], London, 26 May 1713.
3 Holmes, *British Politics*, pp. 83–7, 97–108, 221–46.

monarch support and protect the Church of England. In theory, and often in practice, the Tories were as hostile to catholics as the Whigs. The key difference was that the Tories were just as hostile to other religious groups they believed posed a more immediate threat to the anglican ascendancy. Thus whereas the Whigs presented themselves as the champions of the protestant cause, the Tories presented themselves as the champions of the *anglican* cause. In addition, the Tories may generally be characterised as favouring a more emphatically traditionalist approach to society and the economy, and a more chauvinistic approach to foreign relations than the Whigs.[4]

Overlaying these two basic alignments was a loose commitment on the part of almost all politicians to either 'Court' or 'Country' values. Those described as 'Court' tended to be sympathetic to the government of the day (whatever its political complexion) on the grounds that the monarch's business had to be done, and the administration of the country carried on whoever was in charge. Though there were, doubtless, principled adherents of the Court position, it always contained a high percentage of 'placemen', i.e. officeholders, who were viewed as valuing their jobs more than their principles. It was certainly a convenient ideological position for a placeman to hold. Even so, modern research has conclusively demonstrated that while those who adhered to the Court would generally support the day-to-day business of government, most of them realigned themselves with their Tory or Whig confrères whenever great party battles over particular issues erupted in Parliament.[5] Likewise, those who described themselves as adherents of 'Country' values affected a non-partisan, patriotic approach to the issues of the day. They were against political corruption (in all its forms, from bribing electors to buying votes in Parliament with jobs), social disruption and the intrusion of extravagant, foppish foreign mores. There were occasions when Country members of both parties would come together on particular issues, such as their common hostility to placemen, but these were few and far between. By and large, both 'Court' and 'Country' are best used as terms more precisely to describe the attitudes and values of particular Whigs and Tories.[6] To take the subject of this book as a case in point: Lockhart was a Country Tory to his fingertips.

To further complicate matters, however, there were hidden ideological and factional undercurrents that must be borne in mind when studying the politics of the period 1708–1714. By 1708 the Whig party was dominated by a 'Junto' of Whig aristocrats: Lords Somers and Halifax and the Earls of Orford, Sunderland and Wharton (George's uncle). This group provided the party with some central direction and a generally coherent political strategy. Through their electoral influence and connections, they also gave the party a stronger sense of discipline

4 Holmes, *British Politics*, pp. 87–96, 101–4, 247–84.
5 Holmes, *British Politics*, pp. 224–9, 253–7.
6 Holmes, *British Politics*, pp. 116–47, 221–3, 249–52, 340–1.

than was to be found in its Tory counterpart.[7] Their hegemony over the party did not, however, go unremarked or unresented, and by 1710 individual Whigs, such the Dukes of Shrewsbury and Argyll (who sat in the English Parliament by virtue of his English title, the Earl of Greenwich), were often proving contrary.[8] On the other side of the political divide the Tories were inherently far more faction-ridden. They had no central leadership as such, but many rather adhered (more or less strongly depending on circumstances) to individual chieftains such as the Earls of Rochester and Nottingham and Robert Harley. Whoever got himself appointed to the most senior ministerial post tended to assume a commanding role within the party, but there was always a certain amount of implicit feuding going on between these chieftains.[9] Hence the only way accurately to describe the political allegiance of a Tory like William Bromley of Baginton would be to label him a Country Tory friend of Robert Harley.[10] To complicate matters still further, there was a covert Jacobite tendency among the Tories.

For a good part of this century there has been a historiographic debate on the question of whether or not the Tory party was fundamentally Jacobite.[11] Which side a historian comes out on intrinsically affects his/her interpretation of politics and society, because if there is one thing that is generally agreed, it is that the mass of the political nation (and quite possibly the nation as a whole) was pro-Tory.[12] It is also indisputably the case that some Tory M.P.s were in at least intermittent contact with the Jacobite court at St Germain and sincerely wished to see the restoration of the main Stuart line. The question thus resolves itself into: 'How many were Jacobites?' And since few Jacobites were considerate enough either to have a large 'J' tattooed on their foreheads, or, as in Lockhart's case, to leave us manuscript evidence of their treason, this is ultimately an unanswerable question. By sifting through the veiled allusions and covert connections of those Tory M.P.s who sat in the Parliament of 1710, the present author arrived at an estimate of between 41 and 53 Tory M.P.s and 16–18 peers.[13] Since

7 Holmes, *British Politics*, pp. 235–45, 288–91.

8 G. Holmes, *The Trial of Dr Sacheverell* (1973), pp. 208–9, 226–7.

9 Holmes, *British Politics*, pp. 259–79.

10 Holmes, *British Politics*, p. 277.

11 K. G. Feiling, *A History of the Tory Party, 1640–1714* (Oxford, 1924), pp. 424–93; *The Second Tory Party, 1714–1832* (Oxford, repr. 1951), pp. 1–12; Sir Charles Petrie, *The Jacobite Movement* (1932), pp. 67–176; B. W. Hill, *The Growth of Parliamentary Parties* (1976), pp. 171–93; E. Cruickshanks, *Political Untouchables. The Tories and the '45* (1979), *passim*; Colley, *In Defiance*, ch. 2; Langford, *Polite and Commercial People*, pp. 16, 197–203; Szechi, *Jacobites*, pp. 1–6.

12 Holmes, *British Politics*, p. 248.

13 These figures are based on Szechi, *Jacobitism and Tory Politics*, pp. 200–3, but with certain individuals (Colonel George Douglas, Lieutenant-General Charles Ross and the Duke of Hamilton) excluded as a result of further research by the History of Parliament Trust and especially the work of Dr David Hayton of Queen's University, Belfast, who has convinced me that I was mistaken to count them as Jacobites. I am indebted to Dr Hayton for our long conversation on the subject.

the 1710 election returned some 332 Tories, this puts the Jacobites amongst them
at between 12% and 16% of their total strength in the Commons and 9–10% in
the Lords.[14] They were therefore clearly a minority within the party. Moreover,
in 1708 they were far from being a united minority. Their Court or Country
attachments and their friendships among the Tory chieftains generally had more
practical implications for their voting behaviour than their Jacobitism.[15] Nonetheless, their presence implicitly restricted the chieftains' room for maneuvre (if
they hoped to carry the whole party with them) and allowed the Whigs to smear
the whole party as Jacobite.

The addition of 61 Scottish representatives to the pre-1707 English Parliamentary structure added the final level of complexity to the basic dynamics of
Westminster politics from 1708 to 1714 that we need to take notice of here. For
the Scots truly had their Scottishness in common. Many English M.P.s and peers
regarded all Scots with contempt, and viewed their Parliamentary representatives
as simply importunate, irritating beggars.[16] Hence virtually all Scots M.P.s and
peers must have encountered some degree of anti-Scottish prejudice while living
and working in London. And, naturally enough, they resented it. This common
experience of discrimination in turn fuelled episodic fits of unity which cut across
party lines on particular issues, usually where English indifference or hostility
towards Scotland threatened to hurt Scottish economic interests.[17] Therefore, in
addition to all the other influences on the allegiance and voting pattern of
Scotland's representatives at Westminster, a basic 'national' pull must be taken
into account.

Lockhart's return to Westminster in the 1708 general election thus projected
him into a highly stratified and complex political situation for which he was
barely, if at all, prepared. He was, however, clearly determined to get into the
House of Commons, as may be seen from the fact that because he was uncertain
of his support in Midlothian, which had not been to the polls since 1702, he took
the precaution of standing both there and in Wigton Burghs. This was one of
the collective Burgh seats established by the Act of Union and was at this time
dominated by George's in-laws, the Galloways. In consequence, he appears to
have been returned unopposed.[18] George nonetheless chose to serve for Midlothian, the more prestigious of the two seats, when he won there by a sizeable
majority (by Scottish standards). According to Sir John Clerk, George owed his

---

14 W. A. Speck, *Tory and Whig. The Struggle in the Constituencies 1701–1715* (1970), p. 123.

15 See, for example, LP i. 441–2.

16 BL, Blenheim Papers 61461, ff. 107, 141: Arthur Maynwaring to the Duchess of Marlbo-
    rough [26? Dec. 1710 and 8 July 1711]; LP i. 330; Colley, *Britons*, pp. 11–13, 105–17.

17 See, for example, SRO GD 45/14/352/10: Lord Balmerino to Harry Maule [London],
    2 June [1711].

18 CJ, xvi. 7: 23 Nov. 1708; R. Sedgwick (ed.), *The House of Commons 1715–1754* (2 vols, 1970),
    i. 404.

victory to the support of the minor heritors and a split Whig ticket; an analysis that is certainly supported by the voting figures: Lockhart 27; Lord Charles Ker 17; Sir William Baird 12.[19] Nonetheless, Lockhart's success in 1708 seems to have given him a clear ascendancy in the county, and in consequence he was not to face a really serious challenge again until 1715. He was though, a rare bird in the 1708 Parliament. Because most Tories in Scotland sensibly chose to keep a low profile in the general election so as not to draw the wrath of the Whig administration upon themselves so soon after the invasion attempt, George was one of only five resolutely Tory M.P.s returned for Scotland in 1708.[20]

In terms of the alignments described above Lockhart was a Country Tory friend of the Duke of Hamilton with Jacobite sympathies, and in the political context of 1708 that put him firmly in the political wilderness. Queen Anne's first English ministry had been basically Tory, and was headed by the Duke of Marlborough and Lord Godolphin, ably backed in the Commons by the Speaker, Robert Harley (who also doubled as a Secretary of State). Unfortunately for the Tory party, Marlborough and Godolphin (the Lord Treasurer) were old-fashioned Court Tories, with the emphasis definitely on the 'Court' part of the equation. They saw the winning of the War of the Spanish Succession as their primary task, and were moderate in their anglicanism. This did not sit well with the Country Tories. They wanted to win the war too, but favoured naval campaigns directed at Bourbon colonies rather than an expensive land war on the Continent. Moreover, they had hailed the succession of Queen Anne as a golden opportunity to pass legislation restricting the burgeoning power – as they saw it – of protestant dissenters. They were correspondingly increasingly angered by the lukewarmness of the ministry on the issue and its determination to fight Louis XIV's armies in the most heavily fortified area in Europe outside the Balkans: Flanders.[21]

By 1705 clashes over these and related issues had led to an estrangement between the ministry and its erstwhile backbench supporters. From then on, as their war-weariness grew (and certainly by 1708), the Country Tories steadily moved into virtually constant opposition to the Marlborough-Godolphin ministry. Their place was taken by the Whigs. Between 1702 and 1706 the Junto deftly manoeuvred itself into a position where the putatively Tory ministry was reliant on the Whig voting bloc to get legislation passed. The Junto then used their indispensability to bargain themselves and their followers into office. Harley sought to oppose this trend and was finally ousted from office for his pains in 1708.[22] Thus after the election of 1708, in which the Whigs did very well as a

19 SRO GD 18/2092/2: Sir John's spiritual journal for 1699–1709, 1 June 1708.
20 LP i. 294–5, 301.
21 Gregg, *Queen Anne*, pp. 151–98; H. Horwitz, *Revolution Politicks. The Career of Daniel Finch, Second Earl of Nottingham, 1647–1730* (Cambridge, 1968), pp. 167–204.
22 Gregg, *Queen Anne*, pp. 199–259; Horwitz, *Revolution Politicks*, pp. 204–14.

result of having successfully portrayed the Tories as politically unreliable in the aftermath of the attempted Franco-Jacobite invasion, the ministry had effectively metamorphosed from Tory to Whig.[23] Hence Country Tories like Lockhart were definitely on the outside looking in.

Consequently George's first session at Westminster (1708–9) was a frustrating one. The Scots Tories had no independent plan of campaign, so he simply aligned himself with the English Country Tories. Given the party's overall minority status, however, and the additional numerical insignificance of the Scots Tories, this was of little consequence to either side.[24] Besides which the mass of the Country Tories were suspicious of the Scots, and since Lockhart and his fellow Scots Tories were the first of their ilk the English Tories had encountered (with one exception, the entire Scottish representation at Westminster in 1707–8 had been pro-Union and mainly pro-Court), they had to prove their *bona fides*.[25] This may have been especially difficult for George, given his Wharton connection and the fact that early in the session he was nominated to two business committees of middling importance to the administration: that set up to look into the Royal Navy's finances and the regular committee 'to inspect the laws expired, and near expiring'.[26] This almost certainly occurred with the consent of the government and suggests its managers in the Commons may initially have believed that as Wharton's nephew he was 'safe'. The upshot was that Lockhart found himself *de facto* excluded from the management of the Tory party in the Commons and at the same time outwith the ministry. Correspondingly the only disputes which impressed themselves on him in 1708–9 were Scottish national ones, in which the Scottish M.P.s united more or less irrespective of party affiliations.[27]

The most important of these from his perspective was the Scots representatives' joint opposition to the ministry's proposed new treason act. This measure sought to align Scotland's distinct and more humane treason laws with England's draconian legislation on the subject.[28] The move stemmed from a 'not proven' verdict by a Scottish jury in the case of three Stirlingshire Jacobite lairds who had jumped the gun and taken up arms in 1708 before the French invasion force actually landed.[29] Lockhart obviously had a stake in the kind of treason laws he might eventually breach, but it appears that many Whiggish Scots M.P.s were uncomfortable at the prospect of importing the savage English version of

23 Speck, *Tory and Whig*, pp. 85, 86, 91, 123.
24 LP i. 295, 301.
25 R. R. Walcott, *English Politics in the Early Eighteenth Century* (Cambridge, Massachusetts, 1956), pp. 233–5.
26 CJ, xvi. 19, 25: 26 and 29 Nov. 1708.
27 LP i. 295–309 *passim*.
28 LP i. 300.
29 Gibson, *Scottish Card*, pp. 144–5.

these laws too.[30] In the end, however, the Whig/Court majority in the Lords had its way and English-style treason laws were introduced into Scottish legal practice, albeit with some ameliorating amendments.[31] George drew what little comfort he could from the Scots Whigs' chagrin at their failure to stop the bill and the fact that many 'now saw that the Union would not prove as they had been made believe and expected'.[32] The only legislative success of the session, in Lockhart's opinion, was the passage of an act funding the payment of drawbacks owed to Scots merchants on exports of salted goods, in which, it is interesting to note, he and other opponents of the Union were quite happy to cite its terms to browbeat the government into conceding a point that favoured Scottish economic interests.[33]

The interval between sessions in 1709 was a busy one for some of the Jacobites among the Scottish Tories because St Germain, at the behest of the French government, sent over several agents in the spring and summer to sound out the possibility of a renewed Franco-Jacobite invasion attempt. Lockhart makes no mention of these discussions in his memoirs, though he and the Hamilton group feature prominently in the final report and proposal for an invasion presented to Louis XIV and his Council.[34] Instead he seems to have spent the recess ingratiating himself with his constituents by presiding, as 'chancellor' of a jury, over an attempt to circumvent customs regulations banning the import of French wine and taking care 'to let the nation know how they were used in Parliament, and what they were to expect from the Union'.[35] Whatever the reason for George's apparent ignorance of or indifference to the conspiracy, the plot came to naught due to the desperate straits the French army and navy had been reduced to by the summer of 1709. The bloody and inconclusive stand-off the French army achieved at the battle of Malplaquet in September – the first time it had proved capable of standing up to Marlborough and Prince Eugene since 1704 – subsequently revived the hopes of Louis XIV and his ministers that conventional operations might yet save them and led to the shelving of all plans for an invasion.[36] In any event it was soon displaced in the minds of its potential Scottish participants by the furore surrounding the impeachment of Dr Henry Sacheverell.

Sacheverell was an anglican clergyman of the most zealous kind, and as part of a general Tory campaign to discredit the Whig ministry 'out of doors'

---

30 LP i. 301.
31 Ferguson, *Scotland. 1689 to the Present*, pp. 57–8.
32 LP i. 301.
33 LP i. 299–300.
34 *Correspondence of Colonel N. Hooke*, ii. 539–58, esp. 544–5, 554.
35 Blairs Letters 2/159/6: James Carnegy to Thomas Innes [Edinburgh?], 24 Nov. 1709; LP i. 309.
36 Chandler, *Marlborough*, pp. 201–68.

(i.e. among the electorate) he preached several inflammatory sermons in 1709, in which he alleged the Church of England was in danger of being undermined by the favour the government was showing to the dissenters.[37] George believed Sacheverell did so at the behest of Harley, who was at the time intriguing to bring down his old colleagues and their new Whig allies by persuading the queen that the way they were treating her was demeaning.[38] There is no evidence for such a connection, and in any case Sacheverell and his like needed little encouragement to attack the ministry and proclaim that the Church was in danger. Indeed, the rhetoric Sacheverell deployed had first been used by him in attacking the ministry when Harley was a part of it.[39] And had the government just ignored him Sacheverell's famous sermon 'In Peril Amongst False Brethren', preached before the Mayor and Aldermen of the City of London on 5 November 1709, would barely have made a footnote in history, there were so many like it at the time. For once, however, the fiery Sacheverell hit home – the quietly devout Lord Treasurer Godolphin (referred to in the sermon by his well-known nickname 'Volpone') was hurt and offended, and thus easily led into a Junto proposal to deter further attacks by impeaching Sacheverell.[40]

There could have been no better proof, as far as the mass of the population was concerned, that the blessed doctor's charges were well-founded, and the impeachment's progress provoked rioting in London of an order not to be seen again until the Gordon riots in 1780 and demonstrations in Sacheverell's favour that steadily spread outward from the capital as Tory propagandists fanned the flames of popular outrage.[41] Unfazed, the Whigs pushed the process forward to its conclusion, which was a vote in the Lords on whether or not the Commons' managers had proven Sacheverell guilty of 'high crimes and misdemeanours'.[42] At this point both parties mobilised their best effort to ensure the maximum possible vote for or against the doctor. And the Tories duly sicced Lockhart (by now rated 'a judicious young fellow' by one critical observer[43]) on Hamilton. The Hamilton connection had been giving mixed signals as to its political inclinations since 1708. Hamilton himself had carefully kept a foot in both camps, as had his following: thus one brother, the Earl of Orkney, continued to pursue an essentially apolitical career as a professional soldier, another brother, Lord Archibald Hamilton, had thrown in his lot with the

---

37 Holmes, *Trial of Dr Sacheverell*, pp. 47–75.
38 LP i. 310.
39 Holmes, *Trial of Dr Sacheverell*, p. 20.
40 Holmes, *Trial of Dr Sacheverell*, pp. 68–9, 76–89.
41 G. Holmes, 'The Sacheverell Riots: the Crowd and the Church in Early Eighteenth Century London', *Past and Present*, 72 (1976), pp. 55–85; Holmes, *Trial of Dr Sacheverell*, pp. 156–76, 234–9.
42 Holmes, *Trial of Dr Sacheverell*, p. 279.
43 Blairs Letters 2/159/13: James Carnegy to Thomas Innes, Edinburgh, 11 Mar. 1710.

Whigs, and his friend George Lockhart ran with the Tories.[44] Hence he was one of the few peers of whose votes the leaders of each party could not be reasonably certain. Despite his contempt for Sacheverell, whom he recalled as a 'poor despicable clergy man ... scarce worth their minding',[45] Lockhart vigorously lobbied the duke, but ultimately remained uncertain of the outcome and was probably very relieved when Hamilton voted for Sacheverell's acquittal.

Technically, all the Tories' efforts to save the doctor came to naught, in that he was convicted of high crimes and misdemeanours. But in fact they scored a tremendous moral victory by running the Whigs very close on the final vote and then convincing enough Whig peers to vote with them on the question of punishment to secure a very mild sentence.[46] It was a blow from which the ministry never recovered. The queen percipiently noticed that public opinion was moving against them and began to pay closer attention to Harley's assurances that he could construct a moderate Tory government that would negotiate an honourable end to the War of the Spanish Succession and treat her with more respect. The first tangible token of a shift in royal favour came with the appointment of the maverick Whig Duke of Shrewsbury to the influential office of Lord Chamberlain in April 1710. This was followed by the dismissal of the Earl of Sunderland as Secretary of State in favour of the moderate Tory Earl of Dartmouth in June and culminated in the dismissal of Lord Treasurer Godolphin in August. Harley and his closest allies were then brought into office to replace the rest of the Whig ministers, who resigned in protest.[47]

The successful unfolding of Harley's intrigues over the spring and summer of 1710 was, of course, 'most agreeable' to the Scots Tories.[48] They were, however, neither directly involved, nor necessarily the likely beneficiaries of these developments. Harley had only indirect links with Hamilton by 1710 and the central thrust of his planning for the new ministry was implicitly opposed to the inclusion of the more zealous Scots Tories such as Lockhart and his ilk. What Harley and his colleagues wanted (and had told Queen Anne they could secure) was a moderately Tory ministry, including many Court Whigs, that would be able to hold its own against both the Junto Whigs and the Country Tories if that should prove necessary.[49] George's associates among the Scots Tories were therefore not the kind of people the new ministry wanted to see returned for Scotland. Instead the ministers sought to ensure the survival and expansion of the old Court interest, who were most likely to provide the kind

44 *DNB*, xxiv. 157; *House of Commons*, ii. 98–9; LP i. 313–14.
45 LP i. 318.
46 Holmes, *Trial of Dr Sacheverell*, ch. 9.
47 Gregg, *Queen Anne*, pp. 309–23.
48 LP i. 315–18.
49 C. Roberts, 'The Fall of the Godolphin Ministry', *Journal of British Studies*, xxii (1982) 78–9.

of biddable lobby-fodder the government was going to need to carry off its balancing act.[50]

The problem with this approach was that unless the ministry enjoyed solid support from the Tories it was going to find it difficult to secure a majority in Scotland, particularly in the vital Representative Peers' election, and the only coin Lockhart and his colleagues would accept was power in the form of representation and places.[51] As early as August Mar warned Harley that Hamilton had to be gratified, for 'you see by our accounts from Scotland how necessary it is at this time to have him'.[52] The new premier minister was reluctant to accept this and prevaricated about authorising his agents in Scotland to make the necessary deals. Meanwhile Hamilton, who fully grasped the government's predicament, had ordered his understrappers in Scotland, such as Lockhart, to send round circular letters mobilising the Scots Tory interest.[53] Only when the Scots Tories began negotiating with the Squadrone to carve up the Representative Peers' election could Harley finally be persuaded to give way to the pleas of his managers in Scotland and commit the ministry to bringing in a significant tranche of Hamiltonians and Tories.[54]

Hamilton's success in forcing the ministry to deal with him over the Representative Peers' election did not extend to enforcing the Court's cooperation in elections to the House of Commons. Predictably, the Squadrone were soon charging the Scots Tories with aiming at restoring the Old Pretender and overthrowing the religious settlement of the Kirk: accusations that George pooh-poohed in an anonymous pamphlet he wrote and published in support of the Tory campaign.[55] The Scots Tories' overt platform meanwhile focused on a commitment to securing an episcopalian toleration act and compensation for those lords incarcerated in London but never charged after the failure of the 1708 invasion attempt. Their covert agenda, however, as George recalled, was indeed that 'now or never was the time to do something effectually for the King, and by restoring him dissolve the Union'.[56] And as a notorious zealot for the Tory (and Jacobite) cause, Lockhart duly found himself singled out for denunciation by the presbyteries of Dalkeith and Edinburgh, who enjoined their flocks 'to use their utmost interest' against him.[57] It was to no avail. Lockhart and several others were triumphantly returned with thumping majorities despite

50 HMC *Portland*, iv. 558–9: Lord Dupplin to Harley, 8 Aug. 1710.
51 LL, pp. 40–1, 41–2: GL to the Earl of Breadalbane and Harley, Dryden and Edinburgh, 7 and 9 Sept. 1710.
52 HMC *Portland*, x. 330–1: [21 Aug. 1710]; x. 333: 25 Aug. 1710.
53 LL pp. 40–1: GL to the Earl of Breadalbane, Dryden, 7 Sept. 1710.
54 Szechi, *Jacobitism and Tory Politics*, pp. 64–5.
55 LP i. 319; i. 509–20: *A Letter to a Lord of Session*.
56 LP i. 319.
57 Christ Church, Oxford, Wake MSS xvii. 262: Richard Dongworth to Bishop Wake of Lincoln, Edinburgh, 10 Aug. 1710.

everything the Squadrone could do.[58] Overall the elections were a stunning success and greatly boosted Hamilton's reputation as a political manager as well as finally eclipsing that of his old rival, Atholl.[59] And as a leading lieutenant of the triumphant magnate, George may well have quite reasonably hoped he could look forward to influence, if not office, under the new dispensation.

Such rewards, however, were to prove very slow in coming. Next to his acute understanding of English politics, Harley's greatest gift as a politician was his ability to lie with every semblance of sincerity.[60] Even after they had been comprehensively duped by 'the Wizard' for years, experienced politicians like Lord Lansdowne and the Earl of Orrery would continue, pathetically, to believe in his goodwill towards them.[61] And Harley had no intention of binding himself hand and foot to the Tory party by prosecuting the former Whig ministry and stuffing his administration with wild men from the sticks.[62] Instead he deployed a kind of Fabian approach towards his own backbenchers' demands for patronage and legislation: he obfuscated, prevaricated and delayed action interminably, presumably in the hope that they would get tired of it and give up asking. Hence for a while after the opening of the new Parliament the ministry was able to proceed with its business on the basis of the political equivalent of promissory notes.[63] The problem with this approach was that the new cohort of Country Tories were genuinely committed to an agenda that included investigating and prosecuting the legions of corrupt placemen they were convinced had staffed the previous administration, and just as sincerely believed that they should now monopolise all governmental offices themselves (thereby, of course, protecting the public from fraud and corruption in the future).[64] The two positions were not reconcilable, nor could the Country Tories be put off forever, as Harley was to discover.

Lockhart's experience of Harley's way of dealing with the importunate back-bencher was typical of many. As a lieutenant of Hamilton's with impeccable Country Tory credentials George considered he had the right to recommend clients and friends for minor government office. Correspondingly, he wrote to the premier in September 1710 politely asking that a distant kinsman (one Thomas Lockhart) working in the Customs service be promoted to Auditor.[65] Harley

---

58 LP i. 319; SRO GD 18/2092/3: Sir John Clerk's spiritual journal for 1710-Apr. 1712, 8 Nov. 1710.
59 Szechi, *Jacobitism and Tory Politics*, pp. 66–7.
60 Szechi, *Jacobitism and Tory Politics*, p. 121.
61 E. Handasyde, *Granville the Polite* (1938), pp. 112, 117–18, 123–4, 133; HMC *Portland*, v. 368, 369: Orrery to Robert Harley, Earl of Oxford, 2 and 3 Dec. 1713.
62 PRO, SP 34/13, f. 138: [memo on plans for the session, Harley to Queen Anne] 30 Oct. 1710.
63 Szechi, *Jacobitism and Tory Politics*, pp. 70–3.
64 Szechi, *Jacobitism and Tory Politics*, pp. 73–5.
65 LL, pp. 41–2: Edinburgh, 9 Sept. 1710.

apparently replied in the negative. Doubtless disappointed, but nothing down-hearted, Lockhart tried again in January 1711, this time on behalf of another Scots Country Tory's brother, and, further, shyly asked if he himself might receive 'some mark of her Majestie's favour', on the grounds that 'I have all alongst stood firm to the partie and principles that happily now prevaill, and therby dissoblidged some of my nearest freinds, who both coud and woud have done for me, woud I have enterd into ther measures'.[66] Despite the fact that George may have been hinting at something as cheap as a knighthood, Harley appears not even to have replied. Somewhat annoyed at being ignored, Lockhart ventured only one more recommendation, this time of one of his constituents, then kept silent for over a year.[67] In May 1712, however, he somewhat more pointedly asked Harley (by then Earl of Oxford) to arrange for a purge of the Midlothian Commission of the Peace in favour of selected constituents of his, of whom he thoughtfully provided a list.[68] No action was taken, so George resumed his suit in December, forthrightly opening his letter with the reminder: 'I have sevrall times presumd to speak to your Lordship concerning the Com-missions of the peace in Scotland, but not having ane opportunity to give your Lordship so full ane account of the matter, as I find needfull, since all the applications that have been made to my Lord Keeper have had no effect ...'[69] Receiving no reply, Lockhart wrote again 'with the greatest reluc-tancy imaginable', in January 1713 to press once more for a purge of the Commission of the Peace, and angrily pointing out:

> The want of a new Commissions of the Peace being a genrall loss, it were improper to mention anything particularly prejudiciall to my own interest as ane arguement to induce your Lordship to give them, and yet I cannot altogether pass over in silence, that Sir David Dalrymple's agents in the Countie of Edenburgh, urge as a reason for choosing of him and laying me aside att the next elections that I have not been able to get one Justice of the Peace named since the change of the ministry.[70]

Oxford's tergiversations had clearly already put George in a very embarrassing situation with his constituents, many of whom had deposited their clerk's fees with him in anticipation of being made magistrates two years before.[71] This letter finally elicited a response. In his inimitable fashion Oxford blandly passed over his prevarications up to this point, slyly implying any delay was Lord Keeper Harcourt's fault, then urged George to 'hasten up al your friends both Lords

---

66 LL, pp. 43–4: London, 6 Jan. 1711.
67 LL, p. 44: GL to Harley [London], 19 January 1711; LP i. 370–1.
68 LL, pp. 59–60: GL to Oxford, London, 10 May 1712.
69 LL, p. 61: London, 23 Dec. 1712. 'Lord Keeper' was Lord Harcourt.
70 LL, p. 65: Edinburgh, 27 Jan. 1711.
71 LL, pp. 65–6: Edinburgh, 27 Jan. 1713.

and commons' in anticipation of the session, and solemnly instructed him to come up to London 'fully intrusted about justices of the peace and al other matters requisite for the repose of your country'.[72] A new Commission of the Peace finally materialised in the summer, though it was not fully empanelled until November.[73]

Wringing this little piece of patronage out of the government seems to have emboldened Lockhart to ask for another small favour: the appointment of two of his constituents to minor sinecures in the Scottish administration. Both places were held by Whigs, though one was a Court Whig. By this time, having experienced the Harley technique of delay and obfuscation at first hand, George wrote in the first instance to Lord Keeper Harcourt, who passed it on to Oxford, and made it clear that what he wanted most of all a straight answer: 'Next to the granting of my request the greatest obligation will be to let me know what I'me to expect, for if this shall be thought too great a favour, I must cut my coat according to my cloath'.[74] On this occasion Oxford granted Lockhart's request and in July his constituents duly presented themselves at the Scottish Exchequer for payment of their salaries – only to find that though their appointments were valid Oxford had somehow neglected to issue warrants for them to be paid.[75] Despite further prodding on the subject the two sinecurists had not been added to the civil list for payment by October, at which point George exploded:

> Had it been thought expedient to reject my request at first, or had I myself been only concerned in the matter I would not have troubled your Lordship so often about it, but after the 2 commissions past the Queen's hand and that I pretended to some merit amongst the honest gentlemen of the Countie, I am out of countenance that the salarys of the offices shoud not be allowed.[76]

Lockhart, like many of his peers, found dealing with Harley a frustrating and annoying business. In the long term the endless delays and mendacity that were a commonplace of Harley's dealings with the Country Tories more than negated the positive effect of any patronage they ultimately extracted. His 'masterly' mode of political operation was thus ultimately short-sighted and bound to fail. For when no-one was any longer willing to allow him to secure their support on credit, he was doomed; the only question was when, not if, his political credit would run out.

As far as we can tell, however, Lockhart, like most of the new cohort of Country Tory M.P.s, nonetheless turned up at Westminster in November 1710

72 BL, Portland Loan 29/150/3: 9 Feb. 1713.
73 HMC *Portland*, x. 306: Mar to Oxford, Edinburgh, 3 Nov. 1713.
74 LL, p. 67: GL to Harcourt [London], 21 Mar. 1713.
75 LL, p. 82: GL to Oxford, Edinburgh, 7 July 1713.
76 LL, p. 88: Edinburgh, 24 Oct. 1713.

full of praise for Harley, and it took a while before he became irritated enough with him to turn against the ministry.[77] Early in the session Lockhart and an inner core of Scots Country Tory M.P.s (John Carnegy of Boysack, the Hon. James Murray, Sir Alexander Areskine of Cambo and Sir Alexander Cumming of Culter) were in any case busy setting up a semi-secret steering committee to monitor Parliamentary affairs and organise united – or as near united as they could manage – voting by Scots M.P.s on issues affecting Scotland. The group was secretive about its activities because its agenda was distinctly hostile to the Scots nobility, the committee being resolved, as George recalled: 'to shake off that servile dependance which the Scots Peers expected and had too much enjoyed from the Commons, wherby they rendered themselves more significant to the Court and promoted their designs, which for the most part were prejudicial to the interest of the countrey'.[78] Moreover the initiative was successful. Lockhart and his friends were soon being consulted by the ministry on matters concerning Scotland.[79] George's involvement in the formation of this little group of patriot activists was thus a turning point in his career as a politician, representing as it did the first steps in his emancipation from magnate influence and, in particular, the Duke of Hamilton.

It also led to his first direct clashes with the ministry. The new government had committed itself to a continued military offensive in Flanders and the other theatres of war in 1710, while the Earl of Jersey and later Harley secretly negotiated a separate peace with France.[80] In order to fund the continued war effort various new taxes were passed, one of which laid a 32-year impost on exports of linen. Linen production was one of the most important sectors of the Scottish economy and so Lockhart and his confrères promptly organised a joint campaign of opposition with the Scots Squadrone M.P.s, and succeeded in somewhat softening the impact of the tax.[81] In the course of a debate on the linen duty in the Committee of Ways and Means George also clashed personally with Harley, who had airily asserted that England had bought Scotland and the right to tax the Scots with the Equivalent. Lockhart adroitly responded by turning the debate into an attack on the Union:

> I took him up and said that I was glad to hear a truth, which I had niver doubted, now publickly brought to light and owned, for the honourable gentleman acknowledged that Scotland was bought and sold; but I much admired to hear from one of his experience in business and who had so great

77　Szechi, *Jacobitism and Tory Politics*, p. 69.

78　LP i. 338.

79　LP i. 339–40; LL, pp. 56–7: GL *et al* to Attorney-General Sir Edward Northey [London], 19 Jan. 1712.

80　Gregg, *Queen Anne*, pp. 334–5.

81　LP i. 326–8. I am grateful to Dr David Wilkinson of the History of Parliament Trust for explaining the sequence of events herein to me.

a hand in the purchase, that the equivalent was the price, it being as certain as it was no secret that the equivalent arose and was paid to Scotland on account of a sum with which the Scots customs and excise were to be charged towards paying debts contracted by England before the Union, so that the English got ane equivalent for this sum paid to Scotland, and therfore if Scotland was bought and sold, it must be for a price not yet come to light, and I woud be extremlie glad to know what this price amounted to and who received it.[82]

George then followed up this propaganda success by turning another debate, on a bill to regulate the linen industry in Scotland, into a swingeing attack on English partiality (this time in favour of Ireland over Scotland) and the iniquity of the Union.[83] Within weeks accounts of his clash with Harley were being retailed all over Scotland by opponents of the Union,[84] and when Lockhart returned there in the summer he thoughtfully fuelled the fire with an anonymous pamphlet which described the incident in detail and publicised all the other wrongs inflicted on Scotland during the session.[85]

In the course of these Parliamentary battles and other skirmishes with the ministry, George Baillie of Jerviswood, the Squadrone leader in the Commons, was moved to comment that the English 'were sometimes for acting as if the two kingdoms were united and sometimes as if they were not so'.[86] This was manifestly the case. Yet Lockhart's conduct indicates the Scots Country Tories were not immune to the same kind of political schizophrenia. For the practical politician emerging in Lockhart was perfectly prepared to take advantage of the Union he had just so violently damned when it served his other political ends. Thus when the ministry tried officially to fund all salaries payable to Scotland's administrators preferentially over export bounties and other benefits payable to Scottish merchants (which were limited to the annual yield of Scotland's customs), George attacked the proposal on the grounds that the civil administration in Scotland and England was now one body and could not legitimately be funded solely from Scottish sources. In other words, by the terms of the Union English revenues were required to meet any net shortfall in the expense of administering Scotland.[87]

Even more hard-headed was George and the other Scots Country Tories' cynical exploitation of English ignorance of Scottish affairs to undermine the legal basis of the Kirk's ascendancy in Scotland. In 1711 there was still only one

82 LP i. 327.
83 LP i. 328–32.
84 Blairs Letters 2/168/4: James Carnegy to Thomas Innes [Edinburgh?], 4 Feb. 1711; SRO GD 45/14/352/3: Ann Balmerino to Harry Maule, 30 Jan. [1711].
85 LP i. 529–48: *A Letter From a Scots Gentleman Residing in England to his Freind at Edinburgh*.
86 LP p. 335.
87 LP i. 333–6.

legal church in Scotland: the Kirk by law established. All other denominations (i.e. episcopalians and catholics) were subject to penal laws.[88] In practice, these laws were rarely applied against the episcopalians because they were at least protestants and many heritor families supported and protected episcopalian ministers. In 1710, however, an episcopalian clergyman, one James Greenshields, was imprisoned by the magistrates of Edinburgh for continuing to use the English Book of Common Prayer despite formal warnings not to do so. Greenshields was a highly untypical episcopalian cleric in that he, unlike the vast majority of his brethren, was willing to take the oaths of loyalty to the state enjoined by sundry acts since 1688.[89] Lockhart and the others certainly knew he was a rarity in this, but nonetheless presented him to sympathetic Tories in both houses as an ordinary minister of the episcopalian church persecuted for nothing more than conventional anglicanism by presbyterian bigots.[90] The ploy worked brilliantly. Not Harley's personal intervention in an attempt to persuade Lockhart to drop the matter, nor all the efforts of a delegation from the General Assembly of the Kirk and Scottish presbyterian M.P.s and peers to explain the situation in Scotland were able to defeat the coalition built up by the Scots Tories.[91] George and his fellow episcopalians used the 'persecution' motif so effectively that they convinced not only the Country Tory members of the Lords but also most of the (usually Whiggish) bench of bishops of the Church of England to vote in Greenshields' favour, thereby throwing into doubt the Kirk's right to defend its official monopoly of religious practice in Scotland.[92]

Lockhart then proposed to the Scottish steering committee that they follow up their success in the Greenshields case by bringing in a bill extending formal, legal toleration to the episcopalian church.[93] The ministry, alarmed at the possibility of serious civil disorder if the measure passed, as was being threatened in some hysterical sermonising north of the border, exerted itself to thwart the move. George correspondingly soon found several of his colleagues expressing a reluctance to beard the ministry a second time in the same session, and had to threaten to move the measure independently in order to carry them with him. Before they could move a toleration bill in the Commons, however, Lockhart and Sir Alexander Areskine of Cambo, Lord Lyon King-at-Arms, were summoned into the presence of the Earl of Rochester and the Duke of

---

88 Ferguson, *Scotland. 1689 to the Present*, pp. 102–14.

89 D. Szechi, 'The Politics of "Persecution": Scots Episcopalian Toleration and the Harley Ministry', in, W. J. Sheils (ed.), *Toleration and Persecution, Studies in Church History*, xxi (1984), 280–1.

90 LP i. 348.

91 LP i. 346–8; NLS, Wodrow Letters, Quarto V, ep. 100: Thomas Smith to Robert Wodrow, 3 Mar. 1711.

92 SRO GD 45/14/352/5: Lord Balmerino to Harry Maule, 8 Mar. [1711]; *London Diaries of William Nicolson*, pp. 527, 531, 543, 546, 552–3.

93 LP i. 339.

Shrewsbury, who passed on a personal message from the queen requesting that they delay introducing the bill for one session. The two finally agreed to postpone the measure in return for a solemn commitment on Queen Anne's part that she would support both it and the restoration of lay patronage of Kirk livings next session, and were duly assured of her support in both cases.[94]

George's increasing prominence among the Scots M.P.s did not pass unnoticed among his English Country Tory colleagues. Though he had been appointed to serve on a fair number of Commons committees in 1708–9, thereafter the Whig managers of the house appear to have realised he was an inveterate opponent and he was consequently appointed to the committee of only one bill, and that a private property bill, in 1709–10.[95] In 1710–11, however, he was one of only a handful of veteran Scots Country Tory M.P.s among a host of new boys, which naturally impelled him towards assuming a leading role in implementing their legislative agenda. The fact that few M.P.s were as consistently engaged and ideologically committed as he was reinforced this tendency, and consequently George quickly became one of the inner core of 'active' M.P.s who regularly attended the house and oversaw the passage of legislation, amongst whom Country Tories were a distinct minority. Thus in the first session of the new Parliament, quite apart from his regular involvement in debates, he was appointed to serve on eleven committees and told off to bring in three bills specifically dealing with Commons business.[96] Hence when the English Country Tories decided to establish a Commission of Accounts in March 1711, and the Scottish Tories demanded that a Scot should have one of the seven seats, Lockhart was deemed the only acceptable choice by his English peers.[97]

The Commission of Accounts was a traditional backbench tool, revived, ironically, in the 1690s by Harley, for detecting and punishing corrupt placemen, evil ministers and other *bêtes noires* of Country M.P.s, and in March 1711 the initial legislation setting one up stemmed from a new backbench Tory organisation: the October Club. The October Club was an early product of the same phenomenon of bafflement and mounting irritation with the ministry that George was to experience from 1710 to 1713.[98] While firmly committed to sustaining the ministry in general (out of respect for the queen and in hopes that it would negotiate a quick end to the war), they were determined to force the pace over the investigation of Whig malfeasance and legislation to bolster the authority of the Church of England – both issues the ministry was shy of.[99] The club met regularly in a tavern near the Commons, debated policy among themselves and

94 LP i. 339–40; Szechi, 'Politics of "Persecution"', pp. 281–2.
95 CJ, xvi. 375: 18 Mar. 1710.
96 CJ, xvi. 471–681.
97 LP i. 324–5.
98 Szechi, *Jacobitism and Tory Politics*, pp. 74–6.
99 Szechi, *Jacobitism and Tory Politics*, pp. 76–7.

agreed on joint action in the chamber. At its height the October Club theoretically numbered some 150 M.P.s, but (given the tendency of Country M.P.s in
general quietly to drift home or find other diversions if a Parliamentary session
went on any length of time) it usually deployed only a hardcore voting bloc of
about 80.[100] In a house where it was rare to find over 300 of the 548 M.P.s
present and voting, however, 80 M.P.s was an effective force.[101] Individual
Scottish Country Tories joined the Club and the Scottish steering committee
seem to have entered a semi-permanent alliance with them, but Lockhart's
absence from lists of its members may indicate that he technically stayed aloof,
though it would have been hard to tell this from his voting pattern, political
sympathies and associates.[102]

The Commissioners of Accounts were generally considered to be leading
Country Tories, so it is a token of George's newly achieved prominence that he
was not only the preferred choice of the English Country Tories, but came
second out of seven in the poll with 224 votes.[103] Even so, he subsequently
claimed to be not altogether pleased to be nominated as a Commissioner as he
'forsaw it woud tye me down to a close attendance and almost constant abode
in London, and expose me to the malice and revenge of many who wou'd be
obnoxious to the commission'. When pressed, however, he felt duty-bound to
accept the post.[104]

Thus George committed himself to being 'tyed down to a close attendance
at Essex house' [105] for the next four years. He was very active in the Commission,
and though in retrospect he looked upon its achievements with a jaundiced eye,
the energy he invested in its work suggest that at the time he considered it to
be a worthwhile instrument of reform and retribution.[106] Lockhart's particular
task was investigating the accounts of the Scottish exchequer and administration,
and he spent the summer of 1711 shuttling between formal hearings and examinations in Edinburgh and meetings in London setting in train the administrative
processes for the Commission's investigations.[107]

His first encounters with the officials he was auditing in Scotland were
chastening ones. George initially tried to be reasonable about allowing farmers of
the customs and other officials time to collect their records together, only to find
them deliberately spinning out the process and trying to block his investigations

---

100 H. T. Dickinson, 'The October Club', *Huntington Library Quarterly*, xxxiii (1969–70), 155–74.
101 Holmes, *British Politics*, pp. 249–51, 353–81.
102 A. Boyer (ed.), *Quadriennium Annae Postremum; or the Political State of Great Britain* (8 vols, 1718),
      iii. 117–21.
103 CJ, xvi. 562: 19 Mar. 1711.
104 LP i. 325.
105 LL, p. 66: GL to Lord Keeper Harcourt [London], 21 Mar. 1713.
106 LP i. 349–52.
107 CJ, xvi. 662: 14 May 1711.

by appealing to the courts.[108] Thereafter he became much more inflexible about allowing respondents leeway in any form, as a result of which he ended up offending old friends and colleagues like William Cochran of Kilmaronock and Fletcher of Saltoun, both of whom he named in his reports to the Commission after informants made what later turned out, at least in Fletcher's case, to be unsubstantiated allegations against them.[109] Nonetheless, by the end of 1711 George had become a very effective investigator. The first inkling of the 'bread-money' scandal that was to bring down the Duke of Marlborough came from one of his informants, and his sense that there was something wrong with the price of the forage contract awarded in Scotland in 1708 by the then Minister of War, Robert Walpole, led him to investigate and discover the embezzlement of public funds that was to put Walpole in the Tower for several months in 1712.[110] It is perhaps significant that in the winter of 1711–12 his fellow Commissioners allowed Lockhart the honour of presenting the report indicting both men to the Commons.[111]

If there was one thing that stood out about Lockhart's conduct as a Commissioner of Accounts, however, it was the impartiality of his zeal.[112] Many Tories would, of course, have been happy to take the lead in exposing the iniquity of prominent politicians associated with the former regime such as Marlborough and Walpole, but George went much further. Allowing charges against old comrades in the fight against the Union to go forward in 1711–12 was impressively equitable; even more so his allowing charges of corruption against his own family to reach the light of day in 1713. Lockhart's uncle Wharton, as we have already seen, allowed George's mother, Philadelphia, to take a bribe for peddling her supposed influence over him in 1708–10, while he was Lord Lieutenant of Ireland. Even though both she and Wharton were exempted from prosecution because of the general indemnity act passed in 1709, the report was presented, with Lockhart's formal approval, to the Commons.[113] Hence it is perhaps not surprising that even in the highly charged and very different political atmosphere of 1714, when the Country Tories were split from top to bottom over the succession issue, George received 204 votes (and was returned in 4th place) when he stood again for a seat on the Commission of Accounts.[114]

---

108 LL, pp. 45–50: GL to the Commission of Accounts, Edinburgh and Dryden, 5 and 19 July and 16 Aug. 1711.
109 LL, pp. 54–6, 57–8: GL to Fletcher and Cochran [London, 25 Dec. 1711 and 17 Apr. 1712]; SRO GD 190/3/282/3 (Smythe of Methven Papers): GL to Cochran, Dryden, 8 Nov. 1712.
110 LP i. 361–2.
111 CJ, xvii. 15–18, 28–9: 21 Dec. 1711 and 17 Jan. 1712.
112 Cf. his disapproval of the Country Tories' lack of interest in findingsthatimplicatedanyone other than Whigs: LP i. 352.
113 CJ, xvii. 356: 16 May 1713.
114 CJ, xvii. 689: 18 June 1714.

He had clearly established a good reputation for zeal and effectiveness in the office.

Lockhart's performance as a Commissioner of Accounts in 1711 also immediately boosted his reputation among the Country Tories, as may be seen from his cooption onto the highly influential Committee of Privileges and Elections.[115] And the enhanced respect and influence that flowed from his office and his leading role on this and other committees seems to have encouraged a growing sense of independence and self-confidence. Though he continued to enjoy 'a perfect close correspondence' with Hamilton, he was more and more his own man.[116] Thus from late 1711 onwards George began taking the initiative in organising voting blocs on issues that concerned him.[117] It was, moreover, a propitious time for a determined backbench Tory leader to test his wings, as the Oxford ministry was increasingly forced to seek an accommodation with the Country Tories in the 1711–12 session to secure its own survival against splits in ministerial ranks produced by the controversial nature of the peace it was negotiating with the Bourbon powers.

The epicentre of the ministry's problems was the Peace Preliminaries signed by the ministry in September 1711. These accepted that Louis XIV's grandson, Philip V, would retain Spain and the bulk of the old Spanish Habsburg empire – Britain's treaty obligations and a Parliamentary resolution that no peace could be safe while Spain remained in the House of Bourbon notwithstanding – abandoned several cherished Allied objectives, such as the Dutch Barrier (a chain of fortresses in the southern Netherlands the Dutch Republic had been promised), and gave Britain several commercial perquisites to the exclusion of its allies.[118] Given the political nation's war-weariness and the general mood of hostility towards Britain's allies, who were blamed for reneging on their treaty obligations and leaving Britain to pick up the slack, these peace terms were generally welcomed.[119] A substantial minority of the Tories and all the Whigs, however, found the attendant betrayal of allied interests, to say the least, distasteful. In particular, the Earl of Nottingham, hitherto a ferociously partisan Tory chieftain, was so disgusted with the Peace Preliminaries that he was soon negotiating with the Whigs for a joint campaign of opposition to the ministry.[120] Consequently, as the ministry contemplated the upcoming session it looked to be in dire straits. The impending defection of Nottingham and his connection left the ministry with a very thin majority in the Lords, and one primarily

115 CJ, xvii. 2: 8 Dec. 1711.
116 LP i. 344.
117 See below, pp. 94, 99 and Wodrow, *Analecta*, ii. 44–5: 1712.
118 Gregg, *Queen Anne*, p. 341.
119 Holmes, *British Politics*, pp. 66–70, 77–8.
120 Holmes, *British Politics*, pp. 78–9; Horwitz, *Revolution Politicks*, pp. 229–32

composed of wavering Court Whigs to boot.[121] Meanwhile in the Commons the Country Tories were in no mood to be patient any longer. They overwhelmingly supported the Peace Preliminaries, but were determined to pursue their own religious and Country agenda, regardless of how much this disrupted the ministry's plans.[122]

Crisis management, rather than systematic preparation, was always Oxford's forte and he responded to this one adroitly. To secure his hold on the Commons he surreptitiously arranged for the Jacobite Court to instruct its supporters to back the government and forthrightly cut a political deal with the rest of the October Club (i.e. the non-Jacobite majority): in return for their support the ministry would aid them in cutting back the religious liberty allowed dissenters, pursue Whig malefactors identified by the Commission of Accounts, etc.[123] In the Lords he tried to squeak through with his existing support *sans* Nottingham and his brother Aylesford. This went spectacularly awry when the opposition passed by one vote a resolution that 'no peace could be safe while any part of the Spanish empire remained in the house of Bourbon' and then (in flat contravention of the understandings reached at the time of the Union) denied the validity of the Duke of Hamilton's patent to sit as a British peer on the grounds that as a pre-Union Scots peer he was already represented by the sixteen Representative Peers.[124] Oxford swiftly recouped his position by persuading the queen to create twelve new peers, all stalwart supporters of the ministry, and passing a new resolution negating the one on peace without Spain.[125]

Unlike Hamilton, George believed the peace was 'absolutely necessary', and so openly approved of the October Club's refusal to harass the ministry on the issue that he was named as one of a committee to draw up an address of thanks to the queen for refusing to accede to the Lords' address on peace without Spain.[126] He was, nonetheless, happy to further his own agenda by seizing any opportunity opened up by the ministry's difficulties. His first independent political initiative correspondingly stemmed from an attempt to take advantage of the Hamilton peerage crisis. The initial reaction of the Scots peers had been to seek redress from the government in the form of support for a countervailing procedural vote accepting Hamilton's admission to the Lords as Duke of Brandon. Oxford tried to deliver this, or some acceptable compromise making the Representative Peers seats hereditary, but found himself baffled by a

121 Gregg, *Queen Anne*, pp. 342–3.
122 Szechi, *Jacobitism and Tory Politics*, p. 93.
123 Szechi, *Jacobitism and Tory Politics*, pp. 93–6, 184.
124 G. Holmes, 'The Commons Division on "No Peace Without Spain"', *Bulletin of the Institute of Historical Research*, xxxiii (1960) 223–34; 'The Hamilton Affair of 1711–12: a Crisis in Anglo-Scottish Relations', *English Historical Review*, lxxvii (1962), 257–82.
125 Gregg, *Queen Anne*, p. 350.
126 Szechi, *Jacobitism and Tory Politics*, pp. 93–4; LP i. 366; CJ, xvii. 28: 17 Jan. 1712.

combination of Scotophobia on the part of some of the English Country Tory peers and ethical rigidity on the part of some of the Scots Representative Peers, such as Lord Balmerino and the Marquess of Annandale, who flatly denied that they had the right to bargain away the rights of their constituents (the pre-Union peerage of Scotland) to give themselves permanent seats in the Lords. By the end of January 1712 it became clear that Oxford was not going to do anything to restore Hamilton's rights. The Scots peers consequently began angrily to discuss a boycott of the Lords (which was bound to put the ministry in difficulties).[127] And at this point Lockhart approached Balmerino and told him that some peers were pressuring the M.P.s to quit Parliament at the same time. He then intimated that though the peers had thus far 'slighted' the Scots M.P.s 'yet he has spoke to his brethren on this head and ... they will all desert with our Lords on condition that every [one] give his word of honour not to return without the approbation of the majority of our Lords and commoners as one body'.[128] It is clear that the Scots peers were somewhat taken aback at the proposal, and while they did not spurn it, they responded at best lukewarmly. In the end their own inability to hold together even on an issue affecting them all eroded their boycott of the Lords, and the Scots M.P.s held aloof because the peers refused to accede to their terms; but it was a token of things to come.[129]

For, at the same time as the Scots peers were failing in their efforts to persuade the ministry to redress their particular grievance, the Scots Tory M.P.s were organising their own campaign to get legislation passed granting religious toleration to episcopalians.[130] Greenshields' successful appeal to the House of Lords had stoked the fires of religious bigotry in Scotland, and in the summer and autumn a few episcopalian clergymen had been harassed by Kirk presbyteries. Lockhart published a pamphlet in November 1711 specifically highlighting these cases so as to prepare the way for a concerted push to get a toleration bill through.[131] He and the other Scots Country Tory leaders had also lobbied sympathetic English peers and − most crucially of all − managed to persuade the October Club that such a toleration was a good and anglican measure, thereby guaranteeing its passage through the Commons.[132] Oxford tried underhand to discourage them, but he was not prepared to risk a clash with the October Club on the issue, and thus when formally called upon to deliver the government support promised the previous year by a delegation from the steering

127 Szechi, *Jacobitism and Tory Politics*, pp. 105–6.
128 SRO GD 45/352/15: Balmerino to Harry Maule [London], 31 Jan. [1712].
129 Szechi, *Jacobitism and Tory Politics*, pp. 101–2, 106.
130 CJ, xvii. 33: 21 Jan. 1712; SRO GD 45/14/352/14: Balmerino to Harry Maule, 26 Jan. 1712.
131 LP i. 548–59.
132 Horwitz, *Revolution Politicks*, p. 236; CJ, xvii. 73: 7 Feb. 1712.

committee (including Lockhart), he duly did so, ensuring the bill's easy passage through the Commons.[133]

The only remaining, significant obstacle the toleration bill faced lay in the Lords. There the bill's managers faced a much more tricky situation. Despite Oxford's 'dozen' of new peers the ministry's majority in the upper house was still slim, and Oxford himself, though officially supporting its passage, was patently unenthusiastic about it, which increased the likelihood that Court Whig placemen would oppose it. To ensure its passage the bill therefore had to be acceptable to moderate Court Tories, most of whom were anti-Jacobite. The problem with this was that all these circumstances made it highly likely that some mischievious opponent of the measure would propose an abjuration clause. Such a clause would require all those seeking protection under the terms of the Toleration Act to take an oath denying the right of the Old Pretender to the throne of Great Britain. Since 1702 in England such a clause had been almost routinely inserted in all legislation requiring oaths of loyalty. An abjuration clause of any kind, however, posed a major obstacle for the intended beneficiaries of the bill, the episcopalian clergy, for, apart from an unrepresentative minority (such as Greenshields), they were principled Jacobites who held that the Old Pretender was their only rightful monarch. Hence Lockhart prevailed on the other members of the committee to agree with their presbyterian opponents among the Scottish representatives at Westminster that, in return for allowing Kirk presbyteries to continue imposing penalties on those of their own communion, the presbyterians would only oppose the bill *in toto*, not insert an abjuration clause as a wrecking amendment.[134] Despite this arrangement an amendment stipulating that those wishing to enjoy the benefit of the act must publicly pray for the House of Hanover during their services still got incorporated into the bill, and whether to preserve his influence or his conscience (the latter is unlikely because he was very flexible on the subject of oaths) George saw fit to abstain on the final reading.[135]

When it reached the Lords, however, and seemed set to pass despite the Kirk lobbyists' frantic efforts to stop it, the presbyterians reneged on the deal. At the instigation of Argyll and Islay, a very slightly modified abjuration clause – altered to be acceptable to the more rigid presbyterian conscience – was added to the bill.[136] Lockhart and his colleagues were outraged at this double-dealing, but for the episcopalian clergy back in Scotland it threatened to make the proposed Toleration Act a disaster.[137] For by extending to them a *prima facie* toleration,

133 Szechi, *Jacobitism and Tory Politics*, p. 110; LP i. 378.
134 LP i. 379–80.
135 CJ, xvii. 69: 5 Feb. 1712; Wodrow Letters, Quarto VI, ep. 65: division list of Scots M.P.s on toleration bill, 7 Feb. 1712.
136 LP i. 381–2.
137 Wodrow Letters, Quarto VI, ep. 70: Thomas Smith to Robert Wodrow, 15 Feb. 1712.

which their principles would then oblige them to reject, they would be put in a worse position than having no official toleration at all. In the aftermath of such a public refusal to swear loyalty to the post-Revolution order they would have been subject to renewed harassment by Kirk sessions and would have lost all serious prospect of relief, as, once they realised wherein lay the episcopalians' objections to taking the oath, most moderate Tories and the entire bench of bishops would have washed their hands of them.[138] Consequently the first response of the episcopalian hierarchy in Scotland was to beg the bill's sponsors to allow the measure to drop.[139] It was, however, too far advanced, and the end of the session too far off, for it to lapse by deliberate neglect, and it would have been impolitic to explain why the bill needed to be re-amended to its most influential, and energetic, backers in the Lords: the moderately Tory – but piously anglican – bishops of the Church of England.[140]

Just as the toleration bill could no longer be allowed to die, so it was politically impossible to take out the abjuration clause once it was actually in the bill's text. Lockhart and the Scots steering committee therefore hit on a shrewd, but in Scottish terms effective and vindictive, response. As children of an age of religious controversy they all had a basic understanding of the ideological rigidities and divisions within the Kirk. In particular, George at least well understood that because of the nuances of Scottish presbyterian theology many devout presbyterians would not take any oath that appeared to bind God for the future.[141] The clause that had been inserted was basically the standard abjuration clause, but it had been adapted in one point of its wording (by the substitution of the word 'which' for the phrase 'as it' in the statement on the succession reading, 'as it stands limited') so that it did not suggest that whoever was taking the oath was committing the Almighty to a specific course of action. Lockhart and his associates seized on this minor change for their riposte. When the amended bill returned to the Commons they undercut this conscience-salving adjustment by replacing the bill's abjuration clause with its regular English counterpart.[142] It was then the presbyterians' turn to become alarmed at what the passage of the bill presaged, for it was virtually certain that the English version of the abjuration oath would cause a schism in the Kirk between those willing to take the oath and zealots who would refuse.[143] Pious, but inflexible, nonjurant presbyterian clergymen would thus be as vulnerable to harassment by magistrates of the opposing religious persuasion as pious, but inflexible, nonjurant episcopalians. The Kirk's protagonists therefore tried to get the Lords

138 LP i. 382.
139 Wodrow Letters, Quarto VI, ep. 74: ? to Robert Wodrow, 26 Feb. 1712.
140 *London Diaries of William Nicolson*, pp. 572–4.
141 LP i. 381–2.
142 CJ, xvii. 103–4: 21 Feb. 1712.
143 Wodrow Letters, Quarto VI, ep. 79: Colonel Erskine to Robert Wodrow, 8 Mar. 1712.

to re-amend the wording of the clause back to that originally inserted when it returned there from the Commons. Lockhart and the Scots steering committee neatly checkmated this counter-move by privately lobbying moderate Tory peers and bishops and advancing the argument that adjusting the wording of the abjuration oath to allow mental equivocations was setting a bad precedent. Between the outright Jacobites and episcopalian Scots peers who could be relied on to support the bill in the full understanding of what was going on and the moderate Tories and bishops they managed thus to flannel, the bill's sponsors got the bill through the Lords unamended.[144] Years later George could not recall the moment, and its consequences, without gloating over his success in smashing the 'little chirking jesuitical shifts and evasions' of the 'godly'.[145]

At the same time as the Toleration Act was being manoeuvred through Parliament Lockhart was also closely involved in some internecine quarrelling in the October Club. The Club's alliance with the ministry had paid off handsomely in terms of dissenters struck at with legislation and scores paid off against the former Whig ministers and their henchmen,[146] but there was a substantial minority within it who were uneasy about such a close association with the government. In part this was because of their Country principles, which in theory did not distinguish between the Whig and Tory brands of corruption, iniquity and inefficiency inflicted on the nation by the governments of the era. As far as this minority were concerned the October Club had become 'the creatures and slaves of the ministry'.[147] But the real reason for this minority group's split with the rest of the October Club to form the March Club was a profound difference in attitude towards the succession. The March Club was firmly anti-Whig at its inception, and in favour of Country measures in general, but a major feature of its meetings was an ostentatious Hanoverianism. Club members even criticised the peace terms being negotiated by the Oxford ministry on the grounds that they were alienating the affections of the Hanoverian electoral family.[148] This is not to say that the October Club were all Jacobites – they were not – but such a public espousal of pro-Hanoverian sympathies was increasingly uncommon among the rank-and-file Octobermen because of the Welf dynasty's opposition to the peace terms. They were mostly, in other words, unenthusiastically pro-Hanoverian rather than histrionically so like the March Club M.P.s.[149]

The two organisations consequently clashed almost immediately over an issue felt to have ramifications for the Revolution settlement. One of the objectives

---

144 LP i. 382–3; *London Diaries of William Nicolson*, p. 590: 26 [Feb. 1712].
145 LP i. 383–5.
146 Szechi, *Jacobitism and Tory Politics*, pp. 106–10.
147 LP i. 366.
148 Szechi, *Jacobitism and Tory Politics*, pp. 97–9.
149 Cf. GL's intrinsically guarded description of the majority of the October Club's dynastic sympathies: LP i. 442, 443.

of the October Club since its formation in 1711 had been the resumption of
some of the grants and pensions given away by the crown since 1688. Lockhart
spoke for many when he declared in a speech in 1714:

> I was and will be ever of opinion that the usuall sallarys annexd to the severall
> offices are sufficient to support nay amply reward those ministers and servants
> of the Crown who act with the greatest probity, zeal and success in publick
> affairs; and tis evidently apparent that the great number of these, and for the
> most part very exorbitant, grants, have by the enriching some few private
> familys, extremlie diminishd the revenues of the Crown and given rise to
> impose many otherwise unnecessary taxes on the people, and I coud never
> see any method to stop, nay moderat, such grants, but by reasuming what
> hath past within a certain number of years and giving all manner of discour-
> agement of and opposition to all without distinction that may happen for the
> future.[150]

Moreover, there was a precedent in the successful passage in 1700, under Harley's
auspices, of a bill to resume grants made by the crown in Ireland in the aftermath
of the Williamite conquest. The October Club accordingly backed such a
measure in the 1710–11 session, and got it through the Commons, only to see it
defeated in the Lords.[151] In 1712 Lockhart and two other prominent Jacobites
(Thomas Strangways senior and William Shippen) introduced a new bill establishing a commission to look into a resumption, with the support of the October
Club, and initially engaged the support of the March Club in getting it through
the Commons.[152] Thanks to their better relations with the ministry it also appears
to have been tacitly allowed to proceed unobstructed by the government. When
it came to the committee stage, however, a faction within the October Club
(which if it did not include Lockhart, certainly had his support) proposed that
the resumption bill be 'tacked', i.e. merged, with a government supply bill.[153]
The proposal was founded upon a long-standing procedural custom of the
bicameral English Parliament: that the Lords did not amend bills dealing with
taxation. Thus if the two bills were merged into one the Lords would not amend
it and the ministry would be obliged to exert itself to ensure the combined
measure passed in order to secure the supply it needed to fund its expenditure.
It was a device of dubious constitutional propriety, but it had occasionally,
successfully, been resorted to by the Commons in the past during disputes with
the Lords.[154]

150 LP i. 565.
151 Szechi, *Jacobitism and Tory Politics*, pp. 81–3; H. Horwitz, *Parliament, Policy and Politics in the
    Reign of William III* (Manchester, 1977), pp. 231, 264, 265, 266–8.
152 CJ, xvii. 148: 22 Mar. 1712; LP i. 366.
153 CJ, xvii. 194: 21 Apr. 1712.
154 Horwitz, *Parliament, Policy and Politics*, pp. 74–5, 126–7.

Naturally enough, though it was willing to allow the resumption bill to go forward in the Commons, and even give it some support in the Lords, the ministry did not want a confrontation between the houses (the Lords bitterly resented tacking) and therefore it did its best to undo the merging of the two bills. And, as part of its effort to secure a majority against the device, the government convinced the March Club that the tack was unnecessary because the ministry would support the bill as it stood in the Lords. An unholy combination of the March Club, the Whigs and the ministry then untacked the resumption bill from the supply bill it had been merged with, only for the measure then narrowly to fail in the Lords.[155]

This 'betrayal' angered Lockhart, and seems to have crystallised his dissatisfaction with having to operate through a primarily Country Tory rather than fundamentally Jacobite organisation. He accordingly consulted with English Country Tories he knew favoured a Stuart restoration, and at their behest tried to convince some of the Scots peers that an independent Jacobite initiative in the Lords would best serve the cause because of the ministry's slim majority there. Finding them reluctant, 'so much did they depend on and resign themselves to the ministry, on account of what they either then received or expected in time by preferments', he decided to try and go it alone: 'I did then cast about among the Commons, and finding them well enuff disposed to enter into measures for obliging the Ministry to do what was expected with respect to the King and other matters of moment, wee began to form a party for that purpose and concert measures to be prosecuted ...'[156] The formation of a Jacobite sub-party from the ranks of the Country Tories required, however, one key ingredient: the approval of the Jacobite court. Most, if not all, Jacobite Country Tories at this time believed the queen and her ministers were secretly in negotiation with their king over the water and were loath to do anything that might disrupt their progress. George accordingly sent a message to St Germain via the Jacobite court's Parliamentary agent, John Menzies, asking for its permission to organise a Jacobite breakaway group. After a short interval Menzies returned with a missive from the Earl of Middleton expressing the exiled court's disapproval of the measure and urging the restive Jacobites to continue supporting the ministry.[157] Puzzled, and, if his recollections accurately reflect his reaction at the time, somewhat irritated, George 'told Mr Meinzies that it was my duty to obey, but I was very sorry for this occasion of shewing my regard to the King's commands being now more than ever jealous of the Ministry, at least of the Lord Oxford [the former Robert Harley] ...'[158] St Germain's intervention

155 Szechi, *Jacobitism and Tory Politics*, p. 113.
156 LP i. 368.
157 Szechi, *Jacobitism and Tory Politics*, pp. 102–3.
158 LP i. 369.

having killed the 'bustle' he intended to create, Lockhart withdrew, for a time, back into conventional Country Tory politics.

Though Lockhart knew that the Old Pretender had been sending instructions since the spring of 1711 that his friends in Parliament should support the Harley (now Oxford) ministry, he did not know that the wily premier minister had by 1712 effectively tied the Jacobite court in to support of his government by playing on its hopes of a negotiated restoration. Though they had no grounds at all for the belief other than gender stereotyping, most Jacobites were convinced the queen favoured the succession of her younger brother upon her death. The fact that by 1711 Queen Anne had proved herself a hard-nosed politician with a streak of anti-catholic bigotry a mile wide does not seem to have dented this optimistic assessment of her feelings towards her sibling.[159] And Oxford knew enough about Jacobites and their beliefs to capitalise on their vulnerability. In 1711 Oxford accordingly offered the Jacobite government-in-exile the coin it craved: negotiations for a restoration on the queen's death. Before he could negotiate such a happy event, however, he of course needed to negotiate a profitable end to the War of the Spanish Succession, prepare the way for suitable legislation by subtle intrigue and manoeuvring, etc. In other words, they would have to wait until matters were 'ripe'. In the meantime, of course, the Jacobite court should instruct its followers to support the ministry. There can be little doubt that if Oxford had had his way the interval between the promise of serious negotiations and the materialisation of same would have lasted forever.[160]

The upshot of all this for Jacobite sympathisers like Lockhart was that the exiled court, the true fount of all authority in their eyes, acted as a brake on their gathering hostility toward the ministry. At the beginning of every Parliamentary session from 1711 to 1714 it sent instructions to the Jacobite-inclined M.P.s and peers via Menzies, urging them to support the government.[161] Ironically, the exiled court too grew increasingly frustrated with Oxford's endless prevarications and by 1714 seriously began to doubt his sincerity. But none of their annoyance with the premier minister percolated back to their supporters in Parliament, who, lacking any other information, assumed the Old Pretender had firm promises of a restoration from Oxford and the queen and were therefore fearful of upsetting the applecart.[162] In the end the accumulated suspicion and frustration of St Germain's adherents at Westminster would clear the way for the revival of Lockhart's plans to form a Jacobite squadron of M.P.s, but it was to take some time yet.

Lockhart was in any event soon diverted from the failure of his Jacobite

---

159   Szechi, *Jacobitism and Tory Politics*, pp. 38, 41; Gregg, *Queen Anne*, 15–16, 22, 43–4. See also, E. Gregg, 'Was Queen Anne a Jacobite?', *History*, lvii (1972), 358–75.
160   Szechi, *Jacobitism and Tory Politics*, pp. 39–40, 182–4.
161   Szechi, *Jacobitism and Tory Politics*, pp. 93–4, 124–5, 157.
162   Szechi, *Jacobitism and Tory Politics*, pp. 184–8.

schemes by a personal tragedy: the death of the Duke of Hamilton in a savage duel with the English Lord Mohun.[163] Hamilton had basically dropped out of Parliamentary politics in the aftermath of the failure of the Scots peers' boycott of the Lords over his patent as Duke of Brandon, and instead busied himself with lobbying Oxford for a suitably lucrative official appointment by way of compensation. In June 1712 this finally bore fruit in his appointment as Master of the Ordnance and Ambassador-Extraordinary to France.[164] Because he still required loyal friends at Westminster and in Scotland to guard his back while he was away, however, Hamilton also took care to polish his tarnished image as a Jacobite. Thus he wrote a pleasant but empty letter to the Jacobite court for the first time since the 1690s and took pains to assure old friends like George – with of course as much mystery and obfuscation as he could manage – that he was 'sound' on the issue, and indeed that his appointment as Ambassador also included a secret mission of great import, which of course he could not discuss in detail (but clearly wished Lockhart to understand was the negotiation of a Stuart restoration).[165] Shortly after Lockhart's departure from London, however, Hamilton quarrelled with Lord Mohun during a meeting concerning an inheritance they were both claiming, was called out and fought a particularly nasty duel with the English peer in which Mohun was killed on the spot and Hamilton so badly wounded that he died only minutes later.

In George's opinion there was no question but that the duel had been a put-up job designed to cover a political assassination. The clinching proof for him was the claim by Hamilton's second that the duke was stabbed while he was on the ground by Colonel George Maccartney, Mohun's second.[166] Years later he still burned with anger over the affair and regarded it as a deadly blow to the Jacobites' hopes:

> The more I reflect on this great man's qualifications and disposition to advance that interest, I am the more convinced, that divine Providence, not having as yet poured down the full of that vengeance which this island deserves, permitted this heavy stroak, that we might be therby deprivd of one who was so capable and desirous to promote the true interest of his King and countrey.[167]

And Mohun was indeed a diehard Whig as well as a notorious thug, and

163 LP i. 401–2.

164 Szechi, *Jacobitism and Tory Politics*, pp. 99–101.

165 *Original Papers*, ii. 324–5: Hamilton to St Germain, 19 June 1712; LP i. 407–9. Here I differ with the latest writer on Hamilton, who suggests that he was more sincere in his Jacobitism at this time than I allow, for which see: V. Stater, *Duke Hamilton is Dead! A Story of Aristocratic Life and Death in Stuart Britain* (New York, 1999), pp. 127–9, 197, 209. I am grateful to Prof. Stater for sending me an advance copy of his book.

166 LP i. 401–6.

167 LP i. 409–10.

Maccartney (who was cashiered in 1711 for drinking damnation to the Harley ministry) was pardoned after the Hanoverian succession. Nonetheless, modern research has cast doubt on Lockhart's conviction that Hamilton was murdered as part of a Whig plot.[168] The two noblemen had been bitter enemies for some time as a result of their lawsuit, and Hamilton's Jacobite 'mission', though much speculated upon in London taverns and implicitly believed in by George, in retrospect looks like nothing more than smoke and mirrors deftly manipulated by the duke.

For Lockhart Hamilton's death was, nonetheless, a turning point. Though he had increasingly been pursuing an independent course of action, and was by this time rated a man 'of good sense and probity', by a senior Jacobite agent,[169] George was still in many ways Hamilton's man, and it is doubtful if he could soon have brought himself to oppose his patron and friend. The duke's death thus emancipated Lockhart from his old allegiance. Henceforth he was free to pursue the attainment of his own ideals as he saw fit – and just in time for the development of a major political crisis over the Union.

The crisis developed early in the 1713 session. The terms of the Union laid down that Scotland was to be exempt from the heavy malt tax prevailing in England until the conclusion of the War of the Spanish Succession.[170] This was the most the English negotiators would concede in 1706, but many Scots hoped that in view of the greater significance of malt in the Scots economy the exemption would be continued after the war ended. The English Country Tories had other ideas. They too disliked the tax, but they disliked the heavy land tax even more, and they hoped that if they equalised the tax across the whole of Great Britain they would be able in the short term to justify the reduction of the land tax and in the long term coerce the Scots into aiding them to abolish the malt tax.[171] Accordingly, and despite impassioned protests from Lockhart and the other Scots M.P.s, prominent Octobermen began systematically to intervene in the supply bill containing the malt tax in order to ensure Scotland was taxed as heavily as England. The ministry could do little to redress the situation: once the Country Tories enforced the reduction of the land tax to one shilling in the pound, the ministry had to take its revenue where it could

---

168 H. T. Dickinson, 'The Mohun-Hamilton Duel: Personal Feud or Whig Plot?', *Durham University Journal*, 57 (1965), 159–65. Professor Dickinson's careful analysis of the incident has for a long time convinced most scholars in the field, including myself, that there was no Whig plot. His interpretation has, however, recently been challenged by Stater, *Duke Hamilton is Dead!*, pp. 209–13, who suggests there may truly have been a conspiracy by Mohun and Marlborough to kill Hamilton.

169 Blairs Letters 2/173/20: James Carnegy to Thomas Innes [Edinburgh], 1 Nov. 1712.

170 *English Historical Documents*, p. 683.

171 J.J. Cartwright (ed.), *The Wentworth Papers 1705–39* (1882), pp. 336–7: Peter Wentworth to the Earl of Strafford, 26 May 1713.

find it.[172] Oxford was also becoming more and more obscure in his conduct and conversation so as to hold off the hordes of disappointed place-seekers who now thronged about him, and was correspondingly less and less effective as a Parliamentary manager.[173] By May it was clear the Scots were going to have to find some means of stopping the tax without ministerial help.

And it was George who first proposed the formation of a united bloc of Scots representatives in Lords and Commons, to bargain with the Whigs and harass the ministry.[174] By 1713 Lockhart was an experienced backbench leader, so he must have been well aware that arithmetic told against any prospect of Scots success in the Commons. Even if all the Scots M.P.s had been willing to stand together in the national cause and cast their lot with the Whigs in order to block the malt tax, the Tories would still have had enough votes to overcome their joint opposition, and a number of Scots placemen, such as John Pringle of Hayning, were in any case unwilling to part company with the ministry. So what was George aiming at? In his memoirs he forthrightly stated: 'I believd this affair of the malt tax, as it toucht evry man's copyhold and was a general grievance, woud be the best handle to inflame and keep up the spirit and resentment of the Scots against the Union; the effects wherof ... I did conclude woud certainly tend to advance the King's interest'.[175] Thus it appears that he saw the Commons' Scots bloc principally as a lever to get the peers to act collectively.[176] If all sixteen Representative Peers plus the Duke of Argyll, who sat as Earl of Greenwich, defected to the Whigs, there was a serious prospect of overcoming the ministry's slim majority in the upper chamber, defeating the malt tax and possibly striking a blow at the Union.[177]

If this was Lockhart's plan, it worked well. He personally led a band of Scots Country Tories into a voting alliance with the Whigs in the Commons, and spoke forcefully in favour of a matching association in the Lords at joint meetings held between the Scots Lords and Commons at the Blue Posts tavern in Westminster.[178] When the malt tax passed the Commons in spite of the Scots' efforts there, George was also ready with a further proposal that neatly capitalised on the anger and disgust English arrogance regarding Scotland's economic

172 Szechi, *Jacobitism and Tory Politics*, pp. 128–30. For a different interpretation, see: G. Holmes and C. Jones, 'Trade, the Scots and the Parliamentary Crisis of 1713', *Parliamentary History*, i (1982), 48–9, 52–3.
173 *Original Papers*, ii. 505: Galke to Jean de Robethon, 29 Sept. 1713.
174 LP i. 418–9.
175 LP i. 418.
176 LL, pp. 72, 73–4: GL to the Earl of Loudon, 7 Apr. and 23 [May] 1713.
177 As may be seen from the closeness of the votes in the Lords on Findlater's motion to dissolve the Union and on the malt tax bill (the ministry won by less than ten votes in packed houses on three separate occasions): Holmes and Jones, 'Trade, the Scots ...', pp. 58–60.
178 LP i. 420–3, 429.

problems had aroused in the course of the malt tax debates: the dissolution of the Union.[179]

This had of course been a long-standing Scots Jacobite objective, but, recognising political reality, George had not before sought to introduce legislation realising it. Given the fact, however, that the battles against the malt tax (and their own personal grievances with the ministry) were moving even two of the Union's foremost architects, Argyll and Islay, to 'roar and exclaim bloodily against the Union', the time was clearly ripe.[180] After taking some soundings that led to an abrasive encounter between himself, Speaker William Bromley and Sir Thomas Hanmer (both prominent Tory ministerialists at this time), who threatened him with the Tower if he persisted in the measure, Lockhart accordingly proposed that the Lords introduce a bill dissolving the Union and negotiate with the Whigs for their support.[181] His proposal was duly accepted and his leading role in the nascent Scots bloc was signalled by his fellow Scots' choice of him as one of a delegation of four sent to inform Queen Anne that they intended to move the dissolution of the Union.[182]

Unfortunately for George and the other anti-Unionists the crisis roused the Lord Treasurer from his lethargy. Oxford threw himself into a frantic round of arm-twisting, cajoling and bribing to ensure a Scots defeat in the Lords. This bore fruit in a narrow victory by four votes against a Whig-Scots proposal to take the Union under consideration on 1 June, followed by a second, narrower one, by two votes (76:74) in a packed House of Lords on 5 June in a division on whether to give the malt tax bill a second reading. Thereafter the opposition-Scots coalition collapsed.[183] Ironically, this defeat in the Lords rescued Lockhart from a predicament. Up to the middle of June he appears to have been able to overlook the fact that the Old Pretender had asked his friends in Parliament to support the ministry, presumbably on the grounds that the erstwhile monarch was far away in Lorraine – under the terms of the Peace of Utrecht the Jacobite court was required to leave France; it accordingly moved to Bar-le-Duc in Lorraine in 1713 – and was thus unaware of the affronts his loyal Scottish subjects were suffering and the opportunity this offered to advance the Jacobite cause by demolishing the Union. Hence Lockhart's and a number of other Scots Jacobite M.P.s joining with the Whigs and anti-ministerial Tories in several votes against government measures.[184] In mid-June, however, a letter arrived from the exiled court directed specifically at Lockhart:

179 LL, p. 75: GL to Maule(?), London, 26 May 1713.
180 LL, p. 80: GL to ? [London], 28 May [1713].
181 LP i. 428, 429.
182 LL, p. 77: GL to ?, London, 26 May 1713.
183 Holmes and Jones, 'Trade, the Scots ...', pp. 57–60; Szechi, *Jacobitism and Tory Politics*, pp. 133–4.
184 LL, p. 81: GL to ? [London], 28 May [1713]; LP i. 437.

I am ordered to tell you, that Francis [the Old Pretender] thinks it may be for his service, that all Stirling's relations [the Scots], who have any interest in Mr Porter [the Parliament], should join in every thing with Mr Cant [the Tories]. You are desired, therefore, to recommend this particularly to Cary [Lockhart], King, and others of your acquaintances that deal with Porter.[185]

Even if George had chosen to ignore the order, it was certain many of the Scots Jacobites he was leading would not. Hence he seems to have bowed to the inevitable and given ear to Oxford's promises that, despite the equalisation of the malt tax, the ministry would mitigate its impact on Scotland by lax collection.[186] Hence by the end of the session Lockhart and the other Scots Country Tory Parliamentarians were back on the Tory side of the house.[187]

For all that the Scots Parliamentary mutiny fizzled out so disappointingly, the ructions of the 1713 session significantly enhanced George's reputation among Scotland's Jacobites. During the winter of 1712–13 he took the lead in organising a secret subscription among the wealthier Jacobites to provide a supplementary pension for the Jacobite Court's Parliamentary agent, John Menzies.[188] It is noteworthy that at the beginning of the 1714 session of Parliament, when a delegation of Country Tory Jacobites was sent to inform Oxford's main rival within the government, Viscount Bolingbroke, of their friends' increasing irritation at the snail-like pace of the Tories' advancement in terms of government and court posts and their legislative agenda, Lockhart was one of those chosen.[189] Even while he was enthusiastically cooperating with the Representative Peers during the malt tax crisis, George was determinedly pushing through a bill to curtail the influence of Scottish peers on elections to the House of Commons by the creation of bogus votes.[190] He took a quiet pride in the fact that the noble lords did not like the measure but could not prevent it, 'forseeing that the Commons would carry it over ther bellys'.[191] By the end of the malt tax crisis the Jacobite court began to direct its instructions specifically to him, and by the end of the year the influential Scottish catholic priest and Jacobite agent, Fr James Carnegy, was recommending that he be ennobled:

Some think it might do well because ther are few worth anything of that rank, and he may com to be what Patrick [Hamilton] was and what some would have Louis [Atholl] to be: chief of Mark's family [the Scottish Jacobites].

185 *Original Papers*, ii. 416: David Nairne to Henry Straton, Commercy, 8 June 1713 ns.
186 LL, p. 83: GL to Oxford, Dryden, 30 July 1713.
187 Szechi, *Jacobitism and Tory Politics*, pp. 138–9.
188 Blairs Letters 2/173/20: James Carnegy to [Thomas Innes] [Edinburgh?], 1 Nov. 1712.
189 LP i. 441–2.
190 CJ, xvii. 315, 389, 403, 405, 440: 6 May and 3, 5, 6 and 25 June 1713.
191 LP i. 437–8.

I intreat you'll get Mr Debrie's [Fr. Lewis Innes's] answer and thoughts upon this, for Magnes [Lockhart]is not only to be managed as a true freind of Ned's [the Old Pretender's], but he has in his hands 12,000 marks of Rosline's [?] money which we may get or loss as he is freindly.[192]

Carnegy's proposal was not acted on, but when he returned to Scotland with orders to sound out the Scots Jacobites' attitude toward a planned rising to be led by the Old Pretender, it was to Lockhart and Henry Maule of Kellie that he directed himself when he discussed the project with Lowland Jacobites.[193]

Despite the zealous Carnegy's description of him as 'active and indefatigable', George ultimately gave a more cautious response than Carnegy would have liked. The Jacobite agent's report ends by disgustedly portraying Lockhart's position as 'pusillanimous and inactive', because he wanted to 'sit still and do nothing for John Gray [the Pretender] tho Benjamin's wife [Queen Anne] faill, but let all be done that can in favours of Philip Nortoun [Hanover]'.[194] From which, given the context (Carnegy's enthusiastic espousal of a Jacobite insurrection), it is evident that George still favoured a Parliamentary rather than a military solution to the problem of achieving a Jacobite restoration. In the interim, he urged the Old Pretender via Carnegy to establish a Jacobite steering committee with authority to oversee and organise Jacobite affairs in Scotland. And, of course, Lockhart was to be one of the committee.

Indeed, George's dislike of military adventurism was already manifest in his plans for the new Parliament. The general election of October-November 1713, which had been fought by the Tories principally on the platform of their having successfully negotiated the Peace of Utrecht, had resulted in a thumping victory for the party in England.[195] In Scotland, however, something very unusual in post-Union eighteenth-century politics occurred: an established government interest and those deemed to be its supporters were resoundingly defeated in elections to the lower (but not the upper) house. In part this was owing to the late defection of Argyll and Islay to the Squadrone, but its main ingredient was undoubtedly the voters' hostility toward anyone associated with the ministry which had allowed the malt tax to be imposed on Scotland.[196] The Squadrone, in a cool *volte face*, now proclaimed themselves to be the anti-Union party, and old, true anti-Unionists like George had correspondingly to fight to retain their credibility on this score. Pro-ministerial Scottish Tories were thus the main casualties in the government's rout; well-known Country Tories like Lockhart

192 Blairs Letters 2/181/16: James Carnegy to Thomas Innes, 'Quelbeuf', 4 Nov. 1713 ns. Lewis Innes was Queen Mary of Modena's Almoner.
193 Blairs Letters 2/181/20: Carnegy to Thomas Innes [Edinburgh], 1 Dec. 1713.
194 Blairs Letters 2/188/3: Carnegy to Thomas Innes [Edinburgh], 19 Jan. 1714.
195 Speck, *Tory and Whig*, pp. 113, 123.
196 Ferguson, *Scotland 1689 to the Present*, p. 62.

and his ilk by and large survived. The upshot of all this was that the Tories' share in Scotland's representation in the lower chamber declined to about sixteen M.P.s, of whom perhaps twelve were Jacobite sympathisers.[197]

The political situation, moreover, changed dramatically during the winter of 1713–14. During the Christmas holidays Queen Anne became seriously ill, and at one point seemed likely to die. Her eventual recovery was slow and incomplete. It was all too clear that the crisis Tories of all stripes had long wished away was finally upon them: the last of the protestant Stuarts was about to die and her lutheran, German, pro-Whig cousins were poised to succeed to the throne.[198] If the Old Pretender was to be peacefully restored by Parliamentary means it had to be soon. In addition, the sudden downturn in the queen's health precipitated a struggle for ascendancy within the ministry. The ambitious Bolingbroke, bouncing back from a failed intrigue to sideline Oxford in September 1713, began openly to enlist support against the premier minister, arguing that his refusal to entrench the Tories in every government office threatened the party's future. Oxford, by this time bereft of political credit and down to a faithful few friends on whom he could count, sought support wherever he could find it in a frantic effort to bolster his position. Meanwhile the opposition was wooing the pro-Hanoverian Tories and fanning the flames of public alarm with some highly effective pamphlet and newspaper propaganda declaring the protestant succession to be in danger.[199]

Given these circumstances, the fact that both Oxford and Bolingbroke independently contacted the Jacobite Court in February 1714 and offered to restore the Old Pretender to the throne if he would convert to anglicanism would seem ample confirmation of the opposition's charges. If, however, the detail of both men's proposals is examined, the picture becomes much more ambiguous. For both politicians wanted James Stuart to convert, but then leave Lorraine and move to Switzerland, or, preferably, Italy, after entrusting his political supporters to his 'friend' in London.[200] Both men were also simultaneously reassuring the Hanoverian Tories and the Welf dynasty of their undying devotion to the protestant succession. Both also had enough knowledge of the ins and outs of Jacobite politics to know that the Old Pretender was a devout catholic who had resolutely resisted previous demands that he convert.[201] The overall effect of securing the Old Pretender's departure from Lorraine in line with a Parliamentary

197 Szechi, *Jacobitism and Tory Politics*, pp. 147–51, 200–2.
198 Gregg, *Queen Anne*, pp. 374–5.
199 Szechi, *Jacobitism and Tory Politics*, pp. 154–5, 161–5.
200 University of Pennsylvania Library, MS French 139 (Gaultier Papers), ff. 195–7, 334–6: Abbé Francois Gaultier to the Marquis de Torcy, Feb. 1714; H. N. Fieldhouse, 'Bolingbroke's Share in the Jacobite Intrigue of 1710–14', *English Historical Review*, lii (1937), 457: Marquis d'Iberville to Torcy, London, 18 Feb. 1714.
201 Szechi, *Jacobitism and Tory Politics*, pp. 20–6, 185–6, 190–1.

resolution passed at the tail-end of the 1713 session, would have been to boost the credit of the politician who achieved it in the eyes of pro-Hanoverian Tories.[202] If at the same time the politician in question had had the Jacobite faction among the Tories in Parliament instructed to support him, he would have been in a commanding position. Hence it seems likely that Oxford and Bolingbroke's celebrated overtures to the Old Pretender were nothing more than an offshoot of their power struggle.[203] Both wanted the Jacobites silenced and added to their respective supporters, and were willing to dabble in a little treason to get it.

Lockhart, of course, knew nothing of all this high political manoeuvring. His eyes were on the urgent need to overturn the Hanoverian succession in Parliament before it was too late.[204] He correspondingly appears to have been closely involved in pushing forward a plan to force the issue. Part of the legislation enacting the Hanoverian succession was a provision for the Elector of Hanover to nominate seven additional members to the committee of regents who were to act in his name during the interval between the death of the queen and his arrival in Britain (the others were to be the ministers in power at the time acting *ex officio*).[205] This list of supplementary regents was kept locked and sealed in an official 'black box' in the possession of the Hanoverian Ambassador. What the originators of the plan, Sir John Pakington and Sir William Whitlock, seem to have envisaged was a Parliamentary resolution to open the box and examine the list. When, as they confidently (and correctly) expected, it was found to be stuffed with hardcore Whigs, they planned to capitalise on the Country Tories' fear and outrage to propose the repeal of the Act of Succession in favour of leaving the question of who should succeed her to the queen herself.[206] With the help of English Country Tories, the black box proposal was actually put forward and discussed at a meeting of the October Club in April 1714. The silence with which most Octobermen greeted it was a token, however, of a change in their attitude toward further provocative moves with regard to the ministry. In the political confusion and uncertainty that characterised Parliamentary politics in 1714 they preferred to await the outcome of the contest between Bolingbroke and Oxford for control of the ministry. Lockhart and his allies were thus forced to shelve the plan for the foreseeable future.[207] Ironically, with hindsight, we know that the plan would have been moot even if Pakington and Lockhart had carried it off. As Edward Gregg has convincingly shown, Queen Anne remained personally committed to the Hanoverian succession to the very

202 Szechi, *Jacobitism and Tory Politics*, pp. 138–9.
203 For a different (and more generally accepted) interpretation see, Gregg, *Queen Anne*, pp. 363–4, 375–7.
204 LP i. 441.
205 *English Historical Documents*, viii. 141.
206 *Original Papers*, ii. 427–8: 'Mrs White' to St Germain, 7 Aug. 1713; Blairs Letters 2/188/6: Carnegy to Thomas Innes [Edinburgh], 16 Feb. 1714.
207 Szechi, *Jacobitism and Tory Politics*, pp. 125–6, 159.

end, despite her irritation with individual members of the Electoral family and its servants, so that even if she had had a free choice of her successor she would certainly have chosen one of the Welf dynasty.[208] Nonetheless, and given that George and his colleagues were under a potentially catastrophic misapprehension (from their point of view) regarding the queen's feelings towards her brother, the 'black box' scheme had a practical cogency that is quite striking.

In addition, George sought to exploit the general dissatisfaction felt by the Country Tories to pursue a specifically Scottish agenda: that the Scots should 'revive and pursue' the proposal to dissolve the Union.[209] To get this project moving he obviously needed to win over a substantial bloc of Country Tories, and he began by trying to enlist the aid of the Scottish steering committee. At this point, however, he encountered a serious obstacle: Bolingbroke, described with 'warmness' as 'a good man and a wise man' by them, had got to his friends before Lockhart had. All but one of the original steering committee (Lord Lyon) were reluctant to back an independent initiative of any kind, and were instead inclined to stake everything on Bolingbroke's success in his contest with Oxford.[210] George, the Lord Lyon and several others angrily broke with them on the issue, and though he cooperated with the committee over various pieces of legislation, most notably a bill to resume the lands previously held by Scotland's bishops in order to use the revenues to support the episcopalian clergy, Lockhart's relations with them never recovered.[211]

Meanwhile the contest between the rival ministers and the battle between the ministry and the opposition had reached new heights of passion even for an era of intemperate politics. In March in the Commons opposition claims that the protestant succession was in danger persuaded nearly 50 'Hanoverian' Tories, led by the Speaker, Sir Thomas Hanmer, to vote with them against the ministry in what was tantamount to a vote of confidence.[212] In a packed house the government only managed to secure a majority of about 50, despite a theoretical Tory superiority of over 150 M.P.s. The opposition followed this up by trying to get the Electoral Prince of Hanover (the future George II) summoned to England to sit in the Lords as Duke of Cambridge, in spite of the queen's directly expressed wish that they should not do so.[213] In Scotland and on the Continent Whig partisans were making secret preparations for an uprising supported by a foreign invasion in the event of a Jacobite succession.[214]

208 Gregg, *Queen Anne*, pp. 380–2.
209 LP i. 443.
210 LP i. 444; LL, p. 91: GL to Harry Maule [London], 7 Mar. [1714].
211 LP i. 445–51.
212 Szechi, *Jacobitism and Tory Politics*, pp. 170–1.
213 Szechi, *Jacobitism and Tory Politics*, pp. 171–2.
214 E. Gregg, 'Marlborough in Exile, 1712–1714', *Historical Journal*, xv (1972), 609–10; Blairs Letters 2/188/2, 5, 11: Carnegy to Thomas Innes [Edinburgh?], 5 Jan., 11 Feb. and 6 Apr. 1714.

George naturally flourished in such a partisan political atmosphere. He was present and spoke in favour of the government in the Commons debate on the state of the nation, where he denounced the Whigs as 'men who are by principle enemys to Monarchy, and never to be more dreaded than when they pretend respect and zeall for the service of the Crown', and publicised their attempts to accumulate arms and men in order to resist a Jacobite restoration.[215] Lockhart also joined enthusiastically with Bolingbroke's supporters among the Country Tories in passing the Schism Act, a populist measure designed to prevent dissenters from educating their children in their faith.[216] When Oxford's supporters, along with the opposition and the Hanoverian Tories, tried to get the monies owed Hanover for the troops it had loaned Britain during the War of the Spanish Succession, George was there and was one of the Country Tory and Bolingbrokite majority that rejected the proposal.[217] He was also very active in trying to get a bill to resume episcopal lands in Scotland through the Commons, and was only with great difficulty persuaded to drop the measure when the Secretary of State for Scotland, the Earl of Mar, begged him in the name of the queen (and with the threat of a royal veto) to do so for fear that it would provoke a presbyterian rebellion.[218]

It would be a mistake, however, to assume that close association with and joint endeavour alongside the English Country Tories was by this time deracinating Lockhart in the same manner as some of his fellow Scottish Tories. For him Scottish interests were still paramount and his interpretation of Scotland's advantage in any given situation remained his guiding light – even if he found himself pursuing it in isolation. Hence he was closely involved in the cross-party campaign by Scots M.P.s to prevent additional taxes being laid on the soap used for the preparation of Scots linen, cooperated with Whig enemies such as Sir Gilbert Elliott of Stobs and Sir William Johnstone of Westerhall to oppose the Court over the disbursement of Equivalent monies and stood out alone against the rest of the Scots Tories over the militia bill.[219] George's reasons for opposing the militia bill are particularly revealing, as they highlight his ability to see beyond immediate party advantage. The bill was intended to remodel Scotland's militia after the English model and to facilitate the disarming of Scotland's Whigs, and on those grounds alone it drew overwhelming Scottish Tory support. Lockhart seems to have been the only one to realise that 'sauce for the goose

---

215 LP i. 561–4; History of Parliament Trust transcripts, Blackett Diary: 15 Apr. 1714.
216 LP i. 569–74; Wodrow Letters, Quarto VIII, ep. 82: Thomas Smith to Robert Wodrow, 19 May 1714.
217 Szechi, *Jacobitism and Tory Politics*, pp. 173–4; LP i. 467–70.
218 LP i. 448–51; CJ, xvii. 638: 22 May 1714.
219 Szechi, *Jacobitism and Tory Politics*, pp. 158–9; LL, pp. 102–3, 106–7: GL to Harry Maule [London], 8 and 24 June 1714; Wodrow Letters, Quarto VIII, ep. 91: J. Erskine to Robert Wodrow, 18 June 1714.

would be sauce for a gander' as he tartly told Mar,[220] and that swingeing statutory powers of search and seizure in the hands of an inimical government (and in this context it is worth noting that he believed all British ministries were hostile to Scotland) could hurt the Scots Tory and Jacobite interest as badly as the Whigs. As far as he was concerned:

> I would never consent that such a power over me or those I represented should be lodged with any fellow subject; they might be friends now, but we did not know how long, and if we were to judge of futurities from what had happened, there was little reason to expect that such persons, even at this time, would be named as were agreeable to our friends: for since the Ministry thought fitt to continue and supply vacancies in the standing army with Whigs, there was no ground to believe they would act otherwise in the militia. As for disarming of the Whigs, such a measure would infallibly encrease and continue our divisions at home, which we shoud prevent as much as possible, seeing England had aimd at nothing so much, and had therby oppressd us these hundred years by past. Besides, I did firmly beleive if right measures were taken, allmost all Scotsmen would unite against the oppressions and hardships they were exposed to by the Union, and therfore I wisht every Scotsman was armd, being perswaded that sooner or latter both the King and countrey woud find the benefit of it.[221]

From which it is apparent that although George's opposition to the bill was helpful to his friend Argyll (who was liable to lose his hereditary authority over the Argyllshire militia), its mainspring was deeper than many of his peers allowed.[222] In any event, Lockhart's developing skill as a Parliamentary tactician was successfully deployed against the bill, and as a result it failed to complete its passage through the Commons before the session ended.[223]

The *piéce de résistance* of the session, and indeed George's parliamentary career, however, came in the aftermath of a blow to the Jacobite cause. In late May, as a result of political manoeuvring on the part of Oxford and Bolingbroke, the cabinet agreed to issue a proclamation offering a £5000 reward for the apprehension of the Old Pretender dead or alive should he land in Britain. Seizing the opportunity, the Hanoverian Tories successfully proposed an address thanking the queen for the proclamation and supplementing the size of the proffered reward to increase it to £100000.[224] Lockhart and the other Jacobites among the Country Tories were 'enraged', and with the help of Sir John Pakington, the veteran Jacobite M.P. for Worcestershire, George was able to use their anger

220 LP i. 456.
221 LP i. 454.
222 LP i. 454–7.
223 LP i. 457–8; CJ, xvii. 712: 30 June 1714.
224 Szechi, *Jacobitism and Tory Politics*, p. 168.

finally to achieve one of his long-cherished ambitions: the formation of an independent Jacobite club, 'solemnly engaging to take and follow joint measures'.[225] At the head of this group of 30 or so M.P.s Lockhart and Pakington had a field day at the end of June and early July disrupting and delaying government supply bills while the opposition was attacking Bolingbroke's reputation over his involvement in corrupt dealings associated with the Spanish Commercial Treaty of 1714.[226] By the closing week or so of the session Lockhart was sufficiently prominent and well known as a leader of the Jacobites in the Commons to be summoned to Bolingbroke's office and pleaded with to persuade his friends to desist in their attacks on vital government taxation,[227] and, in addition, effective enough for the opposition to consider it worth investing money in forcing him out of conventional politics.

Lockhart's career as a constitutional politician came to an end as a result of an error of judgement on the part of one of his friends. During the 1714 session Lockhart shared lodgings with John Houston jr, one of the new cohort of Scottish Jacobite Country Tory M.P.s. They got on well, and in strict secrecy George showed him an early draught of his *Memoirs Concerning the Affairs of Scotland*, which he had written in 1707–8. The book was, of course, chock-a-block with sedition and outright Jacobitism, and Houston apparently liked it sufficiently to arrange for a transcription to be taken without asking Lockhart's permission.[228] Unfortunately for Houston the copyist, one William Brown, recognised the import of what he was transcribing and showed the manuscript to James Anderson, a presbyterian minister, who advised him to make an additional copy for himself. Brown, who considered Houston had underpaid him, then made further multiple copies from his illicit transcription and gave these to various prominent Whigs, including Sir John Cunningham, Lord Somers, Lord Halifax and Sir James Stuart, the Scottish Advocate General.[229] They circulated their copies of the manuscript further still, and by the end of June even Oxford had a copy, which he showed to a delighted Jonathan Swift:

> it is a history of the last invasion of Scotland, wrote just as plain, tho not so well, as another history which yow and I know, with characters of all the men now living, the very names and invitation that was sent to the pretender. This by a flaming Jacobite that wonders that all the world are not so. Perhaps it may be a Whig that personates a Jacobite. I saw two sheets of the beginning which was treason every line. If it go's on at the same rate of plain dealing, it is a very extraordinary piece, and worth your while to come up to see it only.[230]

225 LP i. 472–3; LL, pp. 105–6, 108–9: GL to Harry Maule [London], 24 and 26 June [1714].
226 Szechi, *Jacobitism and Tory Politics*, pp. 160, 169.
227 LP i. 476–8.
228 LL, p. 110: GL to Harry Maule [London], 29 June 1714.
229 SRO GD 220/5/108: Deposition of William Brown, 6 Nov. 1714.
230 *Correspondence of Jonathan Swift*, ii. 58.

Finally, in August, Lockhart's chief political rival in Midlothian, Sir David Dalrymple of Hailes, arranged to have it published.[231] George discovered what was afoot too late to pay off the copyist and was forced to watch helplessly as the book went into print.[232] It was, of course, a sensation, as Lockhart had spared neither friend nor foe in his excoriating analysis of Scottish politics in the period 1703–7. And though Dalrymple did not feel quite confident enough of his legal situation directly to accuse George of being the author, it was well known that he had written it.[233]

Lockhart was forced to resort to jesuitical denials of his responsibility for the text in frantic efforts to avoid prosecution for sedition, treason or an action for *scandalum magnatum* on the part of the numerous Scots peers whose reputations he had blasted.[234] And though the circumstances in which the text had reached Dalrymple ultimately did not lend themselves to proving George's authorship at law, as a consequence of which (and doubtless the influence of friends and family) he escaped prosecution, the book exposed him to legal harassment and acute political embarrassment at home in Scotland.[235] It also soured his relations with a number of powerful Scottish politicians, one of whom at least, the Duke of Atholl, made the opening moves in challenging George to a duel for what had been said about him in the *Memoirs*.[236] The upshot of all of which was that Lockhart's political career, in any case jeopardised by the death of Queen Anne in August and the succession of George I with its attendant return of the Whigs to office, was ruined.

Lockhart initially refused to accept his political demise and resolutely advanced his candidacy for Midlothian in the 1715 election. There, however, he found himself facing a reinvigorated opposition which focused directly on his authorship of the *Memoirs* and, by implication, his Jacobitism (something it is worth recalling he had never advertised among his constituents).[237] Even so, his anti-Union credentials bade fair to enable him to make a good showing in the wave of agitation against the Union that accompanied the electioneering in Scotland in

231 LP i. 20–1.
232 SRO GD 220/5/108: examination of Colonel Walter Douglas, 3 Nov. 1714.
233 SR, pp. 262–71 *passim*; LL, p. 115: Atholl to GL, London, 13 Oct. 1714.
234 LP i. xvii (title page); SR, pp. 273–89; LL, pp. 110–13, 114–15, 115–16: GL to Maule and Atholl, London and Dryden, 29 June, 3 July and 3 Nov. 1714; Wodrow Letters, Quarto VIII, ep. 131: John Williamson to Robert Wodrow, Edinburgh, 24 Sept. 1714.
235 SRO GD 220/5/331/7: Adam Cockburn of Ormiston (Lord Justice Clerk) to the Duke of Montrose, Edinburgh, 11 Nov. 1714; SRO GD 220/5/434/2, 11: Dalrymple to Montrose, Edinburgh, 2 and 18 Dec. 1714.
236 LL, p. 115: Atholl to GL, London, 13 Oct. 1714.
237 Wodrow Letters, Quarto VIII, ep. 163: John Williamson to Robert Wodrow, Edinburgh, 23 Dec. 1714; SRO GD 18/2092/2: Sir John's Clerk's spiritual journal for 1699–1709, 9 Feb. 1708.

1714–15.[238] One forecast by the opposing side, indeed, predicted he would still draw 20 sure votes against his opponent's certain 36, thus leaving the outcome (at least theoretically) in the hands of 19 undecided voters.[239] Personal interviews with both Dalrymple, the Lord Advocate, and Montrose, the Secretary of State responsible for Scotland, on the eve of the election, however, seem to have finally dissuaded him from taking his candidacy to a poll.[240] Since the legal authorities were privately expressing doubts about the strength of their case in the event of a trial, and nothing further is heard of indicting him for the *Memoirs* after the election, it seems likely that he was offered a deal: if he would desist, they would drop the case.[241] Despite his withdrawal, George remained a formidable enough force in Midlothian politics even in the aftermath of the '15 rebellion for it to be worth another Lord Advocate, Robert Dundas of Arniston, making a private arrangement with him not to run in the next election (1722) in return for showing leniency to some of his friends who were implicated in the rising,[242] and the Campbell brothers (who seem not to have been in the least offended by his characterisation of them or their father in the *Memoirs*) tried to persuade him to run with their support in 1718.[243] To all intents and purposes, however, the conventional, legal chapter in Lockhart's career had come to a close.

238 Wodrow Letters, Quarto VIII, ep. 164: M. Wood to Wodrow, Edinburgh, 29 Dec. 1714; Quarto IX, ep. 32: ? of Williamwood to Wodrow, Williamwood, 16 Feb. 1715; SRO GD 220/5/434/11 and -/453/10: Dalrymple to Montrose, Edinburgh, 18 Dec. 1714 and 18 Jan. 1715; SRO GD 220/5/454/4: Lord Justice Clerk Adam Cockburn of Ormiston to Montrose, Edinburgh, 8 Jan. 1715.
239 SRO GD 18/3163: 'List of the barons in the shire of Lothian who were in being 1715'.
240 SRO GD 18/2092/4: Sir John Clerk's spiritual journal for Apr. 1712–1715, 1 Mar. 1715.
241 SRO GD 220/5/434/11: Dalrymple to Montrose, Edinburgh, 18 Dec. 1714 ; SRO GD 220/5/454/3: Lord Justice Clerk Ormiston to Montrose, Edinburgh, 4 Jan. 1715.
242 LL, p. 132: GL to Mar [Dryden?], 28 Mar. 1718; LL, p. 179: GL to the Old Pretender [Carnwath?], 23 Apr. 1722.
243 LL, pp. 132–3: GL to Mar [Dryden?], 28 Mar. 1718.

CHAPTER SIX

Revolutionary Jacobite, 1715–1727

Though he had been involved in the Hamilton group's preparations for the abortive 1708 rising, Lockhart was by no means an experienced conspirator. Nor was he fundamentally inclined towards violent measures. As we have seen, he discouraged planning for a Jacobite insurrection in the event of Queen Anne's death early in 1714. His public notoriety in the immediate aftermath of publication of the *Memoirs* in any case made him highly unsuitable for a leading role in any uprising, and moreover, many prominent Jacobites were doubtless offended at his sharp characterisations of themselves or their relations.[1] George corresondingly found himself largely excluded from the plotting that preceded the Jacobite rising of 1715.[2]

This was probably one of Lockhart's luckiest breaks. The historical consensus on the 1715 rising has shifted over recent years, and it is now generally accepted that the '15 was potentially a far more serious challenge to the nascent Hanoverian regime than the much more dramatic rebellion of 1745.[3] Regardless, and notwithstanding its latent power, the '15 was also one of the most incompetently conducted, half-cocked, botched-up jobs ever set in motion by a group of plotters throughout the long eighteenth-century (1660–1832). It redounded to no-one's credit, but because Lockhart escaped with his fortune and reputation (relatively) intact, he was left in a good position to move into the leadership vacuum created by its ignominious collapse, and the flight of most of Scotland's leading Jacobites, in 1716.

The reason the rising was such an abject failure was the half-heartedness of its organisers. At the core of the conspiracy was a group of worried Tory ex-ministers, among whom the former Commander-in-Chief of the army, the Duke of Ormond, the former Secretary of State for Scotland, the Earl of Mar, and Sir William Wyndham, the former Chancellor of the Exchequer, took the lead.[4] None of them had ever shown much, if any, inclination towards serious Jacobitism before 1715, though equally, none of them had been averse to tactical political alliances with well-known Jacobites when it served their turn within

---

1 For examples of which see: SR, pp. 34 (Earl of Balcarres), 85 (Earl of Mar), 111 (8th Earl Marischal).
2 LP i. 484.
3 Lenman, *Jacobite Risings*, pp. 153–4, 257–9; P. Langford, *The Eighteenth Century 1688–1815* (1976), p. 71; Langford, *Polite and Commercial People*, p. 199.
4 Szechi, *The Jacobites*, pp. 74–6.

internal Tory party politics.[5] What alarmed this group of professional politicians into embarking on such a risky venture was the apparent determination to 'get off some heads' of the Whig-dominated ministry installed by George I soon after his arrival in September 1714.

The Whigs undoubtedly had some scores to settle with the former Oxford ministry, but it was strategically unwise to try to do so in the manner that they did. Capitalising on their thumping victory in the 1715 general election, which the Whigs won through overt government and royal intervention on their behalf (which was so gross as to be unsettling even to the handful of Tories who had followed the Earl of Nottingham into office in 1714), in April 1715 the ministry began a formal investigation of the negotiations leading to the peace of Utrecht.[6] This was clearly intended to amass sufficient evidence for a series of impeachments of the leading ministers of the former regime. Bolingbroke promptly fled to France before the process against him could be inaugurated and was ultimately condemned *in absentia*. The first to be formally accused was former Lord Treasurer Oxford. Ormond came next and the Earl of Strafford, a former plenipotentiary to the peace talks at the Hague, soon followed.[7] It seemed as if anyone who had been involved in the peace process was liable to be prosecuted, and any Tory leader who had had dealings with the Jacobites (on however cynically tactical a basis) had cause for serious concern, for who knew what might come out in the process of a trial? The Whig majority in the House of Lords who would judge the case were not likely to be impressed with arguments about the political necessity of encouraging Jacobites to believe a given politician was 'sound' even if he was demonstrably not a Jacobite himself.

The upshot was that Mar, Ormond, Wyndham and their close associates within the Tory party began making serious overtures to the exiled Jacobite court, which had been expelled from France as part of the terms of the peace of Utrecht and by 1715 resided at Bar-le-Duc in Lorraine.[8] Like most amateur Jacobite conspirators resident within the British Isles, they assumed the Old Pretender secretly enjoyed close, friendly relations with the government of France, and that Louis XIV could provide him with an army at the drop of a hat. Their plans, such as they were, therefore revolved around large numbers of Tories and Jacobites assembling in arms at various rendezvous in order to join a French invasion force, which would do the real fighting.[9] Unfortunately for them, their assumptions had no basis in reality. The Old Pretender did have friends at the French court, most notably his illegitimate half-brother the Duke of Berwick,

---

5 Szechi, *Jacobitism and Tory Politics*, pp. 39–40, 100, 159, 174, 183.
6 Colley, *In Defiance of Oligarchy*, pp. 177–87; W. Michael, *England Under George I. The Beginnings of the Hanoverian Dynasty* (Westport, repr. 1981), pp. 122–5.
7 Michael, *Beginnings of the Hanoverian Dynasty*, pp. 125–9.
8 E. Gregg, 'The Jacobite Career of John, Earl of Mar', in *Ideology and Conspiracy*, pp. 181–2.
9 J. Baynes, *The Jacobite Rising of 1715* (1970), pp. 21–2; Szechi, *The Jacobites*, p. 57.

who was a naturalised Frenchman and a senior commander in the French army. The problem here was that the ailing Louis XIV was weary of the endless importunities of the exiled Stuarts and sceptical of their assurances of support.[10] Moreover, France's economy had been badly affected by the War of the Spanish Succession and neither the French king nor his ministers were willing to contemplate the renewed war that would inevitably follow overt French intervention in support of a Jacobite rising.[11] Indeed, the French government was so averse to the project that it specifically forbade Berwick to take part in any rebellion even in a private capacity.[12] The death of Louis XIV on 21 August/ 1 September 1715 removed any hope of overcoming this official hostility by pressure on the king.[13] The Duke of Orléans, who became Regent in the name of the old king's infant great-grandson, was also his ward's next heir – provided the terms of the Peace of Utrecht (by which Philip V of Spain, the nearest relation to Louis XV, renounced his claims to the French throne) were upheld. He therefore had no interest in destabilising the Hanoverian regime, and in 1716 took France into an alliance with Britain dedicated to the maintenance of the Utrecht settlement.[14]

All of which meant that Mar, Ormond and Wyndham were barking up the wrong tree. Bolingbroke, ever the opportunist, entered the service of the Old Pretender shortly after he arrived in France and soon realised the chimerical nature of his friends' plans. He manfully sought to change the French government's attitude towards the conspirators, but his efforts were unavailing.[15] Meanwhile the relentless process of impeaching the former ministry disrupted the progress of the conspiracy back in Britain.

Ormond, the key conspirator in English Jacobite plans for a rising, brazened it out until the end of July 1715, then fled to France in early August. His flight was precipitated by the government's official revelation of its knowledge of the conspiracy in the course of a speech by George I to Parliament requesting its support in whatever measures were necessary to thwart the Jacobites' plans.[16] The wave of Tory, and not infrequently explicitly Jacobite, rioting that swept England in the summer of 1715 heightened the atmosphere of crisis and apparently justified the swingeing measures to restore order introduced by the Whig

---

10 C. Nordmann, 'Louis XIV and the Jacobites', in R. M. Hatton (ed.), *Louis XIV and Europe* (1976), pp. 99–100; L. B. Smith, 'Spain and the Jacobites, 1715–16', in *Ideology and Conspiracy*, p. 161; Michael, *Beginnings of the Hanoverian Dynasty*, p. 144.
11 P. Goubert, *Louis XIV and Twenty Million Frenchmen*, transl. A. Carter (New York, 1970), pp. 267–8; J. J. Murray, *George I, the Baltic and the Whig Split of 1717* (1969), p. 207 n. 1.
12 Baynes, *Jacobite Rising*, p. 20.
13 H. T. Dickinson, *Bolingbroke* (1970), p. 139.
14 Szechi, *The Jacobites*, pp. 90–1.
15 Dickinson, *Bolingbroke*, pp. 138–9.
16 Michael, *Beginnings of the Hanoverian Dynasty*, pp. 144–6, 148–9.

regime (of which the most enduring legacy was the Riot Act).[17] In any event, these demonstrations were construed by both the Jacobites and their opponents as tokens of a substantial degree of plebeian support for the cause of the exiled Stuarts and seem to have persuaded the last leader of the conspiracy still at liberty in Britain, Mar, that they should try to go it alone in the first instance.

Mar had fled London for Scotland on 1 August and retired to the Highlands. From there he summoned the leaders of the Jacobite clans and some of their Lowland counterparts to his home at Kildrummy for two great hunts, under cover of which he consulted with them about the feasibility of a rising.[18] Convinced by his assurances of French support if only they would show their mettle, they agreed to prepare their clansmen and tenants to rise in early September.[19] The authorities in Scotland meanwhile were well aware that something serious was in the offing and began to arrest every leading Jacobite they could find; one of the first was George Lockhart.[20]

After being browbeaten into withdrawing from the election for Midlothian in March, George had maintained a low profile for some months. Only in the summer of 1715 did he begin to receive hints that a conspiracy was afoot. Quite apart from a rising being the ultimate proving ground for a man of his principles, a Jacobite rebellion obviously offered Lockhart the opportunity to re-establish his *bona fides* with the rest of the Jacobite connection in Scotland and he therefore began to buy arms and horses and to enlist suitable recruits for a troop of cavalry. Unfortunately for Lockhart, however, the solidly presbyterian inclinations of the population around Carnwath and Dryden's proximity to Edinburgh (another bastion of Whig support) meant that he had, 'severall neighbours who were spys on me', and these activities did not pass unnoticed.[21] In addition, 'that reservedness' with which he was now regarded by old comrades such as Captain Straton led to a delay in his being informed of Mar's flight to the Highlands. Consequently he was caught unawares and was thus one of the first Jacobite leaders to be arrested and incarcerated in Edinburgh castle in the government swoop that followed. According to his own account at least, George was even deemed sufficiently important to merit a warrant sent up from London personally signed by the king.[22]

Argyll had, however, been appointed Commander-in-Chief of the government's forces in Scotland and after, somewhat defensively, consulting with his friends and securing their approval, George appealed to him to intervene on

17 Monod, *Jacobitism and the English People*, pp. 179–94.
18 Baynes, *Jacobite Rising*, pp. 27–31, 32, 34–6.
19 Michael, *Beginnings of the Hanoverian Dynasty*, p. 155.
20 Baynes, *Jacobite Rising*, pp. 31–2; Wodrow Letters, Quarto IX, ep. 125: Charles Erskine to Wodrow, Edinburgh, 18 Aug. 1715.
21 LP i. 484; J. Maidment (ed.), *The Argyle Papers* (Edinburgh, 1834), p. 134.
22 LP i. 485–6.

his behalf, on the grounds that there was no evidence of his involvement in any conspiracy.[23] While he was waiting for a response, Lockhart energetically involved himself in the Jacobite attempt to seize Edinburgh castle by a surprise attack to be carried out by Jacobite conspirators within the city. Having sounded out several of his guards, George felt sure he could bribe the porter – appropriately named Charles Stuart – to leave the main gate unlocked on the night of the attack.[24] He informed the plotters, but they apparently decided in favour of an escalade instead, which was foiled on the night of 8 September.[25] Luckily for him, Lockhart was not compromised by this fiasco because Argyll had by then successfully intervened on his behalf.

Released on a surety of 6000 marks (approximately £333 sterling) on 2 September, George immediately retired to Carnwath and took up where he had left off preparing for a rising. After consultation with the few neighbouring lairds and noblemen there and in Midlothian and Tweeddale who favoured the Jacobite cause it was agreed that they would only come out in arms in the event of Mar's army (which had openly mustered at Kirkmichael in Braemar on 6 September) passing the Firth of Forth or the Old Pretender landing in Scotland.[26] George also assumed the role of coordinator and liaison between this network and another being organised in Clydesdale by Sir James Hamilton of Rosehaugh and Lord Blantyre, while at the same time busily continuing to gather arms and horses for his own uprising.[27] Philip Lockhart, who was with his brother throughout this period, meantime used his old military connections to recruit half-pay officers in Glasgow.[28] By October Lockhart had thus become the lynchpin of a small network of Jacobites waiting to rise in Midlothian, Tweeddale and Clydesdale.

Inevitably such busy treason soon came to the attention of the authorities, and early in October Argyll ordered George to take up residence first at Dryden and subsequently in Edinburgh, the better to keep an eye on him. On his return to Midlothian the 'official' Jacobite organisation tacitly signalled Lockhart's rehabilitation by summoning him to a secret meeting called to coordinate a general rising in the lowlands south of the Forth of which Viscount Kenmuir was to be the commander.[29] George had already made it clear that he was opposed to precipitate, independent action and argued for delaying such a rising until Mar's army approached Edinburgh, on the grounds that the networks of Jacobites he had organised would take time to contact and had in any case

23 LP i. 486–7; LL, pp. 118–19: Edinburgh Castle, 18 Aug. 1715.
24 LL, p. 257.
25 A. and H. Tayler, *1715: the Story of the Rising* (1936), pp. 55–9.
26 LP i. 487–9; SRO GD 18/2092/4: Sir John Clerk's spiritual journal for Apr. 1712–1715, 3 Sept. 1715.
27 LP i. 488–9.
28 LP i. 489–90; SRO GD 1/616/11: list of officers who deserted to the Jacobites (including 5 from Philip Lockhart's old regiment, Lord Mark Kerr's Horse).
29 LP i. 491–3.

already agreed only to turn out when Mar was south of the Forth or the Old Pretender arrived.[30] Nonetheless he promised that his own troop of horse at Carnwath would support anything agreed to at the meeting. Kenmuir's rising accordingly began with a rendezvous at Biggar which Philip Lockhart joined with the troop George had gathered at Carnwath. Lockhart of course immediately denied any involvement in Kenmuir's rising and reiterated his promises of good behaviour, then asked if he might be allowed to move from Edinburgh to Dryden. Before leaving the city, having received permission to do so, he strictly enjoined Straton to let him know as soon as any of Mar's forces crossed the Forth so that he could hide from the inevitable search party that would be sent after him and then mobilise his Midlothian,Tweeddale and Clydesdale networks.[31] On the night of 12/13 October William Mackintosh of Borlum and a substantial force of Highlanders duly crossed the Forth, outflanking Argyll's army at Stirling and threatening Edinburgh.[32] If all had gone according to plan, George should by then have been summoning his friends to rise. Either because he had no advance warning of Borlum's imminent arrival, or because he still did not trust Lockhart, Straton failed to alert him.[33] Consequently George was seized a second time on the morning of 13 October and all hope of a rising in Midlothian collapsed.

Lockhart's participation in the '15 ended frustratingly but harmlessly (as far as he personally was concerned) at this point. His brother was not so fortunate. Philip Lockhart loyally stuck by Kenmuir, despite the disappointing response to his call to arms, and marched south into England with the combined forces of Borlum, Kenmuir and the handful of northern English rebels who had escaped the mass arrests of suspect Tories that effectively destroyed any prospect of a Jacobite rising elsewhere in England.[34] Philip was therefore present at the disastrous battle of Preston on 12–13 November and was one of those caught up in the surrender of the rebels on the 14th.[35] Though he correctly argued his commission had expired with the demobilisation of his regiment in the reign of Queen Anne, long before he turned out to fight against George I, he had not formally resigned from the army and was therefore treated as a half-pay officer still subject to military discipline. Philip Lockhart was accordingly court-martialled and shot shortly after the surrender.[36]

The death of his brother affected Lockhart deeply.[37] In a letter to a friend

30 LP i. 490–1, 492–3; LL, p. 122: GL to Major Simon Fraser [Edinburgh?], 20 July 1717.
31 LP i. 493–4.
32 Baynes, *Jacobite Rising*, pp. 74–9.
33 LP i. 494–5; LL, pp. 122–3.
34 Baynes, *Jacobite Rising*, pp. 83–116.
35 Baynes, *Jacobite Rising*, pp. 117–28.
36 LP i. 497–8.
37 LP i. 496–7. GL also named his 13th, penultimate, child Philip, and the boy became his father's favourite ('a child I love tenderlie', he recorded in his will; LP ii. 429).

two years later he virtually declared himself and his family to be in a state of bloodfeud with the Hanoverian regime:

> I cannot say I am so good a Christian as not to long for a fair occasion to revenge what … [Philip Lockhart] … did meet with, which I cannot nor never will think of but with warm blood. And come of me what will, I hope I shall leave those behind me full of the same resentment and readie to embrace every occasion to prosecute it.[38]

The vehemence of his response owed more than a little to guilt. George's personal fortune suffered somewhat as a result of his involvement in the '15, and he had to endure a tedious incarceration in Edinburgh castle in unhealthy conditions that eventually made him seriously ill.[39] The government also did its best to build up a sufficient case to bring him to trial for his part in the preparations for the rising.[40] But his travails were clearly as nothing compared to the hundreds of his peers who lost their lives or estates for the Jacobite cause during 1715–16. Lockhart as a consequence could not easily bring himself to abandon the Stuart cause even when he became heartily sick of the incessant bickering that characterised internecine Jacobite politics in the 1720s, and depressed by a gathering sense of futility. In effect, then, Philip Lockhart's execution locked him into commitments that were to dictate the course of the rest of his life and cast a shadow into the next generation. This is not to say he would have abandoned the Stuarts without the spur of a personal score to settle with the Whig regime, but rather that the death of his brother for ten years prevented his becoming an armchair Jacobite like most of his peers.

George was eventually released on £5000 sterling (£60000 Scots) bond on 21 January 1716.[41] He apparently took some time to recover from the illness he had contracted during his incarceration, and probably also judged it wise to keep a low profile for a while. In any event, he seems to have spent over a year living quietly at home revising his *Memoirs* and writing the *Commentarys* which carry his account forward to 1715. Only in the summer of 1717 did he begin once again to participate in Jacobite activity.[42] When he did so he comported himself with all the zeal of a man who had something to prove. As indeed he had. Lockhart's neighbour, Baron John Clerk of Penicuik, caustically observed of George's conduct in 1715 that 'his resolution gave way to his fears and

---

38 LL, p. 124: GL to Major Simon Fraser [Edinburgh?], 20 July 1717.
39 LP i. 495–6; LL, p. 131: GL to Mar [Dryden?], 28 Mar. 1718.
40 LP i. 496; HMC *Various Collections* i. (Berwick on Tweed Corporation) 21: examination of Alexander Fleming.
41 SRO GD 220/5/623/3: Hyndford to Montrose, Edinburgh, 21 Jan. 1716. There were rumours as early as December 1715 that Lockhart was about to be released: SRO GD 18/2092/4: Sir John Clerk's spiritual journal for Apr. 1712–1715, 25 Dec. 1715.
42 LL, p. 129; HMC *Stuart* v. 140–1: Henry Straton to Mar, [Edinburgh] 3/14 Oct. 1717.

apprehensions. Tis true he was taken up and put in the castle, but he had time enough to have gone with his friendes if he had had a mind to it',[43] and it appears that a good many other Jacobites who had survived the rising would have agreed with this assessment.[44] Moreover, an opportunity to vindicate himself and re-establish his *bona fides* lay readily to hand. The Jacobite court was by then intriguing with King Charles XII of Sweden's chief minister, Baron Georg Goertz, hoping to persuade the Swedes either to lend them an invasion force, or – even better – for Charles himself to lead an expedition into northern England. Charles XII felt, with some justification, that George I in his capacity as Elector of Hanover had stabbed Sweden in the back in 1712 and 1715 by occupying the Swedish possessions of Bremen and Verden (and subsequently refusing either restitution or adequate compensation). Charles was also in desperate need of ready cash to sustain his war effort against the anti-Swedish coalition he had been fighting since 1700 (by 1716 this consisted of Russia, Prussia, Poland-Saxony, Denmark and Hanover). Negotiations between Goertz and the Stuart court therefore centred on the raising of a large 'loan' by its adherents in the British Isles, which the Old Pretender and his new Secretary of State, Mar, believed would favourably dispose the Swedes towards the idea of a surprise attack on England.[45] And as one of the few prominent young Jacobites willing and able to carry on the exiled Stuarts' business in Scotland, Lockhart was among the first to be drawn into the Scottish end of the plot.

Lockhart's first intimation of what was afoot came when he, the Bishop of Edinburgh and Lord Balmerino were all contacted by Straton with a view to their organising the purchase and export of 5–6000 bolls (c. 80000 litres) of meal to Sweden as a token of the Jacobites' goodwill. George and the others duly looked into the feasibility of the proposal, but ultimately rejected it on grounds of expense and circumspection. The chastened Scottish Jacobite community was determinedly trying not to attract attention to itself at this time, and as a result of government confiscations of property, losses during the rebellion and the need to support those in exile abroad, did not have money to spare to buy meal for Sweden.[46] Nevertheless, when Mar contacted Lockhart again via Straton, requesting that he canvass for pledges to a war chest to be called on in the event of a Swedish invasion, which doubtless would have been diverted towards the Swedish 'loan' if it looked as if the money might crystallise Sweden's commitment to an attempt, George undertook the task of soliciting pledges and, somewhat to his own surprise, secured promises for a substantial sum. Even so, his zeal did not overcome his long-standing determination to protect Scotland's interests;

43 SRO GD 18/6080: p. 190.
44 LP i. 483–4; LL, pp. 122–3: GL to Major Simon Fraser [Edinburgh?], 20 July 1717.
45 Szechi, *The Jacobites*, pp. 104–6.
46 HMC *Stuart Papers*, iv. 439: Mar to James Murray of Stormont, 8 July 1717 ns; LP ii.
     7–8.

hence he also pointedly requested that 'as this country did not abound in riches, and that the loyall party was less now than ever in a condition to raise money, wee were humbly of opinion that nothing of this kind should be demanded ... but when matters were so well concerted and so far advanced, that the main stroke was to be struck'.[47] By the time this response reached the Jacobite court, Mar and the Old Pretender had in any case given up hope of securing Swedish military aid, so the issue became moot.

Nonetheless, his active involvement in the intrigue seems to have rehabilitated Lockhart in the eyes of the Stuart court. Early in 1717 he used Philip Lockhart's former lieutenant in the Carnwath troop, Major Simon Fraser, who had escaped to the Continent after Preston, as a channel for the expression of his goodwill toward Mar (with whom he had not hitherto been on especially good terms).[48] Mar responded courteously, emboldening Lockhart to write a letter justifying his conduct in 1715 (mainly by blaming Straton for everything that went wrong), pledging his continued commitment to the Stuart cause and implying that he would like to be of use to it in Scotland.[49] Mar understood the subtext and duly arranged for the Old Pretender to reply personally but with general pleasantries, then suggested to Lockhart that, as well as securing pledges of money, he might usefully turn his personal connection with Argyll to account by sounding him out regarding the Stuart cause.[50] George suspected Mar was insincere, but he duly busied himself with this, and although the intrigue came to naught (Argyll, recently put out of office, was almost certainly just trying to see if he could whip up some Tory backing[51]), the net effect was fully to restore Lockhart's credibility with the Jacobite network at home and abroad by the end of 1718.[52]

The renewed perception of George as an aggressive and effective proponent of the cause on the part of his fellow Jacobites led to his playing a significant role in the proposed Scottish rising of 1719. This rebellion was envisaged as an ancillary, or diversionary, action to the main operation: a landing by Ormond in south-western England at the head of a Spanish army. It was a truly desperate venture, only embarked upon for lack of a better alternative. The Spanish Bourbons (who were aggrieved over the loss of former Spanish territories in Italy as part of the peace of Utrecht) had been successfully isolated by some adroit British diplomacy in the aftermath of the War of the Spanish Succession. The

47　LP i. 8.
48　LL, pp. 119–21: Fraser to Mar, Verdun near Toulouse, 10 Apr. 1717.
49　HMC *Stuart Papers*, iv. 360: Mar to Fraser, 15 June 1717 ns; LL, pp. 122–3: GL to Fraser [Edinburgh?], 20 July 1717.
50　LP ii. 9–10.
51　Michael, *Beginnings of the Hanoverian Dynasty*, pp. 221–2; Ferguson, *Scotland. 1689 to the Present*, pp. 137–8.
52　LL, pp. 131–4: GL to Mar [Dryden?], 28 Mar. 1718; LP ii. 11–17.

Spanish government, headed by the cunning Cardinal Giulio Alberoni, therefore sought to disrupt the status quo in the hope that matters might fall out to Spain's advantage. In 1717, encouraged by what they thought was a British reluctance to fight to uphold the terms of the peace, Spanish troops were despatched to seize Sicily from its Savoyard owner. Instead of acquiescing, however, the British government promptly fitted out a substantial Royal Navy squadron, invoked the Dutch alliance and destroyed the Spanish fleet at Cape Passaro in August 1718. With the main Spanish army stranded in Sicily and France mobilising forces for an invasion of northern Spain to enforce a return to the Utrecht settlement, the Spanish government was clearly in dire straits. They correspondingly played their Jacobite card.[53]

A treaty with the Old Pretender was rapidly drafted and signed and Ormond was summoned to Madrid from exile in Avignon to command the hastily gathered invasion force he was to lead into England. Due to mishaps and the inevitable delays inherent in throwing such a major undertaking together, however, the unfortunate commander and his main expedition only finally sailed from Cadiz on 24 February 1719 – the stormiest time of year in the north-eastern Atlantic – and, predictably, it encountered a major gale, was scattered and damaged and was forced to return to port. Meanwhile an ancillary expedition under the exiled George Keith, 9th Earl Marischal, had sailed independently from Los Pasajes a day after the main expedition set out, and though it too encountered bad weather, Marischal persevered and reached Scotland on 9 April 1719.[54] Before either expedition departed, Ormond also took the precaution of despatching messengers to Scotland to alert well-disposed clan chieftains and prominent Lowland Jacobites to make preparations for a rising. One of these, Francis Kennedy, secretly contacted the Earl of Wigton (George's future son-in-law) before the Scottish expedition arrived, and he promptly called Lockhart in to consult on joint measures.[55]

Lockhart's response was symptomatic of the general wariness with which the Scots Jacobites greeted the summons to arms. The Jacobites still at large in Scotland were loath to risk a repeat of their premature exposure during the '15, and Lockhart apparently soon persuaded his peers that they should lie low until Marischal or Ormond was in the offing.[56] His caution was further manifested by a refusal, at least on his own part, to recruit the men and accumulate the arms and horses that were the *sine qua non* of a successful rising despite the timely warning he had received. In a letter to Marischal after his landing George then cited this very lack of preparation as one reason why 'it is not to be desired or expected ... [the Lowland Jacobites] ... should rise in arms untill there be such

53 Szechi, *The Jacobites*, pp. 107–9.
54 Szechi, *The Jacobites*, pp. 109–10
55 LP ii. 17–18.
56 LP ii. 18.

a number of forces near them, as can make a stand, and to which they may resort'.[57] In addition, he personally intervened to discourage the Earl of Dalhousie from taking any action to expose himself after Dalhousie and some friends got wind of a false report that Ormond had landed and resolved to fight their way to the West Country to join him.[58] Thus Lockhart was directly instrumental in ensuring that Marischal's offensive in the Highlands elicited virtually no response from the Lowland Jacobites.

As it turned out, this was fortunate for them, as Marischal's little army of Spanish regulars and those clansmen who had rallied to him were soon afterwards cornered and dispersed by the veteran General Wightman and a small government force at the pass of Glenshiel.[59] Nevertheless, the kind of fearful passivity displayed by Lockhart, on the grounds that 'if any appearance should be made for the King in Scotland, and the grand design fail in execution, wee would meet with no quarters from the Government',[60] was a token of things to come. As Whig rule became the customary, normal state of affairs, individual Jacobites throughout the British Isles consciously and unconsciously adapted themselves to it through a complex of personal relationships and private compromises and accommodations. Over the course of time these acquired the inertia of familiarity. Hence the gathering disinclination to take 'precipitate' action against the new order on the part of men, like Lockhart, who remained bitterly opposed to it ideologically.

On the conscious level, of course, George was still as committed as ever to the Jacobite cause, and duly demonstrated his zeal by arranging for financial credit to be extended to the Spanish troops captured at Glenshiel.[61] Since it was by this time apparent the Old Pretender was not about to return to the British Isles in the near future, Lockhart and Alexander Rose, the Bishop of Edinburgh, also revived an old proposal first put forward in 1713 by Fr James Carnegy,[62] that the exiled king appoint a clandestine committee or board of trustees to run his affairs in Scotland during his unavoidable absence. Lockhart believed such a board would impart a sense of direction and organisation to the hitherto inchoate Jacobite movement in Scotland at a time when a good deal of animus was building up between pro-Mar and anti-Mar factions amongst them.[63] According to George's account the bishop wanted to propose him as one of the trustees, alongside such Jacobite luminaries as Edinburgh himself, the Earls of Eglinton and Wigton, Lord Balmerino, William Paterson of Prestonhall

57 LL, pp. 140–1: [Dryden?, Apr. 1719].
58 LP ii. 22–3.
59 Lenman, *Jacobite Risings*, pp. 191–4.
60 LP ii. 18.
61 LP ii. 23–4.
62 See above, p. 106.
63 LP ii. 25–6.

and Captain Straton, but Lockhart refused on the grounds that it was inappro-
priate for the proponent of a scheme like this to nominate himself. He was,
however, clearly hoping James would nonetheless see fit to appoint him, and
was transparently disappointed and annoyed when the Old Pretender blithely
passed him over.[64] Having heard from his father on the subject, George Lockhart
jr, who happened to be in Rome on the Grand Tour at the time and had carried
the original proposal to the Jacobite court, accordingly wrote to the Palazzo
Mutti pointedly to stress with regard to the board of trustees that, 'tho his name
is not in it and thereby he's deprived of the honour of serving your Majesty in
conjunction with the others that are named, yet he will never be wanting if in
any other capacity he can in the least contribute to your Majestie's service'.[65]
James and his ministers quickly took the hint (it would have been difficult to
miss) and the Old Pretender wrote personally to the trustees and George blaming
the oversight on secretarial error and appointing him a trustee forthwith.[66]

In addition, in an earlier conversation with George junior James vaguely
suggested that Lockhart 'write frequently to him, and ... he expected you would
all in general acquaint him of such storys as were writt home and spred abroad
in order to divide his friends and lessen the good opinion people had of his
servants here'.[67] Once he had been appointed one of the trustees, George
interpreted this as a royal mandate to assume the task of maintaining 'a regular
correspondence' with the Jacobite court which the Old Pretender had specifically
requested should be assigned to one of their number.[68] Lockhart had been
impatient with the lack of purpose and the general disorganisation of the Scottish
Jacobites for some time by 1720 and so seized with both hands this opportunity
to turn himself into James's special agent in Scotland.[69] By doing so he assumed
some of the Old Pretender's shadow authority among Scotland's Jacobites, and
in the process boosted his own status among a network of people whose good
opinion he naturally (as a committed Jacobite) craved.

And though the exiled court had almost certainly not intended Lockhart to
play such a role when they established the Jacobite trustees, James and his
ministers do not seem to have been averse to his doing so. For it soon became
apparent that Lockhart was one of the few trustees with the energy and zeal to
do something for the Jacobite cause. Most of the trustees were aged veterans of
the struggle, such as the Bishop of Edinburgh and Straton, who were appointed

---

64 LP ii. 29–31; SRO CH12/12/1911 (Records of the Episcopal Church): the Old Pretender
    to the College of Bishops and others, 15 Feb. 1720 ns.
65 Ralph Brown Draughon Library, Auburn University, Stuart Papers microfilm, 47/65:
    Turin, 9 June 1720 ns.
66 LP ii. 31: 14 June 1720 ns.
67 LP ii. 28.
68 LP ii. 30.
69 Blairs Letters 2/173/20: Carnegy to Thomas Innes, 1 Nov. 1712; 2/188/3: Carnegy to
    Innes, 19 Jan. 1714.

to give the board some political clout. Others were appointed in order to preserve a pro- and anti-Mar factional balance.[70] Moreover, the elevation of certain of their number to positions of special trust offended touchy aristocrats such as the Marquess of Seaforth and the 4th Earl of Panmure.[71] Hence all but a handful of the trustees were from the outset very reluctant to exercise their 'authority' or even meet together to decide common policy or responses to letters from the Jacobite court, and gratefully delegated responsibility for coordinating individual consultations on such matters, and the drafting of letters in response to the Old Pretender, to Lockhart.[72] He took to the role of man of business with a will, even seeking to extend the trustees' authority by setting up a regular correspondence with the Jacobite clans and the English Tories, and the vital nature of his input with regard to the functioning (in any sense) of James's trustees may be seen from the fact that the board rapidly became moribund after he withdrew from active involvement.[73] By 1730 it had become a dead letter.

Even before he had any 'official' authorisation, by 1720 Lockhart had already begun to re-engage with politics at Westminster on behalf of the Jacobite court. Since the death of Queen Anne Scotland's politics had degenerated into a sterile contest for control of the country's meagre resources of patronage between the two main Whig factions, the Squadrone and the Argathelians (i.e. Argyll and Islay's clients and kinsmen).[74] Each sought to win the favour of the ministry in London by showing how it, rather than its opponent, could best keep Scotland quiet, or alternatively, could cause most trouble if not appeased.[75] Superficially, the situation, which guaranteed a disgruntled faction of 'outs' as opposed to 'ins' at any one time, seemed to offer a golden opportunity for the Jacobites to foment trouble. In reality, however, the hostility between the Argathelians and the Squadrone was only skin deep. Either faction was happy to accept Scots Tory support in scoring points against its opponent. Neither was prepared to let the dispute get so out of hand as to allow any Tories into power or office.[76] Both were certain to rally to the Hanoverian dynasty in a real crisis. Hence Lockhart's efforts to exploit the endless intrigues and bickering generated by the great Argathelian-Squadrone treasure hunt were ultimately doomed to failure.

The appearance of a major political crisis over the election of Representative Peers nonetheless managed to obscure these basic truths about the political situation in Scotland. The crisis arose over the attempt by the Earl of Sunderland, George I's favourite and *de facto* premier minister, to restrict the number of future

70 LP ii. 26, 30.
71 LL, p. 156: GL to James Murray [Dryden?], 20 Jan. 1721.
72 LP ii. 34–5.
73 LL, pp. 165, 168–9, 239, 290–1.
74 Lenman, 'Client Society', pp. 69–94.
75 Szechi and Hayton, 'John Bull's Other Kingdoms', pp. 254–7.
76 LP ii. 67.

promotions to the peerage by act of Parliament. The origins of this manoeuvre lay partly in the Whigs' memories of the previous reign, partly in lingering English Scotophobia and partly in the ministry's attempts to insure themselves for the future. One of the great Whig defeats of Queen Anne's reign had occurred in December 1711 when their majority in the Lords was overwhelmed by Queen Anne's mass creation of twelve peers in order to ensure the passage of legislation necessary for negotiating an end to the War of the Spanish Succession.[77] Most English peers suspected that all Scottish peers yearned for a hereditary seat in the House of Lords, and thus, despite the Hamilton peerage case decision of 1711, feared their order was in danger of being overrun by hordes of greedy hireling Scots.[78] And in 1719 Sunderland, who had long since burned his bridges with the Prince of Wales (the future George II), badly needed to safeguard himself against impeachment in the event of his master's death.[79] The problem for the ministry was that the peerage bill threatened virtually to foreclose the secret hope of every landed gentleman: that he or his posterity would one day be ennobled. Hence the introduction of the measure provoked a massively hostile cross-party reaction in the Commons which led to the first bill, introduced in February 1719, never emerging from the Lords and the second being crushingly defeated in the lower House in December.[80]

The specially Scottish aspect of the crisis arose from an ancillary issue addressed by the two peerage bills. As part of the Treaty of Union the Scots peerage had been entitled at every general election to elect 16 of their number as Representative Peers.[81] And despite proceedural humiliations such as automatically coming behind the lowliest English baron in precedence regardless of their rank in the Scottish peerage, a seat among the 16 became a great prize among Scotland's nobility, carrying as it did access to the fount of all patronage at court and in government and a certain, limited bargaining power.[82] The English peerage, however, disliked the institution intensely. Their deep-seated fear of being swamped by impecunious Scottish noblemen had led them in 1711 to exclude the Duke of Hamilton from taking his seat as a British peer by a breathtaking piece of legal chicanery that barred all those who held Scottish peerages extant in 1707 from ever being admitted, on the grounds that they were adequately represented by the 16. But in addition, many English peers found the very elective principle inherent in the return of the 16 at every general

---

77 C. Jones, '"Venice Preserv'd; or a Plot Discovered": the Political and Social Context of the Peerage Bill of 1719', in C. Jones (ed.), *A Pillar of the Constitution: the House of Lords in British Politics, 1640–1784* (1989), pp. 87–94.
78 Jones, '"Venice Preserv'd"', pp. 84–7.
79 Jones, '"Venice Preserv'd"', pp. 80–3.
80 W. Michael, *England Under George I. The Quadruple Alliance* (1939), pp. 280–7, 294–8; Jones, '"Venice Preserv'd"', pp. 95–104.
81 *English Historical Documents*, viii. 687–8: article xxii of the Act of Union.
82 Lenman, 'A Client Society', pp. 82–4.

election extremely distasteful and an affront to the hereditary traditions of the House of Lords.[83] The better to win support for the peerage bill in the upper chamber, therefore, Sunderland ensured that it contained a clause replacing the 16 elected Representative Peers with 25 hereditary ones. Those Scots peers unlucky enough not to be named one of this select 25 were henceforth to be eligible for election to the Commons, but otherwise would lose all meaningful privilege traditionally accorded their rank.[84]

Predictably, many Scottish peers were outraged and alarmed by the proposal,[85] and naturally enough the Argathelians and the Squadrone each sought to use the crisis to their own advantage – despite the fact that both had supported the peerage bills at Westminster. The Argathelians were at this time in the more vulnerable position, as they were engaged in the technically delicate process of coming 'in', having recently been 'out'.[86] The Squadrone, as the current 'in' faction, had political inertia in their favour. To break their rivals' hold on power the Argathelians had, therefore, decisively to prove their superior ability to deliver the political goods in Scotland. This would impress their usefulness on the ministry in London and thus give them the edge in the struggle for power at the political centre. By the early 1720s, however, Scotland's administrators had a firm grip on the electoral process and could ensure that no Tories would be returned to the Commons from Scotland, and also that the 'out' Whig faction would be only minimally represented.[87] Hence the one area of Scottish politics in which the results were not quite a foregone conclusion was the Representative Peers' election. From 1720 onwards (i.e. after the peerage bills had both failed) the Argathelians correspondingly used continued rumours of, and some ministerial inclination towards, a separate, specifically Scots peerage bill to manipulate the fear of loss of status the episode had generated in many Scots peers to try and disrupt Squadrone efforts to manage the quiet, orderly return of 16 pro-government Representative Peers.[88]

Though Lockhart retained an oversanguine belief in the latent power of the Scots Tory interest, he, Harry Maule and the Earl of Kincardine were realistic enough in practice to accept that there was no hope of defeating the Whig party as a whole. Instead, building on the network they had established in working up petitions from the Scottish nobility against the peerage bills, they sought an alliance with the Argathelians which would secure that Whig faction's support

83 Holmes, 'Hamilton Affair', pp. 257–82.
84 Michael, *Quadruple Alliance*, pp. 283–4.
85 Jones, '"Venice Preserv'd"', p. 87 n32.
86 Jones, '"Venice Preserv'd"', pp. 86–7, 98–9.
87 LP ii. 82.
88 Ferguson, *Scotland. 1689 to the Present*, p. 140; Jones, '"Venice Preserv'd"', p. 104; LL, pp. 159–60: GL to Harry Maule, Cumbernald, 12 Apr. [1721].

for a number of Tory Representative Peers.[89] The *quid pro quo* was that the Tories would back Argathelian candidates against Squadrone ones in both the Representative Peers' and Commons' elections. In the first instance, however, it was necessary for the Scots Tories to re-establish their credibility as a political bloc, and, using the threat of the peerage bill to rouse the dormant Tory network, Lockhart, Maule and Kincardine succeeded in mobilising a strong body of support for the Earl of Aberdeen at a Representative Peers by-election in 1721 occasioned by the death of the Marquess of Annandale. Argyll tried at first to go it alone, but when the Squadrone threw its weight behind Aberdeen in order to make sure of thwarting him, he tried to divide the Tory vote in his faction's favour by putting up Lockhart's father-in-law, Eglinton, instead. The ploy failed and Aberdeen was returned.[90] Clearly alive to the prospect of getting frozen out at the general election if the Squadrone secured the Tories' support, Argyll then sent an intermediary to Lockhart with a proposal for an alliance based on an equal division of the Representative Peers' seats. Lockhart agreed, and in addition demanded a public commitment by all candidates that they would oppose a Scots peerage bill and that Argyll himself would support Tory efforts to end official harassment of episcopalian nonjurors. Argyll pledged himself and his faction to abide by these terms, but at this point the government in London intervened.[91] Clearly concerned that Whig faction-fighting in Scotland was getting so out of hand as to lead to the possible return of Tory Representative Peers, the ministry in London demanded that Argyll and the Squadrone support a joint list of 16 candidates, thus freezing the Tories out instead.[92]

Aware that they had been trumped as regards the peers' election by London's intervention, Lockhart, Maule and Kincardine attempted a riposte that would humiliate the Scottish administration by demonstrating its unpopularity and thus imminent inability to keep the country quiet. This took the form of proposing addresses against a Scots peerage bill from the electors of Scotland's shires when they gathered to cast their votes on election day, starting with Midlothian.[93] In addition, 21 Tory peers turned up at the Representative Peers election to register their minority list of candidates and formally protest against any peerage bill. In a letter to the Old Pretender Lockhart claimed that if he could have persuaded 11 nonjurant Tory peers to take the oaths necessary to qualify to vote, enough formerly Tory placemen would have defected from the Whig side to give them

---

89 Ferguson, *Scotland. 1689 to the Present*, pp. 140–1; LP ii. 58, 82–3; LL, pp. 162–3: GL to the Old Pretender [Dryden?], 15 June 1721.

90 LP ii. 58–9; LL, pp. 160–2: GL to Maule and the Old Pretender, 17 May and 15 June 1721.

91 LL, pp. 162–3: GL to the Old Pretender [Dryden?], 15 June 1721.

92 LL, pp. 175–6, 176–7: GL to the Old Pretender, 12 Mar. and 23 Apr. 1722.

93 LP ii. 84–6. GL and Maule had already floated an address and a solemn commitment against a peerage bill to be attested by all candidates in the Representative Peers' elections at the time of Aberdeen's return in 1721: LL, p. 161: GL to Maule, Carnwath, 17 May 1721.

a majority.[94] This seems highly unlikely, given the formidable numbers deployed by the united Squadrone-Argathelian bloc, but it definitely suggests Scottish Tory morale, and George's optimism, were reviving.

Ironically, this occurred at a time when English Tory hopes of electoral success were fading. Given the recent fiascos with which the Whig regime was associated, the South Sea Bubble and the failure of the peerage bill in particular, it did not seem beyond the bounds of possibility in 1720–21 that the Tories might be able to reduce the Whig majority in the Commons and challenge them in the Lords.[95] Personal animosities within the Whig party had also by this time reached such a pitch that Sunderland, now denied the protection against a vindictive monarch that the peerage bill might have offered, had begun wooing the Tories. Part of his approach, like Harley before him, seems to have been to insinuate (without ever committing himself to anything specific or on paper) to acquaintances and clients whom he knew had Jacobite sympathies that he favoured the restoration of the Stuarts. With hindsight we can fairly safely say that this was a tactical move on his part to make his pitch to the Tory party more effective by silencing or even converting an important section of the party to his cause.[96] Nonetheless, the fact that the senior Whig minister was apparently trying to negotiate with them caused considerable excitement in Tory and Jacobite circles.

Lockhart first learned of the intrigue when a formerly Tory client of Sunderland's, Alexander Urquhart of Newhall, sought out him, Maule and Kincardine shortly before the election. They believed Urquhart to be a Jacobite, but 'were infidels with respect to any good intentions from that Lord' and were thus nonplussed when he produced letters in the Old Pretender's own hand asking in general terms that they forward the schemes the bearer was advancing in support of Sunderland.[97] Lockhart was accordingly deputed to consult with his liaison with the English Tories, William Shippen, to find out what was going on. Under cover of an alleged quarrel with Euphemia, George then disappeared for two weeks in September in order to meet Shippen secretly at Newcastle-upon-Tyne to discuss Sunderland's proposals. There the two decided that in a

---

94 LP ii. 86; LL, pp. 176–8: GL to the Old Pretender [Carnwath?], 23 Apr. 1722.

95 Colley, *In Defiance*, pp. 120–2.

96 There has recently been considerable controversy over Sunderland's motives in his overtures to the Tories and whether or not he was involved in plots aiming at a Stuart restoration, for which see: *House of Commons*, i. 64–5; C. Jones, 'Whigs, Jacobites and Charles Spencer, Third Earl of Sunderland', *English Historical Review*, cix (1994), 52–73; E. Cruickshanks, 'Charles Spencer, Third Earl of Sunderland and Jacobitism', *English Historical Review* (forthcoming; I am grateful to Dr Cruickshanks for supplying me with an advance copy of this article). The interpretation advanced here assumes that his involvement with the Tories and/or the Jacobites was simply an aspect of his tactical manoeuvring within Whig high politics.

97 LP ii. 67–8; LL, p. 168: GL to the Old Pretender [Dryden?], 5 Dec. 1721.

matter of such potential gravity they should consult the Old Pretender directly and in the meantime treat Sunderland's proffered alliance very cautiously indeed.[98] In reply, the Old Pretender acknowledged that he had had reports of Sunderland's alleged conversion to his cause, but no direct contact, and urged them to bear his offers in mind while doing the best deal they could with whichever Whig faction offered the highest price for their support.[99] Lockhart and his fellow trustees took these instructions to heart and did their best to play off the Squadrone, Argyll and Sunderland against each other, although, as we have already seen, with ultimately very limited success. And indeed Sunderland's authority in the ministry appears to have been slipping so badly by this time that when he tried to persuade the king that the government should not spend as much as was needed to clinch a Whig victory at the polls and in addition should allow the Tories a share of the Representative Peers' seats, Walpole and Viscount Townshend were able to persuade George I to overrule him.[100] In any event, the future belonged to the Walpole-Townshend faction because shortly before the new Parliament was due to meet Sunderland died.

The premier minister's death immediately produced a struggle to succeed him within the Whig party. The Walpole-Townshend faction were obviously well placed to capitalise on Sunderland's demise, but there were several potential rivals for the monarch's favour who needed to be comprehensively outdone in order to realise the opportunity. To cement their hold on power, Walpole and Townshend needed to both unite the, at that point, badly divided Whig party behind them and secure George I's confidence.[101] They did so through their superbly timed exposure and investigation of the Atterbury plot.[102] Fortunately for Lockhart and the Scots Jacobites, however, no role seems to have been envisaged for them in this intrigue.[103] Consequently they were uninvolved in the preparations for a rising, and so escaped unscathed from the investigation.

The trials of Francis Atterbury, Bishop of Rochester, and other Jacobites involved in the plot nevertheless put a distinct brake on Jacobite activity throughout the British Isles for the next two years, as Lockhart and his confrères sought to avoid attracting the attention of the triumphant Whig regime.[104] Walpole, who was increasingly the dominant figure in the ministry, also deliberately eschewed

---

98 SRO GD 18/2092/7: Sir John Clerk's spiritual journal for 1720–1, 24 Sept. 1721; LL, pp. 168–70.

99 LP ii. 74–5: the Old Pretender to GL, 31 Jan. 1722 ns.

100 LL, p. 174: GL to the Old Pretender [Dryden?], 12 Mar. 1722; *House of Commons*, i. 64.

101 *House of Commons*, i. 33–5.

102 P. S. Fritz, *The English Ministers and Jacobitism Between the Rebellions of 1715 and 1745* (Toronto, 1975), *passim*.

103 The only reference to GL in the papers relating to the investigation is a code name ('Swinton') on a cipher intercepted en route from the Netherlands (Cambridge University Library, Ch. (H) *Papers* 69/8 (Cholomondeley-Houghton Papers)).

104 LL, p. 181: GL to the Old Pretender [Dryden?], 7 Dec. 1722.

controversial policies and legislation while he consolidated his faction's newly established hold on power. Only from 1724, once they were more secure, did the ministry begin again to advance the Whig agenda, thus presenting Lockhart and the trustees with the opportunity to exploit their more unpopular measures.[105]

The most controversial of these from a Scottish point of view was the revitalised malt tax. Though Scotland had technically been subject to the same malt tax as England since 1713, little serious effort was made to collect it. In 1724, however, the ministry decided to sidestep an impost that had in effect become moribund by levying a special sixpence additional duty on ale throughout Scotland and withdrawing the bounty on grain exports – in effect equalising the fiscal burden on the English and Scottish economies in lieu of the dead letter malt tax.[106] This provoked an outcry all over Scotland which the Jacobites gleefully encouraged, and none more actively than Lockhart.

From the outset Lockhart took a leading part in organising the heritors of Midlothian in support of a petition against the levy and a letter of instruction to their M.P., Robert Dundas of Arniston.[107] These declared special taxes levied on Scotland to be a breach of the seventh article of the Union and called upon Dundas to protest against the measure to the Commons and then withdraw from the house if they persisted in it. Both the petition and the instructions were then imitated in a number of consitituencies across the country.[108] This storm of protest had the desired effect in that even Scotland's 'mean spirited mercenary representatives' in Parliament felt sufficiently alarmed by it to bombard the ministry with pleas for the withdrawal of the extra duty. Walpole conceded this, but flintily extracted the Scots M.P.s' agreement to the levy and actual enforcement of a threepence a bushel malt tax (half the English rate).[109] Encouraged underhand by Lockhart and others (far from all of whom were Jacobites), the brewers of Edinburgh declared their intention to resist by giving up brewing until the government relented,[110] and entirely spontaneously a mob in Glasgow attacked and destroyed the home of Daniel Campbell of Shawfield, the local M.P., who was rumoured to be a supporter of the revitalised tax. The administration refused to be intimidated, however, bloodily suppressed the demonstrations in Glasgow, and then broke the Edinburgh brewers' resistance by threatening them with swingeing fines and imprisonment if they refused to

105 Hill, *Parliamentary Parties*, pp. 185–8.
106 Campbell, *Scotland Since 1707*, p. 49; LP ii. 134.
107 LP ii. 134–5; LL, pp. 220, 250: GL to Baron Sir John Clerk, Dryden, 14 Jan. and 4 Dec. 1725; Public Record Office, Chancery Lane, SP 54/16/105 (State Papers Domestic): Ronald Campbell to ? (enclosing two circular letters from GL), Edinburgh, 21 Dec. 1725.
108 LP ii. 135–9.
109 LP ii. 140–1.
110 LL, p. 236: GL to the Old Pretender [Edinburgh?], 25 July 1725.

return to work.[111] It was an object lesson in the inability of Scottish popular protest to deter the British state when it was determined to achieve a particular objective and in the futility of working to broaden the basis of Jacobite support when there was no hope of foreign military intervention to make it amount to anything. And correspondingly the suppression of the malt tax agitation and the passage of the Disarming Act of 1725 appear to have precipitated a gathering despair in Lockhart.

The Disarming Act flowed directly from the government's conviction that the last, best hope of the Jacobite cause lay in the Highlands and that most of the Highlanders were potential Jacobites.[112] It was a view shared by Lockhart, for whom the Highland clans were 'the only remains of the true old Scots blood and spirit'.[113] Consequently the bill originally envisaged would have anticipated much of the legislation that followed on the failure of the '45: Highland dress was to be made illegal, the Gaelic language was to be extirpated, the clans were to be disarmed one and all, and so on.[114] It had, however, been ten years since the '15 and six since the damp squib of the '19 and passions had cooled among the English Whig backbenchers. Hence despite the government's support for the measure and the fact that Scotland's Parliamentary representatives made hardly any protest (indeed, actively forwarded the bill), the act that emerged at the end of the 1725 Parliamentary session was a much milder measure which aimed first and foremost at simply disarming the clans.[115]

The ministry had also laid plans to take a pragmatic, carrot-and-stick approach with regard to its implementation. In 1724 General George Wade and a selected group of staff officers and engineers had carefully surveyed the approaches to the Highlands, the mountain passes and the disposition of clan strength. In 1725, as soon as the Disarming Act was passed, he exploited his new knowledge to station troops across all the major routes of communication through the Highlands and frigates of the Royal Navy at points off the coast from which they could intercept all sea traffic should it prove necessary.[116] After briefly diverting some of his troops to Glasgow to suppress the malt tax disturbances there, Wade then marched north with a substantial force to Inverness and established a large camp outside the town. Thence he proceeded to send invitations throughout the Highlands inviting the chieftains or their representatives to meet him. When clan emissaries duly arrived, Wade was the model of courtesy. While making it

---

111 Lenman, *Jacobite Risings*, pp. 206–13; LP ii. 165–8; SRO GD 1/616/69: 'Act for Preventing the Want or Scarcity of Ale or Beer, and Bread, in the Good-Town of Edinburgh', Edinburgh, 29 July 1725.
112 B. Lenman, *The Jacobite Clans of the Great Glen 1650–1784* (1984), p. 96.
113 LP ii. 161.
114 LP ii. 141–2.
115 LP ii. 159–60.
116 LP ii. 160–1.

clear that he was inflexible on the question of their handing over their arms, he nonetheless offered various douceurs. The most important of these from the clans' point of view was that he was prepared to remit all the arrears of rent the clans theoretically owed the Forfeited Estates Commission but which had actually been paid to the chieftains and clan gentry in exile on the Continent, and he had the authority to offer pardons to clan chieftains whose people in Scotland submitted to the government.[117]

Lockhart and the trustees were greatly alarmed both by Wade's preparations and the terms he was willing to offer to those clans that complied. Given the unfavourable international situation (i.e. little prospect of a major European war), the Jacobite clans were going to have fight the government alone if they chose to resist, and given Wade's careful preparations, such resistance was not likely to succeed. But they were almost equally disturbed by Wade's proposals to the clan elites. If the clans handed over their weapons and the exiled chieftains were allowed home, they would be neither able, nor in all probability willing, to support another Jacobite attempt for the foreseeable future.[118] The upshot was that the exiled court and Lockhart and the trustees both began frantically seeking a way out of Wade's trap that would preserve the Jacobite clans as a viable resource for the Stuart cause.

The Old Pretender duly found himself caught in a dilemma. His more hard-nosed advisers, such as Bishop Francis Atterbury and the Secretary of State, John Hay of Cromlix, Jacobite Earl of Inverness, favoured exploiting the situation to foment a rising, presumably in the hope that something might turn up on the international scene and that it would certainly add to the Jacobites' credibility in negotiations with European powers like Spain and the Habsburgs.[119] Conversely, his own basic humanity inclined him to reject such ruthless adventurism. As he confided to Lockhart: 'It is but too manifest in this conjuncture nothing but a forreign force can doe the work effectually, and to begin it by halfs would be ruining all. It is my freinds bussiness to lie quiet, and to preserve themselves in a condition of being usefull on a proper occasion ...'[120] A point of view with which George and the trustees were entirely in accord. The exiled clan chieftains also had something to say on the matter, and however much, and however sincerely, they protested their unswerving devotion to the Stuart cause, they were not inclined wantonly to throw away their people's lives.[121] What emerged from this complex of conflicting interests was a half-baked plot

---

117 LL, pp. 241–2, 292: GL to Inverness and the Old Pretender, 2 Sept. 1725 and 29 July 1726; Lenman, *Jacobite Clans*, p. 90.
118 As Atterbury, James's agent in Paris, discovered: G. V. Bennett, *The Tory Crisis in Church and State, 1688–1730: the Career of Francis Atterbury, Bishop of Rochester* (1975), pp. 287–8.
119 Bennett, *Tory Crisis*, pp. 285–7.
120 Stuart Papers 81/11: the Old Pretender to GL [Rome], 21 Mar. 1725 ns.
121 LP ii. 192–3; LL, pp. 231–2: GL to the Old Pretender [Edinburgh?], 25 July 1725.

allied to a pragmatic but slow compliance with the demands of the authorities in Britain.

Lockhart and the trustees' first notice of the plan for a rising came in June 1725, when the Old Pretender informed them that he was determined to support the clans if they chose to resist disarmament and that a rebellion might fall out very fortuitously in the current diplomatic climate.[122] George and Kincardine accordingly met with a 'person of distinction' among the Highlanders and hinted that something dramatic might be in the offing. He responded very positively, which was more than could be said for most of the trustees.[123] Maule, indeed, when the subject was raised some time later, 'turned all into a jest, falling afterwards into a passion and swearing that it was madness to propose anything to be done for you, and that none but madmen would engage in such an affair'.[124] Lockhart himself slowly and reluctantly began surveying opinion on the best place for a landing and considering what issues should feature most prominently in any declaration to be issued by the Old Pretender on his arrival in Scotland at the head of the professional troops loaned by the putative European backer. Who this was to be was never made clear, but in view of Atterbury's negotiations with the Russian ambassador to Paris, it was probably hoped the Russians would be the rising's sponsor.[125] Yet at the same time Lockhart showed no compunction about trying to persuade the exiled court that the Highlanders going it alone 'would be a rash and fatal attempt', that the English Jacobites (who he well knew were the movement's weak link) 'should know they have no staff to lean to but their own', and that England would undoubtedly be the optimum target for an invasion: 'the nearer to London the better'.[126] Meanwhile he encouraged the clan elites to comply at least minimally with the Disarming Act.[127] Nor, when the clan chieftains made it quite clear to Atterbury that they were not going to allow their people to be used as a forlorn hope, did Lockhart evince anything other than approval and quiet satisfaction.[128]

Even before the exiled court was obliged to let the proposal for a rising drop, Lockhart had clearly reached a watershed in his commitment to the Jacobite cause. By 1726 George had had enough. Using Alan Cameron, an agent sent over by the Jacobite court to assess the situation in the Highlands, as a conduit, he sent a verbal message to the Old Pretender seeking permission to retire as his agent so that he might visit the Continent and thus 'be free of the vexations that arise dayly to me from the deplorable state of my Countrey, and no prospect

122 LP ii. 169–70: [Rome], 23 June 1725 ns.
123 LL, p. 231–5: GL to the Old Pretender [Edinburgh?], 25 July 1725.
124 LL, p. 255: GL to the Old Pretender [Dryden?], 18 Dec. 1725.
125 LL, pp. 251–4; Bennett, *Tory Crisis*, p. 286.
126 LL, pp. 231, 232, 251.
127 LL, pp. 232–3, 234.
128 LP ii. 192–3.

of relief'.[129] Only a direct request from the Old Pretender, 'that you woud putt off the thought of it at least for this season', dissuaded him.[130]

It was thus at a point when he was feeling tired and disillusioned with the Jacobite cause that Lockhart found himself acting as a lightning rod between the exiled court and its followers in Britain, for close on the heels of the effective demise of the plan for a rising came the Clementina affair. This ostensibly began as a quarrel between James Stuart and his wife, Clementina Sobieska, over the suitability of James Murray, son of Viscount Stormont and Jacobite Earl of Dunbar, to act as tutor to the young Charles Edward Stuart (the future Bonnie Prince Charlie). Clementina's apparent objection: that Murray, a protestant, was not the appropriate mentor for a catholic prince, was shrewdly designed by her *éminence grise*, Cardinal Alberoni (by this time in exile in Rome and in British pay), to camouflage her personal hostility toward James's favourites, Murray and his brother-in-law Inverness, and draw the support of catholic princes and the papal court.[131] This was highly embarrassing for James because the jealously guarded political settlement within the Jacobite movement (hammered out in the 1690s) virtually required that protestants hold all the most important public offices at the exiled court – of which there were few more significant than overseeing the education of the Jacobite Prince of Wales.[132] To further complicate the situation, many protestant Jacobites, in particular the adherents of the disgraced Mar, detested the Hays and Murray too.[133] Clementina's response to her husband's refusal to replace Murray and dismiss Inverness was so dramatic and intemperate that it has been plausibly suggested that she may have been undergoing serious post-natal depression following the birth of her second child, Henry Benedict, in 1725: she fled the Jacobite court and took up residence in a nearby convent.[134] Her flight unleashed a Europe-wide blaze of publicity and speculation about her motives, which she stoked by publicly increasing her demands from the dismissal of Murray to the dismissal of Murray, his brother-in-law Inverness and Inverness's wife (Murray's sister), her senior Lady of Honour – virtually a clean sweep of the currently dominant clique at the exiled court. She even hinted that James might be having an affair with Lady Inverness.[135]

The Whig press of course had a field day with this public humiliation of the Jacobite pretender, and revenged itself for over a decade of Jacobite sneers and innuendoes at the sexual politics of the Hanoverian royal family by gleefully

129 LL, p. 260: [c. 18 Jan. 1726]; p. 287: GL to the Old Pretender [Dryden?], 23 July 1726.
130 LP ii. 287: the Old Pretender to GL, 1 May 1726 ns; LL, p. 287.
131 McLynn, *Charles Edward Stuart*, pp. 17–18.
132 D. Szechi, 'The Jacobite Revolution Settlement, 1689–1696', *English Historical Review*, cviii (1993), 610–28.
133 Gregg, 'Jacobite Career of John, Earl of Mar', pp. 184–93.
134 McLynn, *Charles Edward Stuart*, pp. 14–15, 26–7.
135 McLynn, *Charles Edward Stuart*, pp. 16–17.

(and utterly implausibly) portraying James as a satyr and Clementina as a poor, wronged princess.[136] The princes of Europe were soon drawn into taking sides in the quarrel too, whether out of a wish to demonstrate their superior catholic piety over the others, as with Philip V of Spain and his queen, Elizabeth Farnese, or a genuine desire to reconcile the estranged couple, as was the case with Pope Benedict XIII.[137] Both Clementina and James also appealed to the Jacobites in exile and in Britain to take their respective sides in the dispute, and open letters, replies and answers to the replies were soon circulating widely within and beyond the Jacobite community.[138] This inevitably polarised the community into 'King's' and 'Queen's' parties, with the existing pro- and anti-Inverness factions adopting contrary positions and the pro-Mar faction re-emerging to join in on Clementina's side too.[139] The affair only came to an end after James dismissed Inverness, when the pope, having investigated Clementina's allegations and found them baseless, finally seems to have persuaded her to return to her spouse.[140] By then, however, Lockhart had managed almost completely to isolate and marginalise himself within the Jacobite movement.

In itself, factionalism among the adherents of the exiled Stuarts was nothing new. The struggle between protestant and catholic for control of the court and its agenda; the abiding jealousies and tensions between the English, Irish and Scots Jacobites; the intrigues and counter-intrigues surrounding the only office with any substantive power, that of Jacobite Secretary of State, were all constant themes in the internecine politics of the Jacobite cause.[141] Indeed, the jealousy and backbiting were so irrepressible that Edward Gregg has suggested that the experience of defeat, frustration and exile created an unhealthy 'politics of paranoia' within the movement.[142] Thus Lockhart was not dealing with an intrinsically unfamiliar situation when he found himself being directed by the Old Pretender 'by a publick approbation of my conduct', to counter the charges levelled by Clementina and her supporters.[143] Indeed, he had already spent a fair amount of time loyally upholding the Stuart court's position first against the critics, and then against the embittered supporters, of Mar earlier in the 1720s.[144]

136 Monod, *Jacobitism and the English People*, pp. 57–60, 64; LP ii. 251, 265; LL, p. 269.
137 Szechi, *The Jacobites*, pp. 110–11, 119.
138 LP ii. 246–51, 265–6.
139 Gregg, 'Jacobite Career of John, Earl of Mar', p. 193.
140 McLynn, *Charles Edward Stuart*, pp. 21, 27–9.
141 Szechi, 'Jacobite Revolution Settlement', pp. 613–14, 625–8; *Jacobitism and Tory Politics*, pp. 20–6.
142 Gregg, 'Politics of Paranoia', pp. 42–56.
143 LP ii. 286.
144 See for example the detailed refutation of Mar's attempt to vindicate himself (LP ii. 201–9) supplied to GL, which he used to uphold the Jacobite Court's position: LL, pp. 246–7: GL to the Old Pretender [Dryden?], 13 Oct. 1725.

And though he personally disliked Inverness, he dutifully tried to conceal the fact and work with him.[145]

What made the situation different for Lockhart was a gathering exasperation, itself a product of his own weariness and frustration. Thus instead of simply seeking to persuade his fellow Jacobites to support the Old Pretender in the affair, he began to be independently involved. Had he done so from an overtly pro- or anti-Inverness position he would easily have aligned himself with the burgeoning factions that had already sprung up, and could have drawn support from one side or the other. Instead, when he was dealing with his fellow Jacobites in Scotland he loyally upheld the Old Pretender's position, and sought to isolate and suppress criticism of the Stuart monarch and his choice of Secretary of State, Inverness.[146] In his correspondence with the Jacobite court, however, he took a very different line. For throughout the crisis Lockhart was covertly sympathetic to Clementina (choosing to ignore her religious bigotry) and hostile to Inverness.[147] Hence his first response to the news of the royal couple's separation was to recommend Inverness's dismissal to James:

> Tis an hard case that people suffering in the same cause, and having no prospect of relief but by and through one event coming to pass, should by jarrs or immoderat unseasonable selfish views act diametrically opposite thereto, and if these are the inevitable consequences of ministers of the first rank, it would appear to be your intrest to lay all such aside, and carry on your business by your own directions, through some other, more subaltern, canals, that will be more observant of your orders, and not so high minded.[148]

When it became clear that James was determined to stand by his Secretary of State, George tried another tack:

> The trustees do not pretend to prescribe what methods the King is to take in obtaining the desired issue, but they humbly conceive that the King, in your great wisdom, may fall upon some way or other that may prove successful. And the trustees beg leave with the greatest respect and submission to represent that they beleive this matter to be of such consequence to the King, that in good policy and prudence the King should rather pass by some failings in and make condescensions to the Queen, than not repair the breach, that in all appearance will prove fatal.[149]

Since it was well known by July 1726, when this letter was written, that Clementina's *sine qua non* for a reconciliation was Inverness's dismissal, such a

145 LP ii. 185–6, 251; LL, p. 215.
146 LL, pp. 268, 269, 270, 279, 285, 288, 299.
147 LP ii. 339–40.
148 LL, pp. 261–2: GL to the Old Pretender [Carnwath?], 18 Jan. 1726.
149 LL, p. 284: GL to the Old Pretender [Dryden?], 23 July 1726.

representation was manifestly nothing more than a tactical expedient aimed at achieving the same objective. When the exiled monarch still refused to dismiss Inverness, George signalled his disapproval by declining to comment further, primly declaring that the trustees

> have an absolute confidence that the King's conduct will be consistent with what prudence with respect to the King and your people does call for, and they'll be the last of your subjects that will advise or wish the King to take any step, even in this material article, derogatory to your charecter, or contradictory to the honour and intrest of your royal family. And therefor they have nothing more to say on this subject, but to joyn issue with the King in praying that God may dispose the Queen to harken to good advise ...[150]

In addition, in a personal letter to Inverness he bluntly indicated that as 'a man of honour' he should sacrifice himself for the greater good of the cause.[151] The upshot of which was that George was clearly one of the participants in the 'universall joy' which greeted the fall of the Jacobite Secretary of State in 1727.[152] Underpinning his response to the unfolding crisis there was, however, something new: a gathering, muffled irritation, steadily growing into anger, at James himself.[153] Its final expression came after Lockhart had been forced to flee Scotland and was residing in the Austrian Netherlands.

Lockhart had never been an unquestioning Stuartophile,[154] and consequently when he finally gave vent to an impassioned critique of the Old Pretender it embraced the whole dynasty and its proclivities. James's conduct during his dispute with his wife was taken to task: ''tis time enuff to propale the secrets of your family when all hopes of bettering them [James's relations with Clementina] are intirely blasted'.[155] His choice of servants was condemned: 'in my humble opinion you have been ill served ever since 1716 that you returned from Scotland'.[156] His treatment of those who had endured wounds, exile and loss for him was so short-sighted that he allowed 'your enimys to upbraid your freinds for having adhered to a prince who ... valued their sufferings for him at so low a rate'.[157] And it all stemmed from 'your lodging too much powr and confiding as it were solely in a single person', for

favourites are constantly the bain of those princes by whose authority they

---

150 LL, p. 295: GL to the Old Pretender [Dryden?], 9 Sept. 1726.
151 LL, pp. 269–70, 288–9: 12 Mar. and 24 July 1726.
152 LP ii. 339.
153 LL, pp. 261, 262, 267–8, 278–9, 287, 288.
154 Cf. SR, pp. 248–9; LP i. 475; ii. 420–4.
155 LL, p. 325: [Rotterdam?], 6 Dec. 1727 ns.
156 LL, p. 326.
157 LL, p. 327.

are raised and supported, seing this can't be done but by suppressing others, who belive, and very often have, ane equall if not a superior claim to their soveraign's confidence and bountie and can't bear the insolence that for the most part attends the dominion of these substitute princes.[158]

Moreover, for all of his vehemence, Lockhart had in fact grasped the fundamental weakness of the Jacobite movement under its first two monarchs: lack of authority in the direction of the cause. Like his father before him, James Stuart was a man of no more than average intelligence. In addition, he was formal and shy, and again like his father, he sought to shield himself from his attendant difficulties in dealing with people and complex situations by vesting all his confidence and authority in a selected individual, i.e. a favourite.[159] This was not an uncommon habit among seventeenth- and eighteenth-century European monarchs, and it had a tendency to cause problems for all who inclined to it, but for a monarch-in-exile it created truly pernicious problems. As Lockhart correctly perceived, the only person who could command sufficient obedience to run an underground movement in a context in which all obedience was ultimately voluntary was one whose authority was unchallengeable.[160] For the Jacobites that could only be the Old Pretender. James's reluctance to become, in effect, his own Secretary of State inevitably created intrigue and jealousy. How long Lockhart had recognised the flaw at the heart of the Jacobite ideal is hard to say, but he must have known that so intemperate a critique was tantamount to a political suicide note.[161] By then, however, he no longer cared.

Lockhart's career as a Jacobite agent was finally brought to an end as a by-blow of his involvement in the internal disputes convulsing the contemporary episcopalian church. Until the 1710s the episcopal church, despite its differences with the Kirk regarding organisation, discipline and a handful of other issues, remained close to it in terms of ceremonial, ritual and doctrine.[162] As the generation of bishops in office at the time of the Revolution died off, however, and replacements began to be consecrated from the ranks of those too young to recall the episcopalians' glory days before 1688, a tendency towards doctrinal separatism began to set in.[163] This tendency did not become pronounced until after 1713, when Archibald Campbell, the putative Bishop of Aberdeen, came under the influence of the group of doctrinal and ceremonial innovators centred on Jeremy Collier who were seeking to change the ceremonial and practices of

---

158 LL, p. 326. GL only implies a dynastic propensity to elevate favourites in this letter, but elsewhere (LP ii. 405) explicitly describes it as 'a curse in a peculiar manner entaild on the royal race of Stewart'.
159 McLynn, *Charles Edward Stuart*, pp. 2, 13, 75; Miller, *James II*, pp. 121–3.
160 LL, pp. 261–2, 329.
161 Cf. LL, pp. 326, 331.
162 Clarke, 'Scottish Episcopalians', pp. 3–4, 187, 365.
163 Ferguson, *Scotland. 1689 to the Present*, pp. 127–8; Clarke, 'Scottish Episcopalians', pp. 340–50.

the English nonjuring community.[164] Campbell's goal correspondingly became the introduction of certain new 'Usages', based on Collier's research into the practices of the early Christian church. These included a reversion to the first liturgy of Edward VI, prayers for the dead, the mixing of water and wine in the communion cup, the reintroduction of extreme unction for those who desired it and modifications in the wording of certain ritual prayers and church discipline.[165]

Since the most common charge made against the episcopal church in Scotland by its presbyterian foes was that it was 'popishly affected', it will easily be appreciated that the usages Campbell was proposing were highly controversial. Their introduction would manifestly hand the Kirk an excellent stick with which to beat its episcopalian foes.[166] There was, though, a deeper unease among the episcopalian clergy about the Romanising tendency they seemed to represent. The episcopal church had never officially wavered in its allegiance to the Stuarts. Nevertheless, once the dynasty had gone into exile, the episcopalian hierarchy had quietly begun to ease them out of direct involvement in the church.[167] In part this was obviously for practical reasons: the bishops and presbyters could not consult on the day-to-day affairs of the church with its head when he was resident in France, still less when he was in Urbino or Rome. But it is clear that the catholicism of the exiled royal family also played a part in the quiet attenuation of their authority. The episcopalian clergy were for the most part loyal Jacobites; they were also devout protestants, and they were naturally wary of royal involvement in the church while the dynasty remained catholic.[168] Hence from 1688 to the 1720s the episcopalian hierarchy sought to run their church with as little official input from the Jacobite court as possible. And nowhere was this more evident than in the choice of new bishops.

Until the death of Bishop Alexander Rose of Edinburgh, the last surviving pre-Revolutionary bishop and unchallenged leader (primus) of the episcopalian church, new bishops were chosen surreptitiously and consecrated without reference to the Stuart court. Rose also had the personal authority to persuade even the aggressive Campbell to restrain himself.[169] Correspondingly, the episcopalian church was able to remain united and a powerful Jacobite influence within Scottish society at the same time as doctrinal disputes and schism were tearing

---

164 Monod, *Jacobitism and the English People*, p. 141; Clarke, 'Scottish Episcopalians', p. 406.
165 SRO CH12/12/268: Archibald Campbell to Bishop Rose [London?], 1 Mar. 1718; SRO CH12/12/125: declaration by the College of Bishops, Edinburgh, 11 Feb. 1723.
166 LP ii. 101. And, indeed, many episcopalians do seem to have found them too Romanising, for an example of which see: Wodrow Letters, Octavo XIV, ep. 13: D. Brown to Wodrow, Aberdeen, 17 Feb. 1719.
167 Ferguson, *Scotland. 1689 to the Present*, p. 127.
168 LP ii. 35, 76, 112; LL, pp. 153, 181, 183, 198.
169 SRO CH12/12/274: Campbell to Bishop Rose, 3 Jan. 1719 and [Feb?] 1719.

the English nonjuring community apart.[170] After Rose's death, however, the discipline and consensus he had carefully preserved progressively collapsed, with Lockhart and the Jacobite court playing a large part in the process.

This was not, of course, intentional. It developed out of internal disputes within the episcopalian community over the usages increasingly being urged upon it by Campbell through his Vicar-Depute and eventual successor at Aberdeen, James Gadderar, in which the choice of new bishops came to be crucial. Like most of the opponents of the so-called 'Usagers', Lockhart apparently had no theological objection to the changes they wanted to introduce, regarding them as 'matters indifferent in themselves' that should be left, 'untill the Church and State are so happily restored and settled that such matters can be duely considered and legally determined'.[171] Rather, his opposition stemmed from apprehension as to the use that would be made of them by the Kirk and the need to preserve unity within the episcopalian community during its travails in the wilderness.[172] Hence when Gadderar first began introducing the usages in Aberdeenshire, and persuaded Bishop John Falconar to follow suit in northern Scotland, Lockhart fully endorsed their summons before the irate College of Bishops. There, when Gadderar and Falconar tried to argue the theological case for the usages in the presence of Lockhart and several other trustees, George 'stopt them short', then invoked James's authority before reminding them of the need to maintain 'unity and harmony and to avoid every thing that might give … their enemies a handle to calumniate them', and ended by demanding that they 'would give that obedience to the College of Bishops which they expected from the laicks'.[173]

Yet at the same time Lockhart was willing to connive at the bishops' continuing to avoid having to secure the Old Pretender's endorsement of their election of new prelates. In the aftermath of Rose's demise he went along with Rose's immediate replacement as Bishop of Edinburgh by John Fullarton before James could be consulted, and in 1723 he acquiesced when the bishops unilaterally decided to consecrate Robert Norrie, on the grounds that 'it was not adviseable to delay it, least the clergy had split and divided'.[174] This willingness to acquiesce in the episcopalian church's evading the catholic Stuart shadow-monarch's exercise of his customary rights sprang from the same silent wariness that led the bishops to behave with such pusillanimity in the first place. Lockhart was no favourer of catholicism, for all that he was recorded as having one catholic in his household in 1705 and George junior was caught bringing back some

170 Lenman, 'Scottish Episcopal Clergy', pp. 44–6.
171 LP ii. 123; LL, p. 182.
172 LP ii. 101, 323–4.
173 LL, p. 183: GL to the Old Pretender [Dryden?], 7 Dec. 1722; Clarke, 'Scottish Episcopalians', pp. 408–9.
174 LP ii. 35; LL, pp. 197–8.

'popish trinkets' among his other souvenirs of the Grand Tour.[175] Hence he was distinctly suspicious of James's reluctance to issue an outright condemnation of religious innovation in the episcopalian church despite a direct request for him to do so from Lockhart and the trustees, ascribing it to the fact that 'the King did not incline expressly to condemn tenets and usages near a kin to those of his own church'.[176]

George's status as the Old Pretender's foremost representative in Scotland thus put him in a highly invidious situation. Despite his tacit sympathy with the reluctance of the episcopalian hierarchy to allow James a role in the selection of new bishops he found himself obliged to enforce the exiled monarch's rights. For James was not prepared to allow the practice of selecting bishops without consulting him to continue after Rose's death. His father had gained the right to nominate catholic bishops in all three kingdoms, and by 1720 the Old Pretender had finally secured papal acquiescence in its continued exercise by him.[177] Technically, pre-1689 Scots law (the only law seen as legitimate with regard to church affairs in the eyes of the episcopalian clergy) allowed him the same privilege with regard to the episcopalian church. And James was determined to exercise his right.[178] The first time he attempted to do so was in 1720 when he nominated three new bishops: David Freebairn, Andrew Cant and David or John Lammie. The College of Bishops, abetted by the trustees, prevaricated for two years over proceedural and other difficulties and only finally agreed to consecrate two of them (Lammie refused the office) after Lockhart showed them a commitment under the exiled king's own hand that in all future nominations he would consult with the episcopalian hierarchy.[179] An unintended consequence of this decision was the alienation of the Usagers. Because the nomination of new prelates now lay *de facto* with the College of Bishops and the trustees, a majority of whom were anti-Usager, the Usagers were cut off from all hope of securing sympathetic bishops who would allow them to introduce their innovations by winning over the Old Pretender. They accordingly began to develop theological objections to any lay intervention in the selection of bishops by presbyters, which incensed Lockhart and most of the trustees and certainly won them no friends at the Stuart court.[180] Ironically enough, however, the crisis

---

175 *Miscellany of the Maitland Club, Volume III, Part II* (Edinburgh, 1843): 'Lists of Popish Parents and Their Children in Various Districts of Scotland as Given in to the Lords of the Privy Council and to the Commission of the General Assembly', p. 402; PRO SP 35/23/74: Commissioners of the Customs to Secretary of State James Craggs, London, 1 Oct. 1720.
176 LP ii. 112.
177 Szechi, *The Jacobites*, p. 118.
178 LP ii. 41.
179 LP ii. 53, 76–7; LL, pp. 181–2: GL to the Old Pretender [Dryden?], 7 Dec. 1722.
180 LP ii. 323, 333–4; SRO CH12/12/477/1: petition by the Presbyters of the see of Edinburgh to the College of Bishops, Edinburgh, Oct. 1726; Clarke, 'Scottish Episcopalians', pp. 402–4.

over James's nomination of a bishop that led to George's downfall was entirely his own fault and stemmed directly from an attempt by him to secure a piece of ecclesiastical patronage for an old friend.

The friend in question was his old tutor and chaplain John Gillane. Lockhart went through the correct procedure, and secured Gillane's nomination by a select group of his friends and kinsmen among the trustees and episcopate in 1725.[181] James accordingly nominated Gillane in a letter to the College of Bishops that arrived at the end of August 1726.[182] By the time the royal mandate arrived, however, the Jacobite community in Scotland had been polarised by the Clementina affair, George was under fire from the 'Queen's party' for his efforts to suppress criticism of the Old Pretender, and his own standing at the exiled court was being undermined by his increasingly overt anti-Inverness position. The 'Queen's party' promptly allied itself with the Usagers, who professed to be outraged at Lockhart's blatant interference in the affairs of the church.[183] The trustees also split on the issue with the result that, despite intense lobbying on his own part, Lockhart could not overcome the endless prevarications of the College of Bishops, whose frailer members were under great pressure not to cooperate from a party of the lower clergy organised by the future episcopalian bishops Robert Keith and Thomas Rattray of Craighall (who also happened to be an old confidant of Mar's).[184] Throughout the crisis the Usagers were much encouraged in their opposition by George's former friend Harry Maule (titular Earl of Panmure since 1723), who also helpfully let them know that Lockhart was out of favour at the Jacobite court.[185] The crisis was so public and Lockhart's role so notorious that by December 1726 it was being noised about in taverns and salons all over Edinburgh. And though there is no surviving evidence for it, it is entirely possible that Lockhart was correct in suspecting that the information that led the authorities to intercept a packet of his letters and arrest one of his couriers in January 1727 came from one of his opponents in this affair.[186]

It is certainly interesting to note that the government knew exactly which ship to search and who to arrest.[187] The first of Lockhart's network to be caught was John Strachan. George, the Earl of Dundonald, and Kincardine, promptly

181 LL, pp. 276–7: GL to the Old Pretender, [Dryden?] 30 Apr. 1726. Cf. Clarke, 'Scottish Episcopalians', p. 403.
182 LP ii. 310.
183 LP ii. 323–4; SRO CH12/12/824: Robert Keith to Thomas Rattray of Craighall, Edinburgh, 28 Sept. 1726.
184 LP ii. 329; SRO CH12/12/825, 826: Keith to Rattray, Edinburgh, 20 Oct. and 1 Dec. 1726; A. and H. Tayler, *1715*, p. 189.
185 SRO CH12/12/829: Keith to Rattray, 14 Jan. 1727.
186 LL, p. 308: GL to the Old Pretender, Brussels, 20 May 1727 ns; LP ii. 327; Wodrow Letters, Quarto XVII, ep. 162: John Boyd to Wodrow, Edinburgh, 21 Mar. 1727.
187 Wodrow Letters, Quarto XVII, ep. 133: John Boyd to Wodrow, Edinburgh, 21 Jan. 1727.

supplied him with money and assurances that if he kept his mouth shut he would
be further rewarded and the case must drop.[188] Strachan accordingly tried to
hold out, but further interrogation in London (amounting in all to nearly a
month of relentless pressure), and government interception of a letter by him to
John Corsar pledging his determination to resist, which his interrogators then
confronted him with, finally broke him and he implicated Corsar and Lockhart.[189]
The vital second witness the government needed to convict George was obviously
Corsar, his main courier, but he had been spirited out of Edinburgh into the
wilds of Angus soon after Strachan was sent up to London. Once away from
Edinburgh, however, Corsar became careless. John Drummond, the Lord Provost
of Edinburgh, soon discovered his whereabouts and a party of troops easily
captured him at a tavern he regularly frequented.[190] Corsar was then immediately
transported to London for questioning. And though Corsar had a reputation for
being 'a staunch man, and no baubler', Drummond perceptively noted that 'fear
is his passion easiest wrought on' – an analysis that was to be triumphantly
vindicated when Lord Advocate Duncan Forbes of Culloden, Walpole, Islay and
Townshend set to work on breaking him.[191] Well before then it was clear that
Lockhart was in serious trouble, and he correspondingly prepared an escape
route. Thus as soon as he received a secret warning from Solicitor-General
Charles Erskine of Tinwald that he was about to be arrested, he was able to
flee over the border into northern England and take ship for the Netherlands,
arriving safely at Dort on 15 April 1727.[192]

188 LP ii. 331.
189 LP ii. 398; Ch. (H) Papers 71/1, 2: examinations of John Strachan, Edinburgh, 8 and 10
     Mar. 1727.
190 PRO SP 54/18/12: John Drummond (Lord Provost of Edinburgh) to Viscount Town-
     shend, Edinburgh, 14, 16 and 18 Mar. 1727.
191 LP ii. 398; PRO SP 54/18/12: Drummond to Townshend [Edinburgh], 28 Mar. 1727;
     Ch. (H) Papers 71/4: deposition by John Corsar, Edinburgh, 24 Apr. 1727 (Corsar's
     signature on this document is very shaky, which suggests he may have been frightened
     at the time he signed it).
192 LL, p. 308; LP ii. 331–2.

CHAPTER SEVEN

Retirement and Seclusion, 1727–1731

Lockhart's flight appears to have terminated the government's pursuit of the trustees, though a number of others, such as Wigton, Balmerino, Kincardine and Dundonald, had been identified in the course of its investigation.[1] Because of the apparent imminence of war with the Vienna Alliance (the Habsburgs, Spain, Prussia and Russia), the ministry, it later emerged, had been primarily interested in discovering evidence of Imperial involvement in Jacobite plotting with which to rouse support in Parliament for an aggressive ministerial line towards the Habsburgs.[2] Thus when the investigation discovered there was no active plotting underway and no evidence whatsoever of Imperial involvement with the Scottish Jacobites, the government soon lost interest.[3] According to Lockhart Islay and Forbes privately let him know after he returned that George I had personally ordered the investigation terminated, and that the intervention of 'a certain freind' who was present, then dissuaded the Cabinet from specifically excepting him from any future indemnity.[4] This was very fortunate, because Lockhart had begun the process of disengaging himself from active Jacobitism almost as soon as he found a safe haven in the Habsburg Netherlands.

Good servant of the Stuarts that he was, George nevertheless first sought to tie up the loose ends of his stewardship of the Jacobite cause in Scotland by arranging for his replacement there. Fending off an invitation to visit the Jacobite court with the exiled Lord North and Grey,[5] who was being widely touted as Inverness's replacement as Secretary of State (Inverness had ostensibly retired from court, but in fact only to the position of minister behind the curtain, in March 1727), he set about establishing a new courier route, with new codes and new personnel, and in Scotland he persuaded Dundonald to assume his former role as secretary to the trustees.[6] As a consequence of George I's sudden death on 11 June, which created the strong likelihood of a clutch of royal pardons in celebration of the accession of George II, by the end of July George's friends in Britain, in particular Argyll, Islay and Lord Advocate Forbes, were already holding out some hope of his being allowed to return from exile.[7] Lockhart

1 LP ii. 398.
2 Langford, *Eighteenth Century*, pp. 93–7.
3 LP ii. 332.
4 LP ii. 399.
5 LP ii. 337.
6 LL, pp. 304, 306–7: GL to the Old Pretender, Antwerp and Brussels, 6 and 20 May 1727 ns.
7 LL, p. 312: GL to the Old Pretender [Brussels?], 28 July 1727 ns.

accordingly began keeping as low a profile as possible so as not to antagonise the ministry and undermine his friends' efforts on his behalf, and accordingly moved away from the busy Jacobite exile community in Brussels to the quiet spa town of Aix-la-Chapelle soon after Euphemia arrived to join him there.[8] He was consequently appalled soon afterwards to encounter Alan Cameron at a roadside inn while on his way to Liège to visit an old friend, Colonel William Clephane.[9]

As Lockhart feared, Cameron's presence signalled desparate measures in the offing. The Old Pretender's putative reconciliation with Clementina, the way to which had ostensibly been opened by the 'retirement' of Inverness from the Jacobite court, was not an event James wanted or welcomed.[10] Which may go some way to explain the enthusiasm with which he took up a hare brained scheme, probably originating with Inverness, to throw himself into the Highlands at the head of no more than a few trusted servants.[11] Such a go-it-alone strategy, which eerily prophesied the approach adopted by Charles Edward Stuart in 1745, had been emphatically rejected by the exiled clan leaders in 1725 and, given that Britain was not at war and the Tories were all busily trying to impress George II with their loyalty and pro-Hanoverianism, was foolhardy to the point of being suicidal.[12] Nonetheless the Old Pretender (whose personal courage was never in doubt) was of a mind to try it, and as soon as he arrived in Lorraine he despatched Alan Cameron specifically to find Lockhart and get his opinion as to the feasibility of the operation.[13]

George's response to the Old Pretender, in which he expressed his reasoned opposition to the plan without giving way to the angry exasperation which shines through as a subtext to his recollection of the episode, was plainly a disappointment to James.[14] In conversation with Cameron, however, he gave full vent to his feelings. After Cameron described the plan, Lockhart and Clephane (whom George had insisted on consulting despite Clephane's old connection with Mar) sarcastically asked if he did not think the 'want of arms, ammunition and mony to be transported alongst with the King woud not be ane irreparable impediment?'. When Cameron tried to deny this and claimed that supplies could be brought in after the rising started and that he did not doubt but that the Jacobite clans would 'be able to make a stand for some months at least', Lockhart exploded: 'I told him that I admired how he who knew the state of the Highlands

8 LL, p. 306; SRO GD 3/5/965: GL to Eglinton, Brussels, 10 June 1727 ns.
9 LP ii. 355–6.
10 M. Haile, *James Francis Edward. The Old Chevalier* (1907), pp. 323–4.
11 LP ii. 357–8.
12 McLynn, *Charles Edward Stuart*, pp. 112–16; Colley, *In Defiance*, pp. 207–8.
13 PRO SP 36/2/3: Cameron's instructions from Sir John Graeme, Frouarde, 22 July 1727 ns.
14 LL, pp. 312–13: [Aix?], 4 Aug. 1727 ns; LP ii. 363: Sir John Graeme to GL, Avignon, 25 Aug. 1727 ns.

and the generall concert and resolution of not going to the feild untill they saw England actually engaged, coud advise the King to throw away his person and expose the countrie and his trustiest freinds to certain destruction'.[15] George rounded off by declaring that those who had advised the Old Pretender to try the venture 'either did not know the true state of the King's affairs or betrayd him'. Nettled, Cameron demanded to know if Lockhart would accompany the Jacobite king. And George, having first established that neither Inverness nor Dunbar would be accompanying the expedition, was still loyal enough to pledge himself to do so, 'tho I thought it a rash destructive undertaking'.[16] Fortunately for Lockhart the sheer hopelessness of the project finally seems to have dissuaded James and his advisers, and within a couple of weeks British diplomatic pressure had forced his removal southwards, terminating the episode.

Nevertheless the sheer recklessness of the scheme seems to have frightened Lockhart, and in retrospect he became angry with James and Inverness for having allowed it to go forward at all. The revelation that Inverness's retirement from the Jacobite court had been bogus and that the Old Pretender clearly intended to keep him in the offing until an opportune moment arose to restore him to favour, likewise exasperated Lockhart, and predisposed him toward his later conviction that Inverness had all along been a secret agent of the British government.[17] All of which helps explain the unforgivable intemperance of George's critique of James's conduct and policies since the fall of Mar which he despatched to the exiled monarch in December, soon after James had renewed his public quarrel with Clementina.[18] As he finished the letter Lockhart clearly knew he had gone too far 'by presuming to express my sentiments on subjects too high for me', but resolved to send it, 'as I'me conscious of my own honest intentions and certain that your innate goodness is more than enuff to pardon the failings of your subjects'.[19] In that he was wrong. His plain horror at the prospect of an independent Jacobite attempt and the vehemence of his denunciation of the Old Pretender's conduct finally discredited him with the Stuart court. Hence his last services to the Jacobite cause, passing on information from an inside source in London that the ministry had copies of all the Jacobite codes and arranging a secure courier route to Scotland, went frigidly unacknowledged.[20] So far out of favour did George fall in fact, that when he died in 1731 literally no notice at all was taken of the event at the Palazzo Muti.

By the end of 1727 Lockhart's career as a Jacobite was thus definitely over. Hence it was well for him that arrangements for his return home were on the

15 LP ii. 359.
16 LP ii. 360.
17 LP ii. 359–60, 362, 400–2.
18 LP ii. 379–80.
19 LL, p. 331.
20 LL, pp. 331–7: GL to the Old Pretender [Rotterdam?], 22 and 29 Jan. 1728 ns.

verge of completion. Early in the new year the good offices of Argyll, Islay and
Forbes of Culloden at last produced official permission to return to Britain.
Lockhart promptly made his final farewell to the James, informing them that as
he would henceforth have to live quietly at home, 'with the utmost caution', he
'must be deprived of the honor of corresponding directly with yourself', but that
'my own well rooted principles will never allow me to be any thing but a faithfull
servant to you and your royall family'.[21] There is no record of any reply. In
due course George thereafter secured a safe-conduct, packed up his family (by
January he and Euphemia had been joined by two of their daughters) and
travelled incognito to London.[22] There, for all his disillusionment with the
Jacobite cause, Lockhart still found it embarrassing to have to thank George II
personally for allowing him to return from exile, but his friends and the king
were adamant on the score and he grumpily reconciled himself to 'bowing my
knee to Baal now that I was in the house of Rim'.[23] As soon as possible thereafter
he departed London for Scotland and retirement.

Though lack of evidence precludes any firm judgement on the subject, George's
final years do not seem to have been especially happy ones. His return from exile
had been on condition that he live in retirement at home, which meant that he
had to stay out of politics and the public eye. His old Jacobite friends seem to
have shunned him and he to have avoided them, and though he apparently
remained on cordial terms with several senior Whigs, such as Andrew Fletcher,
Lord Milton, he was too ingrainedly hostile to their politics to have much relished
an unadulterated diet of their company.[24] His father-in-law, the 9th Earl of
Eglinton, died in 1729 and Lockhart dutifully spent some time and energy acting
as an executor and lambasting his sister-in-law, the Countess of Galloway, for
the refusal of her husband the Earl and her son, Lord Garlies, to assume their
designated role as tutors to the young 10th Earl.[25] He obviously also spent some
time shortly after his return home writing a further continuation of his secret
memoirs in the hope of vindicating himself to posterity, but the zeal and fire that
had inspired his earlier works were missing and the resulting *Register* manages at
once to be both bitter and half-hearted.[26] Even a letter to the *Edinburgh Weekly
Journal* in 1729 under the pseudonym 'Scoto-Germanicus', denouncing the social
familiarity and informality of dress allowed by contemporary mores, has an angry,
despairing tone and shows none of the savage wit and verve of which he was
formerly capable.[27]

---

21 LL, pp. 335–6.
22 SRO GD 1/1155/78/5: GL to John Chancellor, Rotterdam, 9 Jan. 1728 ns; LP ii. 396–7.
23 LP ii. 397.
24 LL, pp. 340–3.
25 LL, pp. 337–43.
26 LP ii. 403–5.
27 *Eccho/Edinburgh Weekly Journal*, XXXIV: 27 Aug. 1729, pp. 127–8; LP i. 604–8; [GL], *A
    Letter to Mr George Crawford, Concerning his Book, Intituled, The Peerage of Scotland* (1719), *passim*.

Nevertheless, it is a mistake for a biographer to assume that a subject who dies during a hiatus in his or her life was doomed to remain in what turned out to be their final situation. Lockhart was only 51 years old at the time of his death and though he did experience some health problems in the late 1720s, he had hitherto enjoyed a robust constitution.[28] Had he survived to 1745 he could quite conceivably have joined the ranks of the many disillusioned Jacobite veterans (such as Lord George Murray and John Gordon of Glenbucket) who had lived quietly through the 1730s only to find themselves revitalised by the advent of Charles Edward Stuart. Suffice it to say that Lockhart's personal disenchantment with active Jacobite politics did not transmit itself to his posterity. Though they barely participated in the plotting that preceded the '45, George Lockhart junior and his eldest son (another George) both turned out to fight at Prestonpans, and though Lockhart junior then prudently surrendered himself to the authorities, Lockhart's grandson remained with the Jacobite army all the way to Culloden, afterwards escaping to France, where he died in 1761.[29]

Lockhart's demise was, moreover, abrupt and in a sense accidental. What we know about it is quickly summarised: for some unknown reason an unknown person challenged (or was challenged by) Lockhart to a duel late in 1731. In his usual clear hand, George wrote a set of minor amendments and changes to his will on 14 December. He then wrote a further amendment in favour of his formerly wayward son James 'in a feeble hand' (according to Anthony Aufrere, the editor of the *Lockhart Papers*), at some time before his death three days later, which suggests the duel occurred between 14 and 17 December.[30] The protagonists fought at an unknown place in or near Edinburgh and George received an unspecified, but mortal wound. He was then carried back to his house in Niddry's Wynd and died there on 17 December 1731.[31]

It was, to say the least, highly unusual for someone of Lockhart's wealth and status (however quietly he may have been living in recent years) to die in such obscurity. Neither the newspapers nor his neighbours, nor contemporary correspondents (including estranged family members) make any mention of the duel or its outcome, though his death was noted in respectful obituaries to which they might have reacted.[32] All of which suggests that the family made considerable, successful efforts to hush the whole affair up. Which of course adds to the mystery of Lockhart's end. Why did his heirs seek to keep the circumstances of his death so secret?

28 LL, p. 223: GL to Baron Sir John Clerk, Dryden, 12 Apr. 1725; p. 341: GL to Andrew Fletcher, Lord Milton, Dryden, 15 May 1731.
29 Macdonald Lockhart, *Seven Centuries*, pp. 222–7, 230–3.
30 LEP, Personal Documents 33: Charters and Commissions, Last Will and Testament, Edinburgh, 14 Dec. 1731; LP ii. 430.
31 *Caledonian Mercury*, no. 9413: 20 Dec. 1731.
32 *Caledonian Mercury*, no. 9413: 20 Dec. 1731; *Gentleman's Magazine*, i. 540.

Barring the discovery of further Lockhart material there cannot be a definitive answer to this question. In the light of what we do know of the man, his family and his times, however, we may be able to identify who is likely to have killed him and why. A significant clue is provided by the close, unbroken blanket of secrecy that covered the cause of the duel and the identity of George's opponent. Duelling was certainly illegal, but it was far from dishonourable (except under certain circumstances), so his having fought one is of itself unlikely to have been the occasion of the family's silence. That a man of his age thought it necessary to fight was, moreover, unusual and betokens a special grievance on either his, or his opponent's, part. We know that Lockhart's *Memoirs of Scotland* had offended the Duke of Atholl to the point of his considering a challenge in 1714, and that George junior came close to a duel on the same score with the 5th Duke of Hamilton in 1725.[33] But by 1731 the *Memoirs* were old hat and it seems unlikely that anyone could have got so offended anew as to have killed him over them, and also that the family would have hushed it up so assiduously had the *Memoirs* alone been the occasion of the encounter.

The upshot is that the circumstances of the fatal encounter point toward an apprehension that some dishonour, or scandal was going to attach itself to the family if the cause of the duel and the identity of the opponent were publicly known. George was not a man given to pursuing other men's wives, nor was he a gambler or toper, so probably none of the usual occasions for hushing up affairs of honour applied. Which leaves one strong candidate: that the duel arose from a personal slight given or received by a member of Lockhart's family (in the wider sense of extended kin). For while duelling with strangers, or even former friends, over insults was certainly socially acceptable, killing family members on such grounds was not. And at the time of his death George was involved in two serious disputes with members of his family.

One arose as a consequence of the clandestine marriage of Lady Mary Montgomery to a lowly army officer, Captain David Cunningham of Milncraig (later Sir David Cunningham of Milncraig and Livingstone).[34] Lady Mary was a younger daughter of the recently deceased Eglinton and thus George's sister-in-law. Lockhart had already assumed a leading role in trying to ensure that those named as curators to the 10th Earl of Eglinton by his father's will accepted the duty laid on them, and he now stepped forward to express the family's outrage at the fact that an episcopalian clergyman had officiated at the ceremony, contrary to law and the family's interests.[35] In the course of his

33 Wodrow Letters, VIII, ep. 132: James Erskine of Grange to Wodrow, Edinburgh, 25 Sept. 1714; LL, p. 115: Atholl to GL, London, 13 Oct. 1714; *Notes and Queries*, ser. 3, vol. viii. 64 (*DNB*, xxxiv. 46 mixes up Lockhart and his oldest son and incorrectly states the duel was between Lockhart and Hamilton).
34 Balfour, *Scots Peerage*, iii. 457.
35 LL, pp. 337–40; SRO CH12/12/497: GL to the Bishop and Presbyters of Edinburgh, Dryden, 8 June 1731.

denunciation of the cleric, one Mr Wylie, Lockhart described the match as 'rash' and 'unequall' and declared that 'never did a couple present themselves who required more caution than in this present case'. This by implication impugned the social status of his new brother-in-law. The early eighteenth-century Scottish gentry (Cunningham was heir to his father's baronetcy) were notoriously prickly about such matters, and the elite group in British society most prone to duelling were military officers. Given the fact that the Countess of Panmure's funeral, which virtually every member of the gentry and nobility with any connection to the Panmure family (including Lockhart and Cunningham by virtue of their marriages) was bound to attend, took place on 13 December 1731 and George drew up the amendments to his will on 14 December,[36] we may have an explanation of who killed George Lockhart and why.

The second dispute that might have led to a duel was a long running one. Back in 1723 George had by accident come across a private enquiry sent to Baron Sir John Clerk of Penicuik by the Earl of Galloway, asking if it was true that George Lockhart junior had recently made a dishonourable retreat (i.e. refused to fight a duel) and humorously implying that he might be suffering from an illness that required mercury (i.e. that he had contracted a case of syphilis).[37] Lockhart, who had considered Galloway a friend, was outraged at 'the kind returns he makes to me and mine', and dashed off a reply to Galloway that was truly unforgivable.[38] Galloway's response was predictable:

> Last week I received your impertinent letter, to which I would not [have] thought it worth my trouble of giveing any return, were it not to assure you that when you and I have ocosione to meet, if you think it convenient to talk to me upon the subject of your letter, depend upon it I shall give you my answere soe plain as you shall not want experienced judges to determine my meaning.[39]

Moreover, the two men never seem to have been reconciled.[40] And, as with Cunningham, Galloway was highly likely to have been present at the funeral of the Countess of Panmure on 13 December, which would have given them ample opportunity to renew their quarrel.

It is, of course, impossible to be certain. Given Lockhart's political sympathies,

---

36 LEP, Personal Documents 33: Charters and Commissions, GL's Last Will and Testament, Edinburgh, 14 Dec. 1731
37 LL, pp. 186–8: GL to Baron Sir John Clerk, Dryden, 8 and 13 Mar. 1723; SRO GD 18/5671: Baron Sir John Clerk to Galloway (draft) [Mar. 1723].
38 LL, p. 186; SRO GD 18/5246/1/134: Katherine Galloway to Baron Sir John Clerk, 8 Apr. 1723.
39 SRO GD 18/5246/1/134: Katherine Galloway to Baron Sir John Clerk, 8 Apr. 1723.
40 SRO GD 18/5246/1/190: Katherine Galloway to Baron Sir John Clerk, Glasertoun, 4 Jan. 1729.

his death by violence is perhaps not so surprising, though the time and the place were unusual. It is, however, ironic that the author of such an enormously indiscreet literary legacy should leave the circumstances of his departure so shrouded in mystery as to leave the historian with no other recourse than informed guesswork.

PART II

The Mind of George Lockhart of Carnwath

Introduction

Fully to understand the human dynamics of ages past we must comprehend how our ancestors saw their world.[1] What principles mattered most to them? How did they reconcile their ideals with their reality? Whose conduct did they admire and seek to imitate? What follows is an attempt to answer these and related questions with respect to Lockhart, and through him to see into the heart of the secretive community of which he was a part. By identifying the mainsprings of his conduct this analysis will both open a window into the mind of one important Jacobite and offer an insight into the conduct of his peers.[2]

The principal sources for what follows are necessarily those generated by the man himself. The *Memoirs Concerning the Affairs of Scotland, From Queen Anne's Accession to the Throne to the Commencement of the Union of the two Kingdoms of Scotland and England in May 1707. With an Account of the Origine and Progress of the Design'd Invasion From France, in March 1708. And Some Reflections on the Ancient State of Scotland*, was Lockhart's first major work. It was based on the notes, documents and other materials he garnered while he was a Commissioner in the Scots Parliament from 1703 to 1707, and was written up while he kicked his heels in involuntary retirement at Dryden and Carnwath in 1707–8.[3] George then showed the manuscript to a few select friends, and may have taken in corrections on specific points from them.[4] The pirated edition of the *Memoirs* published in 1714 derived from this first draft. In 1716–17, or thereabouts, he revised his original text, wrote an angry refutation of Sir David Dalrymple's critique in the introduction to the pirated edition and replied to sundry lesser hacks who had attacked the veracity and style of the *Memoirs*. At this point he also boldly proclaimed his authorship on the final manuscript's title page.[5] Probably around the same time (the two

---

1 For examples of the problems and rewards such approaches can offer, see: N. Nichols Baker, *Brother to the Sun King. Philippe, Duke of Orléans* (1989); K. V. Thomas, *Religion and the Decline of Magic. Studies in Popular Beliefs in Sixteenth- and Seventeenth-Century England* (repr. 1982); J. Dewald, *Aristocratic Experience and the Origins of Modern Culture. France, 1570–1715* (Berkeley, 1993); J. Walkowitz, *City of Dreadful Delight: Narratives of Sexual Danger in Late Victorian London* (Chicago, 1992).
2 In theoretical terms what follows is a typical historian's smorgasbord. The discerning reader will doubtless detect traces of Marxisant conceptualisation, vulgar Freudianism, crude Anthropology and hand-me-down literary theory. The guiding light in the foreground, however, is R. G. Collingwood, *The Idea of History* (Oxford, repr. 1978), pp. 214–315.
3 SR, pp. 3–4.
4 LL, p. 111, 112, 114.
5 SR, Foreword by Paul Scott xix–xxviii and pp. 273–89; LP i. 1.

texts are certainly, deliberately dovetailed) he wrote up what was in effect the second volume of his narrative: the *Commentarys of George Lockhart of Carnwath, Esq., Containing ane Account of Publick Affairs From the Union of the 2 Kingdoms in May 1707 to the Death of Queen Anne in August 1714*. At 207 pages, this was considerably shorter, but still much more flowing, than the *Memoirs*. It also covers a good deal more ground. Whereas the *Memoirs* in effect deals with only four years of Scottish history, the *Commentarys* briskly sweep through the years from 1708 to 1715. The bulk of the *Commentarys*, up to the death of Queen Anne, were probably written in late 1714 or early 1715, and the account of Lockhart's part in the rebellion was then tacked on as an afterthought in 1716–17.[6] George wrote the post-1714 section primarily to refute criticism of his conduct during the rebellion by the likes of Sir James Hamilton of Rosehall and Captain Straton, and therefore completely omits any account of politics and his electioneering in the same period.[7] What we may take as the final volume of his account, *A Register of Letters Twixt the King and George Lockhart of Carnwath, Containing Also a Short Account of Public Affairs From 1716 to 1728*, was probably written in 1728–9 after he returned home from the Continent. He was disillusioned and depressed at this stage, and was again writing to vindicate himself to an unknown posterity. Consequently he made very little attempt to digest his raw material (copies and drafts of the correspondence between himself and the Jacobite court) and the resulting text is awkward and unpolished.[8]

George never intended that any of these works should be published during his lifetime. They were left in a sealed chest that he carefully deposited with his relations whenever there was any danger of its discovery by the authorities,[9] and he instructed his heirs:

> The papers contained in the trunk sealed up to which this is annexed are of importance and cannot for some time be divulged without manifold inconveniencies public and private, general and particular. On the other hand the publishing of them may some time or other be proper and useful on several accounts, for which reason it is expedient they be preserved in secret and safety [sic]. In order therto I do leave them behind me, committing them to you with and under the following rules and directions, viz: that you deposite them in some safe secret place, of which none shall be acquainted excepting one trusty person to take care of them in case of your decease. That you communicate their being any such thing left by me to no soul living but that person, under solemn promises of secresie. That you do not out of curiosity or any other motive break up the sealls or open the trunk, but let it remain

---

6 LP i. 291–2, 483.
7 LP i. 484–98.
8 LP ii. 3 and *passim*.
9 SRO GD 3/5/965: GL to Eglinton, Brussels, 10 June 1727 ns.

intire as I have left it to you. That immediately after my death you enclose this within a letter directed to your son and heir renewing and repeating what is here contained, and joining with me in desiring the continuance of the aforesaid care and caution. That what is in this trunk be after this manner concealled and preserved till the year seventeen hundred and fifty, by which time I reckon the inconveniencies attending the publishing may probably be removed. And lastly, if ever they be published I expresslie require that it be exactly, without adding or impairing, conform to the originall manuscripts.[10]

Because of the '45 it was clearly not appropriate for the family to publish the manuscripts in 1750, and they seem to have remained in the sealed chest until 1799, when Count Charles Lockhart (the son of Count James Lockhart, George's grandson) asked his sister Matilda's husband, Anthony Aufrere, to edit the contents for publication. Aufrere was only finally able to settle down to the task in 1814, and they appeared in print in two volumes three years later.[11]

Aufrere was a scholarly dilettante with a modest literary reputation,[12] but he took George's injunction that the manuscripts be published without editing very seriously. Correspondingly, the text seems to have been published warts and all.[13] Comparison with Lockhart's correspondence and other publications (including the early draught of the *Memoirs* pirated in 1714), and cross-checking with the final draughts of his letters preserved in the archives of the Stuart court, all indicate that the text of the Aufrere edition of the *Lockhart Papers* is authentic.[14] This is fortunate, because the original manuscripts probably migrated to Hamburg with Aufrere's son in the 1820s and, if they survived into the twentieth century, were in all likelihood destroyed when the RAF firebombed the city in 1943.[15]

The upshot of all of which is that the *Lockhart Papers* are a superb source of information for an analysis of the *mentalité* of George Lockhart. Precisely because he was trying not to reflect on his own life – though he obviously wanted to be thought well of by posterity – but was instead attempting to explain the events of his own time to a future audience he hoped would both vindicate him and avenge Scotland's wrongs, he reveals far more about his inner world than he ever intended or realised. What he wrote was definitely polemical, but because

10 LP i. xvii; SR, xxxii–xxxiii.
11 LP i. vi, vii.
12 *DNB*, ii. 726–7.
13 LP i. vii–viii.
14 SR, Foreword by Paul Scott, xviii–xix.
15 If anybody reading this book has any further information on the whereabouts of Lockhart's papers, should they still be in existence, I would be very grateful if they would contact me at the Department of History, 310 Thach Hall, Auburn University, Alabama 36849-5207.

of his personal literary ethics ('I do most solemnly declare I have, to the best of my knowledge, neither added to nor impaired the truth' [16]), and the fact that he was writing to inform the future, we can fairly take it that the text expresses his vision of reality. His numerous anonymously published pamphlets [17] certainly reiterate the outlook and expand on the implicit assumptions underlying the text of the *Lockhart Papers*, and likewise in his correspondence, his explanations, analysis and description of events reveal the same themes and patterns of perception.

The analysis of Lockhart's *mentalité* that follows correspondingly reflects his life and times as outlined in Part I. Like (almost) every human being, life put him on an intermittent learning curve. Many of his ideas and beliefs consequently changed and adapted, but, again like most other human beings, the overall pattern remained remarkably consistent. Since this complex of prejudices, beliefs and assumptions was the bedrock of his understanding, it will be dealt with in chapter 8. Chapter 9, by contrast, focusses on Lockhart's political convictions. Here I will deal with the fruits of his education and his response to the great debates of his time. Finally, in chapter 10, I will turn to the network of belief and principle that tied all the foregoing together and, for George, opened the way to the Jacobite moment.

---

16 SR, p. 5.
17 *Letter to an English Lord* (1702); *A Letter to a Lord of the Session* (1710); *A Letter From a Scots Gentleman in London to his Friend at Edenburgh* (1711); *A Letter From a Scots Gentleman Residing in England to his Friend at Edenburgh* (1711); *A Letter From a Gentleman in Edinburgh to his Friend in London Giving ane Account of the Present Proceedings Against the Episcopall Clergy in Scotland, for Using the English Liturgy Ther* (1711); *A Letter From a Presbiterian Minister to his Friend at Edinburgh* (1714); *A Letter to a Minister in the Country, in Answer to a Circular Letter Sent to the Clergy Perswading Them to be Against the Dissolution of the Union* (1714); *A Letter to Mr George Crawford, Concerning his Book Intituled, The Peerage of Scotland* (1719); *A Letter Concerning the Bishop of Salisbury's History of his Own Time* (1724).

CHAPTER EIGHT

Fundamental Beliefs

Personal character traits virtually always influence the way an individual expresses and acts on his or her beliefs and values. Thus fear or a lack of self-confidence can lead someone to suppress the expression of otherwise strongly held beliefs, and rage against, or a wish to please, a given hearer lead to a more vehement commitment to certain concepts and values than might normally be the case. Therefore before exploring the basic beliefs around which Lockhart structured his ideas and conduct, it is appropriate to review those features of his personality which coloured his thinking.

One of the central features of George's character was his stubbornness. From the time we first encounter him in any depth in his writings and correspondence to the very end of his life he was stiff-necked, and on that score his contemporaries found him difficult to deal with.[1] This showed itself most trenchantly in the pride he took in his own consistency and his admiration for the trait in others.[2] In part it may have developed as a defensive response to his youth and inexperience when he first entered the Scots Parliament.[3] Certainly by 1714, when he proceeded alone with the episcopal estates resumption bill despite his Tory comrades' pleas[4] and joined the Whigs in opposition to the Scots militia bill, it had become ingrained. Correspondingly he silently erased his own early associations with the Court party in Scotland when he set out to summarise his career to date in 1717.[5] The corollary of which is that his final passage out of active Jacobitism in response to *force majeure* in 1728 was such an affront to the consistently activist identity he had constructed for himself that it must have hurt him deeply; it went against everything he had prided himself in being for the previous quarter-century. Hence perhaps his choice of the image of the proud Syrian general Naaman – who, though converted to the worship of Yahweh by the prophet Elisha, was obliged to bow to the idol of Rimmon when he returned home – as a metaphor for his own situation after his return from exile.[6]

A related feature of Lockhart's character was his inability to control his

---

1 SRO GD 18/2092/2: Sir John's Clerk's spiritual journal, 1699–1709, 19 Feb. 1699 and
   10 June 1701; LL, p. 294: GL to the Old Pretender [Dryden?], 8 Aug. 1726.
2 LP i. 498; SR, pp. 57, 110–11.
3 SR, p. 3.
4 LP i. 449.
5 LP i. 498; SRO PC 1/52–3: *Acta*, 24 Feb. 1703 – 28 Nov. 1704.
6 LP ii. 397; II *Kings*, 5. I am indebted to Dwayne Waldrup and Dr Kevin Kragenbrink,
   both formerly graduate students at Auburn University, for their help in tracking down
   this reference.

temper when he encountered behaviour he considered outrageous. We have seen how furious he became with his brother-in-law Lord Galloway over a careless remark in a letter.[7] This was but one example of his lapses into absolute fury when those whom he trusted or valued let him down. Part of the reason for this choleric behaviour was that he found it increasingly difficult to comprehend the behaviour of those to whom he was opposed or who opposed him. In an aside in his *Memoirs* during an account of the 1705 session in the Scottish Parliament, for example, George remarked: 'And here I cannot but wonder at the influence he [Queensberry] had over men of sense, quality and estates. Men that had, at least many of them, no dependence upon him, and yet were so deluded as to serve his ambitious designs, contrary to the acknowledged dictates of their own conscience'.[8] In the same vein, he was apparently perplexed (and, significantly, angered) by Sir David Dalrymple's attempts to justify the Union in the preface to the pirated (1714) edition of the *Memoirs*.[9] Lockhart's conviction of the righteousness of his own beliefs (which obviously also owed something to his stubbornness) was the counterpart of this incomprehension and consequently he more and more tended to become ill-tempered with those who opposed him and still more with 'traitors' to the Jacobite cause, as even he recognised himself.[10] Hence when he wrote to the Old Pretender to tell him the 5th Duke of Hamilton had gone over to the government, he remarked that he (George) was going to have to 'keep out of his way, for I am affrayd the regard he [GL] has for his father's [i.e. the 4th Duke of Hamilton's] memory, would get the better part of my patience, and hinder my dissembling with one that acts so poor a part'.[11]

Intertwined with this strong tendency towards self-righteousness was a very stern, even old-fashioned, sense of propriety. Lockhart, had, for example, a dislike of swearing and cursing that would not have disgraced a godly divine. The feature of Queensberry's and Seafield's characters he found most immediately 'horrid' was their propensity to 'swearing and imprecating curses', in order to convince their audience of their sincerity.[12] He expressed this most clearly in a pamphlet he wrote in the 1720s specifically denouncing the practice among the gentry and aristocracy of Scotland:

> Of all the many vicious practices which abound, ther's none so unaccountable as swearing and cursing in common conversation. Ther's something to be offerd (tho indeed, when thorowlie canvassd, but trifling) as ane alurement

7 See above, p. 24.
8 SR, p. 89.
9 SR, p. 274.
10 SR, p. 34; LP ii. 327–9.
11 LL, p. 303.
12 SR, pp. 12, 19.

in most other vices, but in this, not one tollerable pretext can be assigned towards justifying or even excusing the practice. How atrocious it is in the sight of God, how repugnant to the nature and statutes of our holy religion, how pernicious with respect to civill society, are articles I leave to those whose profession and abilitys render them more proper and capable to illustrate. Ther still remains more than enuff to render it detestable in the opinions of all judicious persons, and to perswade the guilty to forbear a practice so inconsistent with common sense and good manners.[13]

In sexual matters too, despite the indications noted above of his enduring and active sexual interest in Euphemia, George was somewhat prissy. The keynote of the negative character he wrote of his old friend Argyll was his 'lewdness' and he seems to have found hints during the Clementina affair that James was having an affair with Inverness's wife Marjory especially distressing.[14]

The final facet of Lockhart's personality that needs to be taken into account is his growing sense of despair as he got older. This gathering hopelessness may well have stemmed from the unusual depth of his historical awareness, for he was, on his own admission, prone to reflect at length on why Scottish history had taken the course it had over the previous century[15] – mute evidence for which can be found in his voluminous writings. By the 1720s, apparently, successive disappointments – and an acute awareness of previous failures – had rendered these reflections morbid. Thus he interpreted the Clementina affair as 'the severest stroke the King's affairs have met with these several years, and will be such an impediment to them that they [the trustees] have much reason to think no circumstance of time, no situation of affairs of Europe, can make amends',[16] which certainly exaggerated its significance. Likewise by the time he finally ceased to be an active Jacobite he clearly despaired of there ever again being any hope of a Stuart restoration.[17] All of which is significant because it went against the grain of most Jacobites' outlook, which tended towards the incurably optimistic[18] – the corollary of which was that George increasingly felt himself to be trapped in a milieu dominated by frighteningly naive fools.[19]

13 LP i. 609.
14 LP i. 32, 109–10; ii. 383.
15 SR, p. 248.
16 LL, p. 284.
17 LP ii. 405.
18 Szechi, *Jacobitism and Tory Politics*, pp. 36–42; J. Black, *British Foreign Policy in the Age of Walpole* (Edinburgh, 1985), p. 138.
19 LP ii. 359–60.

Human Nature

Lockhart's views on human nature were sombre and pessimistic, and thus in accord with general opinion on the subject throughout the British Isles.[20] Like most of his contemporaries, George appears to have derived his assumptions from a lifetime of hearing sermons which assumed the fallen and disgraced state of humankind. 'The state of humane affairs', he wrote in 1729, 'requires that distinction and those degrees of higher and lower ranks which have been hitherto established in all ages and countries'.[21] Strict observance of this social hierarchy in the sense of careful maintenance of a social distance between upper and lower ranks was necessary because 'Mankind are naturally ambitious of powr, and when they attain to more than that to which they have ane inherent title, they think their's no way to secure the posession, but by grasping at more and keeping their fellow creatures at under'.[22] Lockhart's human beings were thus inherently selfish and blindly ambitious; only firm social discipline could restrain them. Though he believed, too, that 'generosity and honour' were 'the strongest of all motives', he regretfully concluded they 'have not a like effect with all men',[23] and was correspondingly highly critical of most politicians' motives. 'Nothing', he declared in the *Memoirs*, 'can separate statesmen from that selfish, ambitious principle that overrules all their projects'.[24] Conversely, in the larger scheme of things, those who, like the Scots, had been 'conquered' by their enemies would in time become natural slaves who accepted their bondage.[25]

These orthodox positions were of a piece with George's thoroughly conventional opinions of the essential nature of women ('naturally timorous and credolous'[26]), and the conviction that royalty were innately different from the rest of the human race.[27] In fact, the only divergence between George's position on human nature and the general consensus among his peers lay in his conviction that the taint of particular sins, and specifically the sin of rebellion, almost indelibly imprinted itself on a man's nature. 'The leopard may change his spots and the Ethiopian his colour', he asserted, 'but it is impossible, at least very rare, that anything will alter a rebel and traitor'.[28] Furthermore, such taints often

---

20 J. A. Sharpe, *Crime in Early Modern England 1550–1750* (1984), pp. 144–5; J. Robertson (ed.), *Andrew Fletcher. Political Works* (Cambridge, 1997), pp. 151, 209; Chevalier de Johnstone, *Memoirs of the Rebellion in 1745 and 1746* (1820), pp. 196–7.

21 LP i. 608.

22 LL, p. 326. GL's views on human nature may have been influenced here by Fletcher of Saltoun: *Fletcher. Political Works*, p. 142.

23 SR, p. 90.

24 SR, pp. 214–15.

25 LP i. 418.

26 LL, p. 330.

27 LP ii. 417.

28 SR, p. 160. See also, pp. 11 (Queensberry), 58–9 (Stair).

became enduringly associated with particular families and were transmitted like a genetic disease from generation to generation. Hence Hugh Campbell, the 3rd Earl of Loudoun, 'being descended of a family enemies to monarchy, and educated after that way ... easily dropt into Court measures', and David Leslie, the 5th Earl of Leven, having been 'born and bred an enemy to the royal family, ... therefore chearfully embraced, and significantly promoted, every thing against its interest'.[29] Which in turn meant that rebellion in one generation was bound to have ramifications for society and the polity in multiple generations to come.

Society

Given this grim view of human nature and the long-term consequences of rebellion, it is not surprising to find that Lockhart favoured strict order and hierarchy in society. This emerged most clearly in his disapproval of what he saw as a contemporary trend towards greater informality in social relations and social mixing at public events:

> too much familiarity begets contempt from the vulgar, a similitude in dress and behaviour lessens the respect justly claimd and paid to those of a superior rank (for visible appearances work powerfully on humane minds) and in time produces that meaness in the one and arrogance in the other, which terminates in ane equality pernicious to both.[30]

Keeping the lower orders under firm control was a social duty necessary for the maintenance of the hierarchical order he believed vital to keeping society on an even keel. As he remarked in the context of his polemic against the practice of cursing and swearing in 1730 'I can't but observe that persons of power and authority are much to blame and accountable for the prevalence of vice in these sort of people, for did they meet with the discouragement and punishment they deserve and shoud be inflicted by their superiors, theyd be less offensive in this particular'.[31] He was correspondingly also upset by anything that fostered independence among the lower orders. The presbyterian practice of involving the whole congregation in the selection of a minister mightily offended him because he believed it slighted the deference to the opinions of their betters he felt was appropriate.[32] Likewise he condemned Lord of Session Sir Gilbert Elliott of Minto's public praise of the Bothwell Brig rebels not because they were (from George's point of view) wicked Covenanters, but because 'such maxims advanced

---

29 SR, p. 60. Fletcher of Saltoun apparently held the same opinion: *Fletcher. Political Works*, p. 135.

30 LP i. 608.

31 LP i. 609.

32 SR, p. 8; LP ii. 126–7.

by judges from the bench may be reckoned by the commons as ane invitation to rebell with authority'.[33] One of the worst things Lockhart could say about the behaviour of his peers, when it met his disapproval, was that it was 'mobbish'.[34]

George was, however, equally disapproving of anything that indicated a breach in the traditional hierarchical order at the other, upper, end of society. Social mobility generally offended him, and he perceived the advancement of men from socially inferior backgrounds to positions of power and authority as a dangerous threat to good social order. Hence he was scandalised by the Commissions of the Peace issued by the Marlborough-Godolphin administration in 1707, in which 'the powr lodged solely in the hands of rigid presbiterians, bitter Republicans and the meanest of the gentry, and in some counties to make up a number, litle countrie lawyers and noblemen's stewards, nay even ther domestick servants were named'.[35] Likewise the Commissions of the Peace for Edinburghshire nominated by the Whig regime in 1725 displeased him because they contained, 'some ... [who] ... were not heretors'.[36]

All this hostility to the sudden rise to power and authority of men from the lower ranks of the elite stemmed from George's belief that those so elevated could only sustain themselves by oppression or pandering to the mob, and in either case were bound to undermine the rightful authority of the great families of the kingdom. Thus in the case of the Earls of Stair and Glasgow he implicitly linked the fact that they and their families 'had rose but lately from nothing' with accusations of avarice and abuse of power.[37] Likewise, since it was composed of 'old, forfeited rebells and gentlemen of no fortunes, respect or families in the kingdom',[38] the Convention Parliament was bound to abuse its trust. Conversely, because the seceders of 1702 stemmed from 'the first quality and best estates in the kingdom', their action assumed a noble and righteous significance.[39] Their political opponents, by contrast, were incapable of negotiating a worthwhile treaty with England in 1702–3 because 'ther are but few of them of our ancient nobility and gentry who have the most intrest and authoritie in the natione, ther being none of the great and ancient names ... among them; wheras ther are 6 or 7 of our modern new raisd families and ther relations'.[40] For Lockhart, right rule was bred in the bone.

George also believed, however, that those born to exercise social authority

33 LP i. 556.
34 SR, p. 165.
35 LL, p. 64.
36 LP ii. 167.
37 SR, pp. 59, 61.
38 SR, p. 8.
39 SR, p. 14.
40 LP i. 280. Generic contempt for 'new men' was quite commonplace in Scotland at this time: see, *Burt's Letters*, i. 97.

had a moral duty to do so responsibly. While chiding his sister-in-law Lady Galloway and her husband the earl over their reluctance to act as guardians for the young orphaned 10th Earl of Eglinton in 1729, Lockhart remarked: 'man came not into this world merely for himself, but to act a sociall part, to assist and releive all mankind as far as he can, and in so far as particular freinds or near relations are concernd to venture and expose himself to certain degrees of inconvenience and danger in their service'.[41] His vision of the ideal relationship between rulers and ruled was classically patriarchal, and in conventional fashion took the elite family as its model. In a long letter to his oldest son, written to be read after his death, George handed down a great deal of advice and direction, and incidentally theorised at length about the nature of society and the reciprocal nature of social obligations:

> In short, familys are petty states and have the same fate, and are subject to the same rules and guided by the same maxims as the most powerfull extensive kingdoms. A family that is divided can no more subsist than a kingdom. Subjects may be compelld by laws and a superior force, but never heartily and chearfully obey and support ther prince that does not cherish and protect them, and they often desert him when he's at a pinch; just so, the nearest blood relations expect mutuall good offices, especially from those that claim a superiority, and when these faill, ther attachment in a short time evanisheth.[42]

Lockhart firmly believed in acting out such a beneficent role toward the world in general – where other considerations did not intrude – but most of all with respect to his blood relations. For his family occupied pride of place in all his social thought.

Family

George was an affectionate father, and very probably enjoyed an affective relationship with his wife, Euphemia. Whether or not this stemmed from the disruption he experienced as a child is hard to say, though, *prima facie*, it does seem likely.[43] We can, however, be certain that, despite his general insistence on strictly ordered social relationships, he sought to create and sustain an indulgent, mutually supportive ethos within the Lockhart household. The most telling evidence for this is in the long letter of advice he left for George junior, in which he briefly theorised about the nature of the family in human society and the vital need for it to remain united and obedient to its patriarch:

41 LP ii. 431.
42 LP ii. 427–8.
43 See above, pp. 20–2, 24–5.

the power and grandeur of a family does not altogather consist in the enjoyment of ane estate, tho ever so great, but in having freinds and depend- ents able and willing to stand by and support it; and from whom can that be expected, in such a measure of zeall and sincerity, as from those blood relations descended from the same originall and partakers of the benefites once enjoyd and handed down by ther common progenitors for the co[m]fort and welfare of the society thus united and tyed togather by the strongest obligations of mutuall love, freindship and good offices? [44]

Accordingly, and albeit with an eye to the patriarch receiving a useful return on his emotional and financial investment, he advised George junior to be unstintingly generous and hospitable:

Let your house be as ane assembly for them to meet frequently and be merry, and ane asylum in case of distress; and wher it happens by misfortunes and not from causes criminall or blameable in them, do not stand upon what patrimony I have alloted them and you perhaps have paid, but generouslie and like a true freind enable them to set out again in the world. Charity requires such kind of aid, in some measure, to all fellow Christians, and much more to such near relations who's low and mean circumstances dart back a reflection on you and the family you represent, and who by being assisted may recover so as to repay what you advance, and return your freindship with interest. [45]

The corollary of this heavy emphasis on the need for family unity and mutual support was that Lockhart was deeply disturbed by behaviour that tended to disrupt his own, or indeed any other, family. His apparent rejection of his mother may have stemmed from the part she played in the instability of his childhood years. [46] He was also very distressed by the Old Pretender's problems with Clementina and in the process of urging their reconciliation revealed a thoroughly pragmatic approach to spousal relations that was at odds with his traditionalist patriarchal theorising. Despite James's status as both patriarch and sovereign, Lockhart felt the Stuart pretender was being unreasonable in the demands he placed on his wife, so that 'the prerogatives of a soveraign and husband are skrewed up to a pitch not tenable by the laws of God or man, or consistent with prudence'. [47] Moreover, George was patently outraged by suggestions orig- inating from Inverness's circle that James might divorce Clementina. By implication James was dishonoured for even giving a hearing to 'this bag of lyes

---

44 LP ii. 427.
45 LP ii. 428.
46 See above, pp. 17–18, 22–3.
47 LP ii. 405.

and nonesence' that struck at his marriage.[48] This was the most serious charge Lockhart could make. For he believed that along with religion, honour constituted the vital bond that held all elite relationships, and thence the whole of society, together.

Honour

Every member of the ruling elite in the British Isles affected to believe in the unwritten code of honour prevailing among them. At its most benign the code carried a public expectation that a gentleman keep his word once pledged. At its most pernicious it demanded that gentlemen duel to uphold their statements when these were challenged and to retain the respect of their peers for themselves and their families. Virtually every heritor was steeped in it from an early age and it strongly influenced the dynamics of their personal relationships.[49]

Lockhart's beliefs on the subject of honour differed from the norm (as in so much else) only in the intensity of his commitment to it. As far as he was concerned the code of honour sustained the moral order of society by tying its rulers to a system of ethics:

> truth and sincerity are so essentiall ingredients of the composition of honor, that without these qualitys it cant possibly subsist nay have a being; and hence it is to insinuate the least doubt of these is the highest indignity and imputation amongst men of true honor, who expecting that what they assert or deny on their simple affirmation or negation shoud be absolutely credited, think the requiring any collateral conviction a reflection on their charactars. And this certainly is a wise and necessary maxim, as the allowing or even supposing it possible for a man of honor and honestie to deviat in the most minute degree from plain naked truth woud render all mutuall confidence in mankind precarious.[50]

Unusually for him, George was even willing to set aside a man's politics and sexual morals when passing judgement upon him. At its simplest, those who maintained their honour were worthy, those who did not were contemptible. Andrew Fletcher of Saltoun, despite being 'an enemy to all monarchical government' and the Stuarts in particular, was held up as the exemplar of the true Scots patriot for all future ages in large part because 'he was a strict and nice observer of all the points of honour, and his word [was] sacred'.[51] Lockhart also profoundly disapproved of the 2nd Duke of Argyll's morals: '[he] succeeded his

---

48 LP ii. 348.
49 V. G. Kiernan, *The Duel in European History. Honour and the Reign of Aristocracy* (Oxford, 1989), pp. 152–64.
50 LP i. 610.
51 SR, pp. 43–5.

father not only in his estate, honours and employments, but likewise in his lewdness and disloyalty, and, if it was possible, exceeded him in them both', but the duke's honourable conduct more than made up for these blots on his character ('his word was so sacred that one might assuredly depend on it').[52] Moreover, George retained his respect for Argyll even when his sense of honour had a direct, adverse effect on the Jacobite cause. For when Argyll refused to be drawn over to the Jacobite side in 1715 Lockhart wholeheartedly endorsed his decision: 'I had such an abhorrence at breach of trust, that had I been the Duke's adviser, it should have been to doe as he did; for 'tho there was nothing I so much desired as to see him engaged in the King's cause, I wisht it done in a way consistent with his honour'.[53] Conversely he remained primly disapproving of those who favoured the Stuart cause when they behaved, as he saw it, dishonourably. When William Cochran of Kilmaronock, a veteran of the anti-Union opposition and a staunch Jacobite, was discovered by the Commission of Accounts to have been involved in a fraud associated with the customs, George not only participated in exposing him, but also came close to duelling with him when Cochran traduced him among their fellow Tories.[54]

The corollary of this heavy emphasis on the social necessity of honourable conduct was that political dealings with the dishonourable were both distasteful and, in most cases, pointless. Chicanery and betrayal by the likes of the Squadrone or the Whigs in general were almost inevitable.[55] How could it be otherwise when one was dealing with men like the Earl of Rothes, who (according to George) was 'false to a great degree, a contemner of honour and engagements ... and scandalously mercenary'? Or the Earl (subsequently Duke) of Roxburghe, who was 'extreamly false and disingenuous, and so indifferent of the ties of honour, friendship, vows and justice, that he sacrificed them all, and the interest of his country, to his designs, viz. revenge and ambition'.[56] The implication was that there should be few dealings and no compromise with them and their ilk.

Honour, moreover, was a delicate plant. It could be compromised by dealing with 'men whom no rules of honour or bonds of society can bind',[57] but equally it could be tainted by false judgement. Though George never comes out and says so directly, he implies that Hamilton's secret dealings with Mar and Queensberry over the choice of commissioners for the treaty of union (in which they, according to the *Memoirs*, manoeuvred him into a false position) led him

---

52 SR, p. 81.
53 LP ii. 14.
54 SRO GD 190/3/282/3 (Smythe of Methven Papers): GL to Cochran, Dryden, 8 Nov. 1712; LL, p. 58.
55 LL, p. 148.
56 SR, p. 64.
57 LL, p. 148.

into behaviour that compromised his honour.[58] More dramatically, the Old Pretender's refusal to accept Clementina's charges against the Inverness connection directly impugned his honour:

> Ther were so many instances givn by persons well affected to the King, from their proper knowledge of the triumvirate's insolence to the Queen and others about the Court, that the same was scarcely to be doubted; but at the same time they [the trustees] endeavoured to suppress such reports, because it was a terrible reflection on the King's honour and judgement not only to allow therof, but even break with the Queen rather than part with these favourites, when she complaind of them.[59]

A man could only retain his honour by rigid adherence to the code, correct behaviour towards others comprehended within it and shunning those who were outwith the system. Hence George's refusal to meet General Wade in 1726: 'Some of my friends blame the part I acted, but I can well enough foresee some inconvenience that might happen if I did not keep myself abstract from these people, and I am sure no benefit would accress from any dealings I could have with them'.[60]

Lockhart's interpretation of the code of honour undoubtedly helped him deal with his circumstances up to 1728. As a Jacobite in a Whig polity he needed some form of ethical bridge to allow him to get through the compromises of everyday life when they clashed with the principles he held so dear, and his adherence to the code of honour provided it. An overriding belief in the importance of maintaining one's honour, however, necessarily carried with it a willingness to vindicate oneself by violence. On one level this belief in the virtues of honourable violence led George to his death in a duel in 1731. On another, more fundamentally, it created in him a fixed belief in the need for, and indeed perverse virtue of, revenge in human affairs.

Revenge

Vengeance as a compelling, often justified, motive for political action is a recurrent theme in all of Lockhart's writings, and one that was close to his own heart.[61] In 1708 he declared of those who supported the Union in the Scottish Parliament: 'it will be as great a pity if sooner or later ... they be not as high erected on a gibbet as the honour and interest of the nation are by their means

---

58 SR, pp. 107–9, 195–6.
59 LP ii. 221.
60 LL, p. 294.
61 See, for example: SR, pp. 3, 227; LP i. 427–8, ii. 140; LL, pp. 75, 81. Such an attitude was widespread in parts of Scotland at least as late as the 1720s: *Burt's Letters*, ii. 257–8, 259.

dejected'.[62] In 1714 he told Secretary of State William Bromley that the Scots Tories 'saw no way left but to be evens with those who thus used us', i.e. the Oxford ministry, for having vacillated and let them down so many times.[63] And in 1725 he and several other prominent Scottish Jacobites carefully subverted James's declared (and probably sincere) wish to allow a full amnesty in the event of a Stuart restoration by adjusting the wording of his intended proclamation so that it would not cover the architects of the Union:

> so ... as to leave a door open to get in upon those perfidious instruments of that unparalelld treacherie to their country, if ever Scotland was so happy as to have a Parliament within herself, that woud do justice to the honour of the nation, by redressing wherin it was scandalouslie violate, and providing against the like for the future; for procuring nothing wherof nothing coud be more effectuall than a publick brand of infamy on those who had the cheif hand therin.[64]

And as we have already seen, George's attitude toward the Whig regime was also profoundly affected by the execution of his brother Philip in the aftermath of the 1715 uprising; thereafter his struggle against the new order had something of the quality of the bloodfeud about it.[65]

The source of Lockhart's conviction that revenge was an appropriate response to defeat or betrayal, as befits a man and a cause that were basically religiously inspired, was a particular interpretation of the role of God in the world. Lockhart's deity was a very interventionist one, who, in Old Testament fashion, constantly manipulated nature and human affairs visibly to punish and reward nations (George's silence on the subject of God's role in shaping the lives of individuals suggests his vision of the divine part therein was more ambiguous). Such retribution can obviously be taken as a form of revenge by the deity, but Lockhart carried it further. In his view, human failure to avenge certain crimes, such as regicide, committed by other humans was directly contrary to the expressed will of God. Such negligence in turn invited divine revenge. This was most clearly demonstrated in George's thinking on the subject of why God had chosen to punish Scotland by subjecting it to England. In the *Memoirs* he advanced two reasons, the crucial one of which concerned the death of Mary, Queen of Scots, at the hands of Elizabeth I:

> The first is, the mean-spirited behaviour of King James VI in not revenging his mother's murder ... And which of his royal progenitors would not have resented it with fire and sword? For my part, I'm afraid the indignation of

62 SR, p. 158.
63 LL, p. 102.
64 LP ii. 236.
65 See above, pp. 120–1.

God was stirred up upon this account against his posterity, and that particularly in the case of his son, Charles I.[66]

Scots involvement in the rebellion that led to the killing of Charles I then
compounded the original offence, but the implication is clear. For George,
revenge was not just a legitimate human response; in certain circumstances,
such as the betrayal of the nation, it was one mandated by a watchful, activist
deity.

Anti-Presbyterianism

Lockhart was a messianic episcopalian Jacobite (the significance of this will be
explored in detail in chapter 10) and it strongly affected his attitude towards
other sections of Scottish society. In the case of Scotland's presbyterians it
heightened his confessional aversion to their beliefs to an intensity little short of
hatred.[67] The 'rotten fanaticks', he wrote in 1708, were Scotland's bane, 'acting
from a selfish principle and conscious of their ill actions and designs, ... like the
devil himself, never idle'.[68] Commenting on recent political events, he characterised them to Mar in 1718 as, 'men ... accustomed to do evill'.[69] Moreover,
throughout his *oeuvre* Lockhart never loses an opportunity to highlight and gloat
over any incident that reflects badly on the presbyterian Kirk and its ministers.[70]
    At the heart of his hostility to presbyterians and presbyterianism lay the belief
that they were created and sustained by the Scottish nation's English nemesis.
Until religious divisions rent the fabric of Scottish society in the sixteenth century,
George believed, Scotland was powerful and respected. But then the rise of the
presbyterian party allowed the English to foment internal strife that prostrated
the nation.[71] Since then, presbyterianism 'was [re]established in a time of confusion and hath ... been protected and cherished by our statesmen, whom the
Presbiterians supported in the managing of the nation; and thus they playd and
I'me afraid do play to one another's hands, contrary to the inclinations of the
people'.[72] The convenience of corrupt court politicians was thus all that sustained
presbyterianism in Scotland down to the eighteenth century, for 'had ... [the
Presbyterian clergy] ... not been supported from England, it had long ere this

---

66 SR, p. 248.
67 This was not uncommon amongst Jacobites in general, as may be seen in: SRO GD
    220/5/455/4: anonymous account of 10 June Jacobite celebrations in Aberdeen, Aberdeen,
    13 June 1715; *Memoirs of the Insurrection in Scotland*, pp. 2, 100; Johnstone, *Memoirs of the
    Rebellion*, pp. 205–6, 209–10.
68 SR, pp. 20, 27.
69 LL, p. 128.
70 SR, p. 135; LP i. 381–2, 383, 524, 561.
71 SR, p. 245.
72 LP i. [5]26–7.

dwindled into nothing'.[73] They were all either witting or unwitting tools of a foreign enemy. Either way, attacking or undermining the presbyterian Kirk was a patriotic and/or meritorious act.[74]

Anti-Catholicism

Lockhart's attitude toward the Roman Catholic church is more difficult to establish. It has long been assumed (probably correctly) that of all the protestant denominations in the British Isles, Scottish episcopalians were liable to be the most sympathetic towards the sufferings of their persecuted catholic fellow subjects. This should not, however, be taken to mean that in their teachings and polemics episcopalians approved of, or did not seek to oppose, the Catholic church.[75] Moreover, this hostility towards catholicism created an abiding source of tension between their duty towards the exiled Stuarts as kings and their suspicion of them as catholics. And Lockhart seems to have been as suspicious of James's catholic propensities as any of his peers.[76]

This silent tension between the loyal, protestant adherents of the Stuarts and their royal master had existed since the 1690s, and for most of the time both parties tried to play down issues and events that might have brought them into conflict.[77] James himself determinedly tried to remain aloof from any religious controversy and pointedly refused to follow his father in seeking to convert his servants. As he observed in 1718:

> Je suis Catholique, mais je suis Roy, et des sujets de quelque religion qu'ils soient doivent etre egalement proteges. Je suis Roy mais, comme m'a dit le

73 LP i. [5]26.
74 Hence GL's public stand against the Kirk on almost every possible occasion: Blairs Letters 2/83/2: Carnegy to Innes, np, 8 June 1703; SRO GD 18/2092/4: Sir John Clerk's spiritual journal for Apr. 1712–1715, 3 Nov. 1712.
75 Clarke, 'Scottish Episcopalians', pp. 5, 27; *Correspondence of Colonel N. Hooke*, i. 294–5, ii. 261, 330–1, 335; Westminster Diocesan Archive, Ep. Var. V, ep. 48: Edward Dicconson to [Laurence Mayes] [Douai], 27 Mar. 1714 ns;SRO GD 220/5/434/5: the heritors of Ruthven to Sir David Dalrymple, Ruthven 12 Nov. 1714; Blairs Letters 2/134/3: Bishop William Nicolson to Thomas Innes [Edinburgh?], 17 Aug. 1706; 2/125/7: Carnegy to Thomas Innes [Edinburgh], 23 Aug. 1706; 2/228/11: Patrick Leith to [Thomas Innes], Edinburgh, 12 June 1720.
76 Hence, too, the enthusiasm with which protestant Jacobites (including GL) seized upon rumours that James had converted: NLS, Wodrow Letters IV, ep. 88: Robert Wodrow to James Wodrow, Edinburgh, 19 Dec. 1706; Blairs Letters 2/173/16: Carnegy to Thomas Innes [Edinburgh?], 16 Aug. 1712; *Original Papers*, ii. 545–6.
77 Szechi, 'Jacobite Revolution Settlement', *passim*; HMC *Stuart*, iv. 349–55: Mar to James [Urbino?], 14 June 1717 ns; iv. 370: Ormond to James, 20 June 1717 ns; iv. 466–8: William Dicconson to Queen Mary [St Germain], 26 July 1717 ns; vi. 165–6: Orrery to Mar, 6/17 Mar. 1718 ns; vi. 133–5, 185–6: James to Cardinal Gualterio [Urbino], 11 and 24 Mar 1718 ns; vii. 533: Dr P. Barclay to Mar, Rome, 12 Nov. 1718 ns.

Pape luy meme, je ne suis pas Apôtre, je ne suis pas obligé de convertir mes sujets que par l'exemple, ni de montrer une partialité apparente aux Catholiques, qui ne serviroit qu'a leur nuire effectivement dans la suitte.[78]

Even so he could not escape having his every move that touched on the religious balance of power within the Jacobite movement intensively scrutinised. Thus in 1720 when the catholic Lady Jean Drummond absconded with the heir to the (Jacobite) Duchy of Perth shortly after his father's death, so as to prevent him coming under the tutelage of his nearest protestant (but also Jacobite) kinsmen, George and the trustees asked James to intervene to have the boy sent home. Lockhart denied any religious motive underlay this appeal, standing simply by the need to respect the laws of Scotland, but his placatory observations – 'as he is young, he has time enough to think of choicing or at least declareing his religion', and that '[James's] interposeing and obtaining a just redress in this matter would be duely improven, and tend much to his advantage' – suggest the implications of James's compliance were obvious to all concerned.[79] James nonetheless refused to get directly involved on either side, though he did quietly pressure Lady Drummond to 'doe what is reasonable upon this occasion',[80] with which George and the trustees professed to rest content.

A far more difficult situation developed as a result of the Usager controversy within the episcopal church. Because the usages were seen by many episcopalians, including Lockhart, as inclining towards popery, they feared that James, who still theoretically retained his full authority as head of the episcopal communion, would secretly favour them. Thus when James, entirely consistent with his long-standing policy 'never to medle in what concerns the religion of any of his friends',[81] refused explicitly to condemn the usages at the behest of Lockhart and the episcopalian conservatives, George transparently distrusted his motives: 'Whither this manner of writing proceeded from no design, or that the King did not incline expressly to condemn tenets and usages near a kin to those of his own Church (on which account I purposely shuned in my letters to make mention of the particulars) I cannot pretend to determine'.[82] Only once did Lockhart in a moment of anger show his dislike of catholicism more openly. He was always contemptuous of conversions to catholicism,[83] but when the Duke

---

78 HMC *Stuart*, v. 515: James to Fr Gaillard (Queen Mary of Modena's confessor), Fano, 28 Feb. 1718 ns.

79 LL, pp. 150–1. The 'capture' of catholic heirs by their protestant relatives was a well-known mode of bringing a family into conformity with the established church in other parts of the British Isles too: S. J. Connolly, *Religion, Law and Power. The Making of Protestant Ireland 1660–1760* (Oxford, 1992), p. 309.

80 LP ii. 47.

81 LP ii. 47.

82 LP ii. 112.

83 SR, pp. 32, 50.

of Wharton announced his in 1726 he could not forbear sharply commenting in a letter to James:

> I'le venture to say he has done you more disservice than it ever was or will be in his power to repair. I should be glad he were truely a Christian of any Church, but if, as most beleive, there's nothing of religion in it, nay suppose it was otherwayes, he has tuned it very ill, for such steps in any about the King, or declaring for the King under the present state of affairs, does you and your cause no small harm.[84]

All of which suggests that George and the other trustees' tacit opposition to James's forthright attempts to assert his authority over the episcopal church owed not a little to a discreet but profound streak of anti-catholicism.[85]

Anti-Clericalism

In part, too (because of the general belief among protestants that all catholics were priest-ridden), Lockhart's dislike of catholicism may have stemmed from the surprising degree of anti-clericalism he consistently displayed. For all his voluntary association with a specifically hierarchical church with an elevated view of the role of the clergy, George was quite forthright in expressing his contempt for those clergymen he considered unworthy. In the *Memoirs* he attacked Archbishop Paterson of Glasgow as 'avaricious' and 'worldly'.[86] In 1717 he dismissed Henry Sacheverell as 'a poor despicable clergy-man', whose famous sermon was only noteworthy for the number of 'railing Billingsgate expressions' it contained.[87] And in 1724 he characterised the bishops of the episcopal church as mainly motivated by 'private views and self interest'.[88] George was also sceptical of doctrinal disputes based on competing interpretations of Biblical texts and strongly implied that he considered such disputes to be merely attempts at self-advancement by ambitious clergymen.[89]

From his other, more general, comments on the clergy, of which his observation to James – 'it is not easie, under any circumstances, to keep [the clergy] in due bounds' – may be taken as typical, it is apparent that George was an out-and-out erastian, at least in the sense that he believed the clergy and the

84 LL, p. 294.
85 See above, pp. 143–4. It should be noted, however, that GL, like many other contemporary Scots, had no problem with employing or sheltering individual catholics even though he disapproved of their religious beliefs: *Miscellany of the Maitland Club, Volume III, Part II* (Edinburgh, 1843), p. 402: 'Presbytery of Dalkeith'.
86 SR, p. 55.
87 LP i. 311, 318.
88 LL, p. 207. Nor did he have a much higher opinion of many of the lower clergy: SRO CH 12/12/497: GL to the bishop and presbyters of Edinburgh, Dryden, 8 June 1731.
89 LP i. 505; ii. 334.

church should be subject to the (rightful) powers that be.[90] This finds further support in his outrage at the Usagers' defiance of the authority of both the trustees and their putative king. When William Keith in 1727 suggested to him that a solution to the dispute over episcopal appointments might be to put the matter to neutral arbitration or else to consecrate one new bishop from each party, Lockhart was outraged: 'I replyd with indignation that the King was not reduced quite so low as to make a reference or composition with a parcell of litle factious preists in the diocess of Edinburgh, who as they were serving the Covenanted cause shoud change their black gouns into brown cloaks ...'.[91] His personal religion, it seems, played a large part in inspiring Lockhart to commit himself to the Jacobite cause, but it never made him any great respecter of the clergy.[92] It also certainly did not extend to putting him in charity with his political opponents.

Partisanship

Given George's vehemence and self-righteousness, it will come as no surprise to learn that he was, and was known to be, absolutely politically intolerant.[93] He was fully aware of this, as is apparent from his attempt to fend off criticism of the *Memoirs* on that score: 'I foresee it may be objected I write too much against a certain party. It is true my indignation against the betrayers of my country is so great I never could, nor will, speak otherwise of them'.[94] Nevertheless, he lost no opportunity to attack his political foes. As far as he was concerned the two components of the Revolution interest in Scotland, the presbyterians and the Court, were uniformly selfish, malicious, mercenary and unpatriotic.[95] Their malevolent solidarity was the polar opposite of the well-intentioned, but disunited Cavaliers:[96]

> But this is a rock often the Cavaliers (but never the Presbyterians) have split upon. And the reason, as I take it, from whence this comes is that the former being (I say it impartially) of generous spirits, and designing good and just things, believe every man is so too, and are not at such pains as is necessary to cement a party's councils and measures together. Whereas the

---

90 LP i. 522, 570, ii. 333; LL, pp. 182, 207.
91 LP ii. 328–9.
92 See below, p. 145.
93 SRO GD 18/3209: James Forbes of Newhall to Baron Sir John Clerk, Newhall, 17 Apr. 1727.
94 SR, p. 6.
95 SR, pp. 28, 58–9, 155, 252–61.
96 Interestingly, this is a classic demonstration of the creation of the 'Other', i.e. an enemy who literally mirrors your own side's virtues and vices, in an attempt to explain the course of events.

Presbyterians, acting from a selfish principle and conscious of their ill actions and designs, are, like the devil himself, never idle, but always projecting, and so closely linked together that all go the same way, and all either stand or fall together.[97]

Placemen and Courtiers, by contrast, were simply 'prostitute[s]', willing to do 'any thing that would procure or secure them in their employments and pensions'.[98] Hence Lockhart's description of them in 1702 as 'ready to sacrifice their honour, conscience and country'.[99] In the same vein, he described the leaders of the Court party and Squadrone, for the most part, as monsters of depravity.[100] Queensberry was 'altogether void of honour, loyalty, justice, religion, and ingenuity; an ungrateful deserter of, and rebel to, his prince, the ruin and bane of his country, and the aversion of all loyal and true Scotsmen'.[101] Roxburghe was 'the very bane and cut-throat of his country, by being extreamly false and disingenuous, and so indifferent of the ties of honour, friendship, vows and justice, that he sacrificed them all, and the interest of his country, to his designs, viz. revenge and ambition'.[102] Stair was simply, 'the Judas of his country'.[103]

These remarks come from the *Memoirs* and are a good indication of how Lockhart viewed his opponents in his early years in politics. But he did not mellow as he got older. In 1722 the Squadrone were willing to 'serve and trukle under him [Robert Walpole] or the devil himself for wages'.[104] The Scots Whig M.P.s of 1724 were 'a parcell of people of low fortunes that could not subsist without their board-wages (which at ten guineas a week during each session was duely paid them) or meer tools and dependents'.[105] And in 1727 the Whigs in general were 'truely mercenary'.[106] Conventional Scottish politics after 1714 were correspondingly, as far as Lockhart was concerned, a contest in servility, as may be seen from his description of their dynamics in 1725:

The government here is entirely in the hands of [the] Duke of Argyle, or rather Lord Ilay, and the Campbels are extremely uppish and insolent. Their merit consists in undertaking to carry through the malt tax, as the Squadrone's was formerly in supporting the Commission of Forefaultrie, so that each party

97 SR, pp. 19–20.
98 SR, pp. 12, 28.
99 SR, p. 10.
100 Though he was willing to concede that some of his less important political opponents, for example Loudoun and Tweeddale, had some personal merits (SR, pp. 60, 66).
101 SR, p. 12.
102 SR, p. 64.
103 SR, p. 58.
104 LL, p. 180.
105 LP ii. 139.
106 LP ii. 404.

raise themselves by alternate hardships on their native Countrey. We were in great hope the Squadrone would have kicked out, but they're a mean-spirited dastardly set, and will come into no measures that may irritate their good masters of England, so as to cut them off from hopes of being taken in again.[107]

The 'vineager of [his] wrath' against those he saw as his political enemies clearly retained its savour for Lockhart throughout his life.[108]

George's bitter hostility towards his political foes should not be taken, however, as blinding him to the mote in his own eye. He intermittently brooded at length on the weaknesses and failures of his own side, and though on occasion he made excuses for them on the grounds of their 'generous spirits', he was also aware of their faults. The problem with the Tories, he reflected in 1723, was that they

> leap greedily at anything to blacken the Character of ther friends and in no way have ... [they] ... since I knew the world done themselves more harm than by cherishing jealousies and propagating lyes of one another. And tis a strange [sic] that fatall experience will not open ther eyes to see the traps laid by ther adversarys to catch them.[109]

It was nonetheless clear to Lockhart where the balance of good and evil lay, and it is indicative of the way his religion suffused his political consciousness and vice versa that he responded by pronouncing the most solemn anathema of the age on the whole parcel of Whigs, Squadrone, courtiers and presbyterians who had combined to pass the Act of Union – he excluded them from heaven:

> It is true that God hath in all ages and countries raised up wicked and tyrannicall princes and rulers, and also rebellious and treacherous subjects, both of clergy and laity, as a scourge to sinfull nations, but their wickedness, tyrannies, rebellions and treacheries were never to be esteemed the less criminal. And if so in preceeding times, those of the present age, when they reflect upon the part they have acted with respect to Scotland, have no reason to expect to be justifyed in this world or that which is to come.[110]

The Jacobite elect, however, suffered from a besetting curse, which George shared in full measure: acute political paranoia.[111]

107 LL, p. 258.
108 LL, p. 106.
109 LL, p. 194.
110 SR, p. 250.
111 Gregg, 'Politics of Paranoia', pp. 42–56.

Paranoia

The classic conspiracy theory maintains that in any political situation those who appear to be friends are secretly enemies who are working behind the scenes to sabotage or undermine group x or y. In Lockhart's case, the conspirators were legion: all English governments, most English politicians, any Scottish politician who collaborated with the English ministers, all presbyterians, even on occasion the French.[112] All of them aimed at subordinating, using or oppressing Scotland. The Union only ever materialised because

> the Scots statesmen and Revolutioners were so sensible ... of their own guilt in betraying their country and acting contrary to its interest these many years by-past, that they thought themselves in no security from being called to account for their actions, unless they removed the Parliament and rendered the nation subservient and subject to a people whom they had served, and from whom they looked for protection.[113]

In part this conspiratorial interpretation of contemporary politics may have stemmed from George's involvement in several genuine conspiracies, and too, from his acceptance of the Tory version of the history of the British Isles since 1640. Many Tories as well as Lockhart matter-of-factly believed that there had been a deep-laid conspiracy against Charles I, monarchy and episcopalianism throughout the British Isles, and it was a plain fact that there had been a conspiracy against James II and VII in 1688.[114] Lockhart also knew for a fact that the Cavaliers and Jacobite Tories generally had had a hidden agenda for as long as he had been associated with them.

Rationalisations of Lockhart's political paranoia can only, however, go so far. Edward Gregg has argued that Jacobitism quickly developed a fully-fledged internal culture of political paranoia; Lockhart's conspiratorial interpretation of contemporary events solidly supports his case.[115] The further he rose within the Jacobite hierarchy, the more paranoid George became. His first letter directed at the Jacobite court after his release in 1716 is mainly concerned with vindicating himself against charges of laxity and cowardice that he believed were being levelled against him by other Jacobites.[116] After he rose to become secretary to the trustees and their chief coordinator he steadily became more and more irrationally paranoid. When he was feeling charitable he suspected Jacobite

---

112 SR, pp. 39–40, 48, 229; LP i. 507.
113 SR, p. 123.
114 See, for example: Holmes, *Trial of Dr Sacheverell*, pp. 52, 53, 64; Colley, *In Defiance*, pp. 88–9; W. A. Speck, *Reluctant Revolutionaries. Englishmen and the Revolution of 1688* (1988), pp. 82–3; J. R. Jones, *The Revolution of 1688 in England* (1st edn, 1972), pp. 222–45.
115 Gregg, 'Politics of Paranoia', pp. 51–2.
116 LL, pp. 121–5.

Secretaries of State of being so incompetent that they were endangering the cause. When he was not, he straightforwardly branded them traitors. James Murray was thus so unsuited by character and ability to run the Jacobite underground that his fall was highly welcome.[117] Mar was of course a proven traitor by the mid-1720s, and as far as George was concerned his eventual successor, Inverness, was a mortal enemy, motivated by 'malicious, villanous treacherie and revenge', who would stop at nothing to bring down honest men like himself.[118] Even the inoffensive Sir John Graeme was implicated in the alleged sale of cyphers to the British government.[119] As for the lesser functionaries of the Jacobite underground – couriers, agents and the like – many of them, too, were incompetent buffoons where they were not double agents.[120]

It is doubtless difficult to work for any length of time in a twilight world of conspiracy, espionage and treason without being consumed by it. Lockhart succumbed, and it is perhaps as well that he passed out of active Jacobitism when he did, because by 1727 he was beginning to see traitors everywhere. Thus the Usagers and their backers among the episcopalian elite, whom he accused of betraying his courier route to the authorities 'are some of the very persons whose factious humours appeared so conspicuous at Perth [i.e. in 1715]'.[121] George's demons were growing too ubiquitous for him to have functioned effectively for much longer.

117 LP ii. 340, 343.
118 LP ii. 186, 401.
119 LP ii. 338; LL, pp. 319–23.
120 See, for example: LP ii. 348–9; LL, p. 321.
121 LP ii. 327; LL, pp. 222, 308.

CHAPTER NINE

Political Principles

The political behaviour of an individual is always a dynamic phenomenon rooted in a matrix of beliefs and values; in essence, the restless, growing child of many fathers. Lockhart's basic assumptions about the nature of human beings and their social interactions were, therefore, always in play with a more coherent, formally logical set of political beliefs. The classical bent his political principles show suggests George acquired them in the course of his education, but it would be a mistake to see them as simply derivative. His ideas and analysis (and thence Lockhart the political actor) were the product of continuous dialogue between his core beliefs and the formal body of political thought he had internalised. It would seem reasonable also to suppose that he selected from his education certain key concepts that helped him make sense of what he saw going on around him and provided him with both ethical guidelines and justification for his own conduct.

Duty

The classics studied by the majority of the Scottish elite in the course of their education [1] taught that participation in the processes of government was a duty incumbent on every civilised human being with the leisure and intellectual wherewithal to do so. Aristotle, Seneca and the other classic writers on the subject all assumed that only through participation in government could a man fully realise his potential virtue, and Lockhart apparently took the lesson to heart.[2] Looking back over his career in 1717, he proclaimed his particular satisfaction that he knew

> that the King's service was the only motive that induced me to be a Parliament man in 1703, and to continue such at a great expence for above ten years, and that I never had a veiw in all the publick transactions and affairs wherin I had any concern, but to advance his interest; and I give all the world a defyance to make one instance when I ever spared my pains or my mony,

1 C. Kidd, 'The Ideological Significance of Scottish Jacobite Latinity', in J. Black and J. Gregory (eds), *Culture, Politics and Society in Britain, 1660–1800* (Manchester, 1991), pp. 110–25.
2 J. Warrington (ed.), *Aristotle's Politics and the Athenian Constitution* (1959), pp. 191–7; J. M. Cooper and J. F. Procopé (eds and translators), *Seneca. Moral and Political Essays* (Cambridge, 1995), xxiii–xxiv.

stood at dissobliding my nearest relations … consulted my private gain, or was backward to enter into any measure when his service was intended and likly to be promoted by it.[3]

Irrespective of its accuracy, this statement reveals that for George a commitment to doing the right thing regardless of the opinion of others was paramount. Hence his frank praise for the merchant 'Lows of Merchiston', whom he had asked for a financial contribution to the Stuart cause. Lows responded generously, but sternly refused any formal recognition or thanks from the exiled court, 'saying what he would doe, was only from a sense of his duty, and he desired neither thanks from the King nor praises from others', making him, in George's opinion, 'an example to others and a reproach to some'.[4]

Doing one's duty with respect to the state and society was, too, more important than any other obligation. Personal fears and feelings were absolutely secondary considerations. Hence when the Galloways baulked at becoming tutors for the young, orphaned 10th Earl of Eglinton for fear of subsequent litigation when he came of age, Lockhart roundly criticised them: 'The danger arising from ommissions is no relevant excuse; it may indeed affect and terrify a formall, narrow-chicken hearted pedant, but it can never penetrate so deep into the mind of a truly generous gratefull soul, as to prevent his performing the most essentiall duty to his deceast freind'.[5] Undutiful behaviour was a scandal as far as he was concerned and strongly coloured his opinion of those he believed were failing to meet their responsibilities. Thus the anti-Gillane group within the episcopal church were 'factious' and 'furiosi' for their defiance of those who had done their duty towards them.[6]

Yet despite his hard line on this issue, George held that duty and obedience were in a reciprocal relationship. Only those who did their duty to society could legitimately expect to receive their due in terms of deference and respect. As he solemnly told George junior:

as, after my decease, you become the head of the family and on that account a respect and regard is, in a more conspicuous degree, due to you from all my younger childeren, than any one of them can claim of another, so are you bound to employ the advantages and priviledges you enjoy for ther support and protection … And therfore as the younger childeren owe a deference and regard more than ordinary to the head of this society, so he again is bound by reciprocall obligations to perform all the offices of ther naturall father, whom he represents.[7]

3 LP i. 498.
4 LP ii. 93.
5 LP ii. 431.
6 LP ii. 326, 327, 333.
7 LP ii. 426.

Which strongly suggests that though Lockhart theoretically saw duty as an absolute, in reality he implicitly regarded it as conditional on the performance of their responsibilities by others. When this was not forthcoming, the individual's obligations towards those who were failing were suspended.

This, in turn, led him to withdraw his own obedience from those who, in his opinion, had failed to meet their responsibilities, and specifically to refuse to accord the Scottish nobility their accustomed due. As a 'humble' laird with conservative views on the social order George should have been willing to follow the lead of his noble betters, but in fact he consistently refused to do so after 1707.[8] His reasoning on the subject is instructive and comes out most clearly in a passage in the *Commentarys* approvingly relating the speech of Dougal Stewart of Blairhall on the 1709 decision by the Commons to exclude the eldest sons of Scottish peers from sitting in the lower house:

> ... to be thus dissappointed and neglected was a terrible mortification to them, and as great a satisfaction to others, who thought they richly deserved such and worse usage, as they had been the chiefe instruments in selling and betraying their countrey ... the Scots Commons did not think their libertys safe in the hands of these persons or their representatives, who to gratify their ambition had ruined the nation and sold their own birthright and priviledges.[9]

By taking this position George was obviously opening the way to the withdrawal of obedience by members of the lower orders who were dissatisfied with the conduct of the elite, but either that did not occur to him or he simply dismissed it. More importantly, it made the proper performance of one's duty even more crucial to good, harmonious social relations.

Disinterestedness

How to do one's duty uprightly and appropriately in a wicked and ungrateful world was a question that had much exercised classical political philosophers.[10] George drew directly on their thoughts on this subject for guidelines for his own conduct, and the key concepts that he seems to have taken especially to heart were disinterestedness, in the sense of a refusal to be swayed by personal motives or ambition, and honesty, in the sense of a selfless commitment to the pursuit of the good.

Thus at the outset of his political career, Lockhart presented himself as a man endeavouring 'to act with that honestie and impartiality towards every one,

---

8 LP i. 326, 338, 424, 437–8, 538; LL, p. 103.
9 LP i. 298–9.
10 See, for example: M. Causabon (transl.), *The Meditations of Marcus Aurelius* (repr. 1935), *passim*; Seneca. *Moral and Political Essays*, pp. 172–80.

that becomes a Gentleman ...' [11] And as it came to a close he clearly felt he had lived up to that ideal: 'I'me sure no part of my behaviour these 25 years bypast, that I enterd into publick affairs, will admit the least shadow of reason to think I postponed your [the Old Pretender's] or my countrie's service to any veiw or interest whatsoever ...'.[12] A self-image that underpinned his breathtaking assertion to Inverness in 1727, 'I thank God for't, I never was, and I beleive never will be of a party'.[13]

Indeed, the core of Lockhart's vision of himself lay in what he believed to be his lofty approach to politics and his selfless commitment to the Jacobite cause. From this Olympian height he felt entitled to judge and reprove the conduct of others, of whatever station. In 1708, for example, he prided himself on remaining committed to turn out as soon as the rebellion began despite the ill-judged sneers and jeers of the Atholl group of Jacobite conspirators, and in 1715 he declared he was not 'in the least disgusted' at having been excluded from the plotting that preceded the '15.[14] When other Jacobites became enmbroiled in factional disputes with each other, George was forthright in his condemnation: ''Tis a melancholy reflection to observe that in no case, even when wee run the most eminent hazard, people will lay asyde their litle partie, selfish ways of thinking and acting'.[15] Those Jacobites who, in his opinion, did not succumb to self-interest were the ones Lockhart most respected and wished to be associated with.[16] Thus despite the fact that Lord North and Grey had converted to catholicism, which as we have seen was not something liable to endear him to George, he praised him for his devotion to James's service and his lack of, 'by veiws'.[17] Even North and Grey's withdrawal from the Jacobite court to take up a commission in the Spanish service was a subject for praise, because thereby North and Grey discreetly veiled 'the unpolitick maxims and measures which the King pursued'.[18]

Lockhart's right to reprove ill-judged actions even extended, in the final analysis, to the highest ranks. He laid it out for Inverness in 1726 in the course of suggesting that since his tenure of the Secretary of State's office was the central issue in the Clementina affair he should resign:

> It is consistent with the rules I have layd down of acquainting the King or his ministers, fairly and without feud or favor, of everything that I think for

11 LL, p. 56.
12 LL, p. 326.
13 LL, p. 270. GL's hero, Fletcher of Saltoun, was similarly hostile to party distinctions: *Fletcher. Political Works*, p. 166.
14 SR, pp. 217–18; LP i. 484.
15 LL, p. 220.
16 SR, pp. 110–11, 133–4, 184.
17 LP ii. 337.
18 LP ii. 338.

his service, and I presume after due reflexion you will think it no disservice
done yourself, since by knowing what's layd to your charge, you may have
an opportunity of vindicating yourself, and at the same time do justice to our
common master.[19]

As far as he was concerned, 'I never will be persuaded that he who's directed
by the smallest selfish view in the present state of affairs, can have the least title
to be reputed an honest or loyall man'.[20] Even James himself was not above
such criticism from someone as morally sound as Lockhart, because 'I can
propose no benefite to my self from what I may represent, as I have not earthly
dependance upon any person or cause but you and yours, and as I can't pretend
any particular dissobligation from any person that has been or may be concernd
in your affairs'.[21] The upshot is that George's conviction that he was a disinterested actor insensibly drew him into the role of censor, which inevitably brought
him into conflict with conventional politics and politicians. It also, however,
almost certainly helped ease his passage out of politics and into retirement. As
far as he was concerned, he withdrew safe in the knowledge that he had done
the right thing, but had been brought down by the 'malice', 'private designs'
and 'faction' that 'predomine so much in all interests'.[22] And, of course, following
the classical precedents he had imbibed, he retired to do what all disinterested
patriots should do: write up his memoirs and reflect on the iniquity of the times.

Honesty

The other half of the dutiful, disinterested actor Lockhart wished to be was a
man who was never afraid to pursue the good even at significant personal cost.
In terms of practical politics, a man showed 'honesty' by honourable, open
commitment to a cause, appropriate gratitude and loyalty to patrons and
thoroughgoing consistency. His justification for such a potentially destructive
position derived from his vision of the history of his own times, as he revealed
in passing in a pamphlet on the Greenshields case in 1711: '[t]he changes and
vicissitudes in this age are so great ther's no sure game but acting honestly'.[23]
The corollary of which was that his assessment of other politicians was condi-
tioned by his opinion of their honesty.[24]

There is, of course, a tension here between the behaviour forced upon George
by his circumstances – he could hardly openly declare his adherence to the

19 LL, p. 270.
20 LL, p. 148.
21 LL, p. 326.
22 LL, p. 300.
23 LP i. 527.
24 SR, pp. 18–19, 34, 42–3.

exiled Stuarts if he wanted to be an effective actor on their behalf – and his ideals. He seems to have squared his conscience on this score by resting on the need for a certain degree of dissimulation in the regrettable situation he found himself in, particularly with respect to the oaths he was obliged to take against the exiled Stuarts. There he chose 'to venture ... [myself] ... in the hand of God rather than of such men as we have to do with'.[25] Which in his own mind justified his assertion in 1714 that he 'ever professt and aimd at one and the same thing, and what it was, was no great secret, and I could not accuse my self of having deviated from a close and steady pursuit of it'.[26] Twelve years later he revealed the same more explicitly to James:

> I'me none of these stingy folks that are affraid to speak above their breath but in a corner, but I endeavour withall, to have dealings with none but people of charactar, and hitherto with so much caution that I have escaped all inconveniencies, tho perhaps as many traps have been laid for me as most men these 20 years bypast.[27]

Lockhart was thus aware that his circumstances precluded him from fully living up to his own ideal of 'honesty'. And this in turn may go some way toward explaining the vehemence with which he condemned other politicians who failed to live up to his standards.

Thus, for example, the character sketch George wrote of Queensberry in his *Memoirs* is based on his own disgust at the duke's lack of gratitude towards James II and VII and his disloyalty in 1688.[28] When the Earls of Balcarres and Dunmore defected from the Cavaliers to the court in 1703, it was their inconsistency and lack of loyalty to their Stuart patrons that most offended him: 'Wretches of the greatest ingratitude! They owed all they had, and much they had squandered away, to King Charles and King James'.[29] Likewise the Earl of Cromarty's political vacillations justified Lockhart's description of him as 'so extreamly maggoty and unsettled that he was never much to be relyed upon or valued'.[30] The interplay between George's partisanship and this ideal of honesty also meant that his political opponents were automatically excluded from being truly honest men, for all that they might be consistent in their principles and grateful to their (antithetical) patrons. The best they could hope for from Lockhart

25 LL, p. 200. The 6th Earl of Home expressed much the same sentiments in 1703: 'My Ld Hume befor he took the oaths said he did great violence to his conscience on that occasion, but that he wold rather trust his soull in God's hands, than trust the Crown of Scotland in the hands of Hanover' (Blairs Letters 2/87/10: Lewis Innes to Alexander(?) Gordon, St Germain, 23 Apr. 1703).
26 LP i. 446.
27 LL, p. 300.
28 SR, pp. 11–12.
29 SR, p. 34.
30 SR, p. 43.

was the grudging admission that they were not personally malevolent. The Marquess of Tweeddale, for example, was 'a well-meaning, but simple, man', and 'the least ill-meaning man of his party, either through inclination or capacity'.[31] And George coloured his description of George Baillie of Jerviswood with unflattering comments about Baillie being 'morose, proud and severe', a 'dictator' to his party, and 'of a rebellious race', despite the fact that he had 'gained a great reputation by standing so stiffly by the interest of his country', during the reign of William III and II and was unflinchingly consistent in his commitment to the Hanoverian succession.[32] Lockhart's admiration for the republican-inclined Fletcher of Saltoun ('if ever a man proposes to serve and merit well of his country, let him place his [Fletcher's] courage, zeal and constancy as a pattern before him'[33]) might seem to contradict this crudely partisan delimitation of the ideal, but George clearly felt able to overlook Fletcher's republicanism for other reasons (see below, p. 209). Overall, it is clear, only those who aligned themselves with Lockhart could ever be truly honest.

In addition, the aspiration to selflessness that was part of George's ideal of honesty acted over time to disgust him with the normal workings of early eighteenth-century politics. Even taking into account his partisanship, his reaction to the behaviour of the Court party in 1703 is illuminating:

> And to see bribing and bullying of members, unseasonable adjournments and innumerable other ungentlemanny [sic] methods made use of to seduce and debauch people from the fidelity they owed to that which ought to be dearest to them – I mean the interest, welfare and liberty of their country and fellow-subjects, by whom they were entrusted in that office. These considerations, I say, enraged and emboldened a great number of members ...[34]

George laid the blame for this sorry state of affairs on the prince's need to corrupt the people's representatives in order to get his legitimate business done in an irresponsible assembly.[35] For even the uncorrupt amongst the mass of backbenchers were for the most part, as far as he was concerned, 'meer tools' who 'give themselves no trouble in business, and have no design in being chosen, even at a great expence, but to have the honour of being called Parliament men', and the pleasure of making 'a hideous noise like so many Bedlamites' on party issues.[36]

Despite this gathering alienation, his belief in 'honesty' could align him with these same irresponsible M.P.s when cross-party backbench measures rooted in

31 SR, p. 66.
32 SR, pp. 64–5.
33 SR, p. 45.
34 SR, p. 40.
35 LP i. 350.
36 LP i. 351.

Country ideals arose. Lockhart was always a supporter of place and resumption bills, and, as we have seen, his staunchness in this respect probably led directly to his being chosen to be a member of the Commission of Accounts.[37] In this area, too, he was occasionally able to see beyond his own political prejudices, and in 1714, for example, spoke against the ministry and the rest of the Tories in the debate on Queen Anne's grant of the Asiento to the South Sea Company on the grounds that:

> It is not any particular grant, out of prejudice to any particular person or party on whom it is bestowd, or by whose influence it is obtaind, that I am for reducing; for if each partie be allowd to support and maintain the grants bestowd under their own influence, the evill will never be remedied, for tho they shoud reduce what was granted by ther predecessors, they will inhance the same to themselves and thus take all, if not more, with one hand, than they give with the other. I am for wholesale work, by reassuming all that have past and discouraging all that may pass for the future, seeing they tend to impoverish the Crown and multiply taxes on the people ...[38]

Which implies that George's belief in honesty was more important to him than his party identity. In general terms his prejudices and partisanship effectively limited 'honesty' at large to those he was aligned with politically (i.e. Cavaliers and Jacobite Tories). But when he applied it to himself his praxis made it act independently of his Jacobite/Tory identity. Moreover, in the event of a clash between the two, the 'honest' George Lockhart could overbear the 'Jacobite/Tory' George Lockhart.

Unity

Lockhart's powerful concept of honesty, however, coexisted with an equally powerful belief in the necessity and virtue of unity and harmony among the Jacobites and Tories. As far as he was concerned, 'Ther is not any thing so essentially necessary for the King's service as a perfect good harmony and close concert amongst his friends', indeed, this was the *'unum necessarium'*.[39]

Throughout his life George took it for granted that he should always seek to act dutifully, selflessly and honestly. But even when he felt he had lived up to these ideals he was in principle prepared to sacrifice himself for what he conceived of as the greater good of the cause, in particular its unity.[40] Thus when the whole concept of a committee of Jacobite trustees acting on James's behalf in

---

37 See above, pp. 89, 91, 98–9.
38 LP i. 566.
39 LL, pp. 148, 244.
40 LL, pp. 24–9; LP i. 325.

Scotland came under severe criticism soon after its inception, Lockhart led the rest of the trustees in offering to give way

> chearfully ... to such other persons as are ambitious of and ... [the Old Pretender] ... thinks fit to employ in their stead, and by their absolute submission to the others' directions evidence to ... [the Old Pretender] ... and the world that they have not the honour which may accress to themselves so much at heart, as the prosperity of his affairs in whatsoever hands he thinks fit to lodge them.[41]

Likewise, he also expected that those whose occupation of positions of authority within the Jacobite court was disrupting the unity of the movement should be prepared to go as willingly as himself. 'The unanimity the King so earnestly recommended to yours here', he told James in 1726, 'is as necessary elsewhere, as all divisions give your enemies fresh hopes and new handles to work on, and mightily discourage those that are most active in your service'.[42] The corollary was that Inverness should forthwith resign his office or be dismissed.

Sustaining the unity of the Jacobite cause was also theoretically more important to George than personal scruples. Analysing the roots of Cavalier failure and presbyterian success in the Scottish Parliament, he observed that in large part these stemmed from the Cavaliers 'being of generous spirits, and designing good and just things, believe every man is so too, and are not at such pains as is necessary to cement a party's councils and measures together. Whereas the Presbyterians, ... [are] ... so closely linked together that all go the same way, and all either stand or fall together'. Consequently the Cavaliers' 'noble' practice 'ought never to be prosecuted until we are convinced of a general reformation of minds and manners. Which I am sure this age cannot in the least pretend to'.[43] In like fashion, though he certainly favoured a pragmatic response to the new oaths imposed in 1723 (i.e. that the Jacobites should resign themselves to the necessity of taking them in order to preserve themselves to overthrow the regime), his attempts to persuade the Old Pretender to intervene in the dispute in principle revolved around unity. 'Whatever course be taken and whatever be the consequences', he told James, 'sure I am a measure shoud be concerted and as unanimouslie as possibly followed, that is wee shoud either all swear or all stand out to the last extremity. For a division and doing things by halves lessen the credit and strength of the partie ...'.[44] Conversely, what he saw as the lack of adherence to this principle among the Jacobite leadership in part provided Lockhart with sufficient justification for his final retirement from an active role

41 LL, pp. 157–8.
42 LL, p. 261.
43 SR, p. 20.
44 LL, p. 195.

in furthering the Stuart cause in 1728. As long as 'subjects of the best quality and merit ... are trampled upon and abused by a parcell of people who never were nor will be capable to do the King any materiall service', those who might have adhered to the cause were 'highlie discouraged', and the cause 'consequently must daylie languish and in process of time be tottally forgot'.[45] Disunity was the mother of disaster.

If the principle of unity in party politics was important to Lockhart, it was, nonetheless, completely overshadowed by the semi-mystical value it acquired for him when national unity was at issue. Even in bitter retrospect in 1708 he was still clearly moved by what he remembered as the united opposition of the people of Scotland to the Union and their desire for a Jacobite restoration. 'For from hence arose that unanimity amongst the episcopals, presbyterians, Cavaliers and many of the Revolutioners, so that, according to the Scots proverb, "they were all one man's bairns", had the same desire, and were ready to join together in the defence of their country and liberties'.[46] Recalling the public reaction to the apparent imminence of a Franco-Jacobite landing in March 1708, he fondly related that 'in every person's face was to be observed an air of jollity and satisfaction'.[47] Indeed, whenever circumstances seemed to suggest that the Scottish nation was uniting behind the national cause George always made a heavy emotional investment in whatever was afoot even when the implications for the Jacobite cause were, at best, ambivalent. In 1713 he scorned the threats of the Oxford administration, which was seeking to deter him from continuing his attempts to work up a Parliamentary offensive against the Union, declaring he would be glad to have the 'honour' of being sent to the Tower because he was sure 'it woud exasperate and cement all Scotsmen that one of their number was so used, on no other account than asserting the rights and appearing in behalf of his countrey'.[48] Similarly in 1724 he was tremendously excited by the national reaction to the renewed malt tax – 'tis impossible to express the resentment of the nation at this measure, all partys seemed reconciled and to unite in opposing what was so pernicious to the country in general ...'.[49] – though the riots and associated agitation were virtually devoid of Jacobite content.

Even for someone as zealous and patriotic as Lockhart the enthusiasm with which he responded to events in 1708 and took up these later agitations is striking, as is the theme of unification which runs through his interpretation of events in general. The reason for his passion is, however, exposed in the course of his analysis of Scotland's downfall. There disunity, fomented by English machinations, was the true engine of national ruin. In the heroic days of yore

45 LP ii. 405.
46 SR, p. 212.
47 SR, p. 227.
48 LP i. 428–9.
49 LP ii. 134.

animosities and feuds proceeded from the quarrels of one family with another, or the ambition of some aspiring great man. But then the authority of the king did dissipate and quash them, and they never, or at least seldom, failed to be suspended when the honour and defence of their king or country required it. And if there was any who on such occasions did continue obstreperous, or side with the enemy, they were esteemed by all their fellow subjects, and declared and treated by the states, as rebels. So that the English seldom or never reaped much advantage of intestine divisions. And to this unanimous and hearty concurrence of all the subjects towards the defence of the country is chiefly to be ascribed the so long continuance and duration of the Scots kingdom and monarchy.

After the Reformation, however, religious divisions disrupted this consensus and the English were able to play upon them to such effect that 'the nation was totally divided and at odds'. The final outcome was that 'such grudges and heartburnings arose as have never been abated, far less extinguished, to this very day, and did at last bring the kingdom to ruin'.[50] Scotland's disunity in the face of the threat of absorption by the auld enemy even became part of the nation's divine punishment for its acquiescence in the killing of Mary Queen of Scots.[51] Reunifying the nation concomittantly acquired a blessed aspect. In George's eyes it would prefigure the (Jacobite) redemption he had worked for for so long. Unity was thus more than a pragmatic political ideal for Lockhart; it offered hope and perhaps even divine forgiveness for Scotland.

Legalism

Lockhart showed a strong inclination towards strict social order and moral propriety throughout his life.[52] In the political arena this expressed itself in a conviction that the law was a transcendent institution. 'We ought strictly', he observed in 1709, 'to obey the letter of the law'.[53] Unusually, moreover, given his customary partisanship, George applied this rule relatively even-handedly. Predictably, governmental legal/constitutional impropriety, such as the Scottish administration recalling King William's Scottish Parliament after the king's death, drew his forthright condemnation because it was 'inconsistent with the very nature and constitution of the Scots Parliament', and an 'overturning and trampling upon the most nice and sacred part of our constitution, the greatest preservative and bulwark of all that is near and dear to a free people'.[54] Likewise

50 SR, p. 245. Harry Maule shared GL's perception of the Reformation: Blairs Letters 2/228/16: Maule to Thomas Innes, London, 19 Mar. 1720.
51 SR, p. 249.
52 See above, pp. 162–3, 165–6.
53 LP i. 504.
54 SR, pp. 10, 17.

he was highly offended by the affront to precedent and equity implicit in the Aliens Act:

> it seems they had not advised with the learned Bacon or Coke, who would have taught them it was the constant unanimous opinion of all the judges and lawyers of England since the union of the two crowns that the *post nati*, that is those born in the other kingdom after the accession of the same monarch to be king of both kingdoms were, by the laws of nature and customs of all nations, freemen, and had an uncontroverted natural right to enjoy the privileges of the natural free-born subjects of the other kingdom.[55]

Yet Lockhart also believed in upholding the letter of the statute even when he fundamentally disagreed with the laws in question. Thus Scotland's technical constitutional position after the Union, in that it was not subject to England but that both kingdoms were dissolved and a new entity, Great Britain, was created, was something Lockhart insisted on respect for, though he sincerely believed that the whole relationship was a mockery.[56] 'Now that wee are united', he asserted in 1709,

> wee should reckon ourselves one and the same people and shun every occasion of giving jealousie to one another, and if wee designe to be happy, keep every article of the Union sacred and unviolable; the Union being like to a vault which is a foundation very strong and capable to bear a mighty structure, but the alteration of the least stone looses and brings the whole to ruin.[57]

And in the same vein George was willing to admit privately that a measure like the malt tax, "tho ... a burden too heavy to bear, ... was not however illegal',[58] and that the opponents of the Union were in the wrong in some of their tactics in 1706–7. 'I must acknowledge', he conceded of the anti-Unionists' plans for summoning masses of demonstrators to Edinburgh to intimidate the Scottish Parliament, 'both the stile and method of giving this advertisement [to go to Edinburgh] were very improper'.[59] Like many of his contemporaries (and much legal opinion since) he was also less concerned with justice than legality. Hence his outrage over the arrest of many leading Scottish anti-Unionists in the wake of the invasion attempt in 1708 and their transportation to London 'merely on account of suspicion and without any accusation or proof against them',[60] even though he knew they were absolutely guilty of treason (as, indeed, he was

---

55 SR, p. 83.
56 LP i. 504–5, 537.
57 LP i. 505.
58 LP ii. 141.
59 SR, p. 187.
60 SR, p. 232.

himself).[61] Similarly, he was outraged by the Whig regime's efforts to circumvent the legal chicanery the Jacobites and their lawyers resorted to in order to block their prosecution in the aftermath of the '15, despite the fact that it followed a major rebellion and the Whigs certainly had ample grounds in equity for seeking both redress and retribution.[62]

Lockhart's fixed belief in the necessity of upholding the law also directly affected his vision of the role of Parliament within the polity (Scottish and British). In almost all circumstances, as far as he was concerned, Parliament had the right and the authority to intervene in the lives of, and dictate to, the Scots and British respectively. He was correspondingly an active proponent of measures designed to override property and customary rights (with respect to coalmining) in the Scottish Parliament and a staunch supporter of English Tory attempts to intervene in the lives and education of the children of religious dissenters.[63] The only set of laws he regarded as unalterable by Parliament were the fundamentals of the polity.[64]

This caveat enabled George to sidestep a severe internal clash between his (basically incompatible) political principles. For while he was in general an uncompromising proponent of the 'awful majesty' of the law, his belief that there was an inviolable fundamental constitution, beyond any written law, saved him from the contradictions with respect to the existing order his political beliefs and commitments should have created. Without it Lockhart could not have operated within the post-Revolutionary polity and still believed himself to be an honest, upright patriot.

Monarchism

Though it is anachronistic in this period to use the term 'monarchism' to describe the instinctive assumption among ninety-nine per cent of British politicians that the core of the English, Scottish, Irish and British states was the monarchy, it is a useful anachronism for the purposes of our analysis here.[65] For in all its successive incarnations, Toryism in the British Isles has always been especially closely associated with what we would now denote as monarchism.[66] The Scottish Toryism Lockhart took up at the outset of his career was no exception. As may

---

61 SR, pp. 213–22.
62 LP i. 497; ii. 5–6.
63 SRO GD 1018: Baron John Clerk to Sir John Clerk of Penicuik, Edinburgh, 7 July 1703; *APS*, xi. 336; LP i. 569–74.
64 SR, p. 277.
65 Clark, *English Society*, pp. 121–98.
66 Clark, *English Society*, p. 52; R. M. Stewart, *The Foundation of the Conservative Party 1830–1867* (1978), xii; M. Francis and I. Zweiniger-Bargielowska (eds), *The Conservatives and British Society, 1880–1990* (1996), pp. 40–1. Also, cf. J. J. Sack, *From Jacobite to Conservative. Reaction and Orthodoxy in Britain, c. 1760–1832* (1993), pp. 112–45.

be seen from the name they adopted to describe themselves, the 'Cavaliers' in the Scottish Parliament[67] clearly wanted to suggest a connection with the Stuart loyalists/monarchists of the Great Civil War.

George correspondingly believed there was a sacred aspect to the institution of monarchy. 'All soveraigns are accountable only to God, ... and being of a rank and degree above the rest of mankind are to be used more tenderlie', he opined in a rebuttal of Salmon's *Review of the History of England*.[68] Through their special relationship with the deity and their supernatural nature monarchs symbolically represented the whole constitution, and a good subject was duty bound to support the institution and its incumbent regardless of personal cost. Thus the loyalists who suffered as a result of their support for the monarchy during the Great Civil War had no specific claim on the monarchy after it was restored 'for as the quarrell was not solely the King's, but equally the people's, in so far as the constitution was invaded and subverted, every member of the society were obliged in duty and interest to contribute in a matter that was nationall and so essentially affected the vitalls of the commonwealth'.[69] And George prided himself on his own record of upholding the institution. In a speech on the Asiento in 1714, for example, he asserted that, 'Ever since I had the honour to be a member of the Scots or British Parliaments, and in every station of my life, I have made it my profession and it has been my practice to support the Crown in all its just rights and prerogatives'.[70]

Implicit within Lockhart's vision of the monarchy is, too, the old medieval doctrine of the king's two bodies, i.e. the monarch who is frail, human and quite possibly erring, and the crown which is perfect and immortal.[71] He accordingly always saw those monarchs he accepted as at least semi-legitimate, i.e. Anne and the Old Pretender, as willing the good, even when their actions and policies met with his disapproval.[72] Anne was for him the 'compassionat Queen' whose indifference towards Scotland and patriotic measures designed to secure Scottish liberties was the result of her being imposed on by evil counsellors.[73] Likewise when the Old Pretender adamantly refused to accept Clementina's demand for Inverness's dismissal, George stalwartly maintained the fiction of his being misled by wicked courtiers as long as he could.[74]

Yet within the statement quoted above there is an implicit limitation. What

---

67 SR, pp. 27–8.
68 LP ii. 417.
69 LP ii. 420.
70 LP i. 564.
71 A. Black, *Political Thought in Europe 1250–1450* (Cambridge, 1992), pp. 189–90.
72 SR, pp. 57, 102; LP i. 425, 480.
73 SRO GD 150/3508/34 (Morton Muniments): GL to Lord Aberdour (son of the 12th Earl of Morton), Carnwath, 'Sunday night, past 11' [May-June, 1704?]; SR, pp. 57, 102.
74 LP ii. 221, 251, 322, 338, 404–5.

exactly were the crown's 'just rights and prerogatives'? In fact, Lockhart, like many other post-Revolutionary Scottish and English Tories, regarded the monarchy as a vital part (even the lynchpin) of the constitution, but still only a part of the whole.[75] Parliament, the church and the law all had a role (however subordinate) to play in the running of the kingdom, and none of them could legitimately be excluded or tampered with.[76] He accordingly viewed the Revolution of 1688 as 'only an alteration of one, though indeed a material, part of the constitution'.[77]

But as a patriotic, historically aware Scot, George could not and did not stop there. Underpinning the generally accepted justification for the Scottish War of Independence among his contemporaries was the belief that beyond the monarchy, and above its authority, was a fundamental constitution.[78] Hence his observation, in the context of a hypothetical situation in which a restored Stuart embraced the Parliamentary Union, that such an action, because it subverted the constitution of the kingdom, *de facto* terminated his allegiance to the monarch in question.[79] This position (which implied that the crown was a revocable trusteeship) owed a great deal to the presbyterian-Whig school of historiography current in Scotland at the time Lockhart was growing up.[80] It is therefore quite striking that he should deploy it as an argument for resistance to the Union, and suggests that his period of presbyterian education had a greater impact on him than might appear at first sight.

Lockhart's very orthodox vision of the monarch's role in the proper order of things in the British Isles was an important component in his political outlook. But its thoroughgoing, albeit not entirely episcopalian, ordinariness implies, too, that it cannot have been the core of his Jacobitism, otherwise staunch upholders of the existing order and the Hanoverian succession like Seafield and Sir Thomas Hanmer would have been Jacobites to the core. For the Jacobite moment that brought these ideas to an energising focus we must look elsewhere, in the complex of history, Anglophobia and patriotism that will be examined in the next section.

---

75 H. T. Dickinson, *Liberty and Property. Political Ideology in Eighteenth-Century Britain* (1977), pp. 28, 42–50.
76 See, for example, his implicit assumption that a future Scottish Parliament would play a major role in constructing a restoration settlement: LL, pp. 141, 252.
77 SR, p. 277.
78 M. Lynch, *Scotland. A New History* (rev. repr. 1994), p. 111; Kidd, *Subverting Scotland's Past*, pp. 17, 19–21.
79 SR, p. 277.
80 Kidd, *Subverting Scotland's Past*, pp. 86–9; D. Allan, *Virtue, Learning and the Scottish Enlightenment. Ideas of Scholarship in Early Modern History* (Edinburgh, 1993), pp. 33–7, 41–2.

CHAPTER TEN

The Jacobite Moment

Viewed in abstract terms, the fundamental beliefs and the political ideals reviewed above were necessary components of Lockhart's Jacobitism. If he had not believed in honour, revenge, honesty, unity, and so on, he probably would not have been a Jacobite. But in themselves they are not *sufficient* to explain him. In particular, they do not explain why he chose to launch himself into the Jacobite wilderness rather than follow his family's traditional path of service to the state. Many of his contemporaries shared his opinions with regard to the nature of society, the family, the monarchy, etc. But they did not become committed Jacobites. There clearly had to be something else in his mentalité that brought him to this pass; some kind of crucial, watershed decision, factor or event in his life. In effect, a Jacobite moment.

The idea of vital, recurring moments/problems in the history of ideas is now common currency. It was first developed by John Pocock, in his enormously influential book, *The Machiavellian Moment*.[1] Since, however, the Jacobite moment I envisage below differs markedly from the development of a secular political self-consciousness in sixteenth-century Florence and its ramifications for Anglo-American civilisation, as outlined by Pocock, my appropriation of the term demands some justification.

Upbringing, education, experience and personal psychology all undoubtedly influence a given human being's choices, but the decision to adhere to one group or another, to act or remain quiescent, etc, are, in the final analysis, personal and individual. If, however, we study a large enough sample of human beings, we may be able to discern a common pattern in the decision-making of particular groups and types among them. This is the essence of the political history of mentalities. And in the Jacobite context I would argue that there was a common body of assumptions and beliefs that created a recurring sense of confrontation and crisis between a section of the Scottish elite and the post-Revolutionary order. This was the Jacobite moment writ large. What follows below is an attempt to identify what lay at the heart of George Lockhart's Jacobite moment.

1 J. G. A. Pocock, *The Machiavellian Moment: Florentine Political Thought and the Atlantic Republican Tradition* (Princeton, 1975), vii–ix.

Religion

It is now generally accepted that the eighteenth century was still an age of faith.[2] Hence the ideology of Jacobitism, with its heavy emphasis on a divinely ordained royal succession, naturally reflected the religious nature of its adherents' commitment to the cause of the exiled Stuarts.[3] Moreover, their (and in particular Lockhart's) deity was constantly involved in and directing the course of human affairs. In conventional fashion, George therefore ascribed generally fortuitous results to divine intervention. Thus several of the great families of Scotland were saved from disaster at Queensberry's hands through the medium of his trumped-up 'Scots plot' because 'the wise providence of God discovered and brought to light the hellish contrivance'.[4] Similarly God's direct intervention was apparent to Lockhart not only in the dreary succession of Jacobite failures from 1689 to 1717 ('they were more occasioned by the immediate interposition of God and visible hand of God than the power and contrivance of their enemies'[5]), but also in the Jacobites' survival. For Lockhart the divisions in the Whigs' ranks that allowed the Scots Jacobite community to escape crippling retribution in the aftermath of the '15 were a clear-cut example of this: 'it pleased God, by their divisions and animosities, to pave a way for the preservation of vast numbers, who, in all probability, would otherwyse have mett with no mercy'.[6]

But Lockhart carried God's role further than many of his patrician contemporaries. In his world omens and indications of divine will were constantly present. In 1703 the rolls were being called in the Scottish Parliament on the question of whether a bill making it high treason to impugn the authority of Parliament or to dispute or seek to change the Claim of Right should pass, when:

> the greatest rain that was ever seen come from the heavens, which made such a noise upon the roof of the Parliament-house (which was covered with lead) that no voice could be heard and the clerks were obliged to stop. Whereupon, as soon as it ceased, Sir David Cunningham of Milncraig took the occasion to tell the house, 'It was apparent that the heavens declared against their procedure'.[7]

Apparently aware that his inclusion of this anecdote invited charges of superstition from his more sceptical contemporaries, George defensively added, 'though this be but a trifle, I inclined not to pass it altogether by'.[8]

---

2 J. Black, *Eighteenth Century Europe 1700–1789* (1990), pp. 187–90.
3 Dickinson, *Liberty and Property*, p. 29.
4 SR, p. 49.
5 LP i. 480–1.
6 LP ii. 4.
7 SR, pp. 36–7.
8 SR, p. 37.

It is clear, however, from their intermittent appearance in something as formal and stereotyped as his personal political memoirs, that in fact such unusual events were more than 'a trifle' to him. Lockhart implicitly believed in portents, apparitions and witchcraft.[9] One of the few occasions when he chose to attend a Scots Privy Council meeting after September 1703, other than those on the Scots plot, came in June 1704, when it met to hear the case for a prosecution of the Pittenweem witches.[10] When George I died suddenly in 1727 a story circulated that on her deathbed his wife, incarcerated since he divorced her on grounds of adultery in 1694, had sent the king a message summoning him 'to appear within the year and a day at the Divine tribunall and ther to answer for the long and many injuries she had received from him'.[11] Lockhart clearly believed the story and recorded it and its alleged provenance in detail.[12] Likewise, though he affected a certain scepticism, he nonetheless solemnly passed on to Sir John Graeme, briefly James's Secretary of State in 1727–28, an account of predictions by 'Meg Malloch', one of which was that George I would soon die and others that events would soon come to pass 'that would make us all rejoice', because, 'taking it altogather, there's something pritty remarkable in it'.[13] Ultimately, as Lockhart declared in 1708, 'I can never suffer myself to despond, or doubt, but that, some time or other, God will bless such resolutions and endeavours [i.e. Jacobite conspiracies] with success by restoring the nation to its ancient rights and liberties', he was predisposed to see and believe in omens that suggested God loved the Jacobites and that a restoration was nigh.[14] When he began to despair of their divine favour and ultimate success, his ability to function effectively within the Jacobite underground rapidly waned.[15]

Lockhart's religious alignment (sincere episcopalianism) also bore directly on his image of himself as an honourable political actor and on his behaviour in that role. Despite his conviction that revenge (the antithesis of the largely conventional Christianity he otherwise espoused) was in many circumstances a divinely approved activity, in his own mind George's honour was closely associated with his religion. This may be seen in the close linkage of the concepts 'Christian' and 'gentleman', which recur in his public and private writings

---

9 Such beliefs were not uncommon among the elite at this time: *Burt's Letters*, i. 241, ii. 15–19, 211–13.
10 SRO PC 1/53: Acta, June 1703-Apr. 1707, p. 245: 13 June 1704.
11 LP ii. 352.
12 LP ii. 351–2.
13 LL, p. 310.
14 SR, p. 5. This was a common trait among episcopalian Jacobites, for examples of which see: Blairs Letters 2/124/11: Carnegy to Thomas Innes [Edinburgh], 19 Mar. 1706; 2/134/3: Bishop William Nicolson to Thomas Innes [Edinburgh], 17 Aug. 1706; 2/211/6: Duke of Perth to ?, 9 Feb. 1716; 2/201/11: Carnegy to Thomas Innes [Edinburgh?], 24 Apr. 1716.
15 Cf. LL, p. 184; LP ii. 405.

whenever he wants to signal the basis of his own honourable conduct or his approval of that of others.[16] But most importantly of all, his conception of honourable religious conduct was centred on a particular, powerful vision of Scotland's part in the divine plan.

Episcopacy played a pivotal role in this vision. Of all forms of church government he believed it to be the most 'agreeable to the word of God', and that it was 'orthodox and primitive' compared to its presbyterian alternative.[17] In addition, he believed the pre-Reformation Kirk to have been superior to virtually every other church in Europe (and obviously in particular to the Church of England): 'Here the Christian religion soon took footing, and was preserved in purity, when most other nations were corrupted. And though in process of time the church of Scotland became, as did the rest of Europe, subject to the Papal hierarchy, yet she was among the first that shaked it off'.[18] Moreover, the special, pure nature of Scottish Christianity had created a bond of cosmic significance with the deity. Lockhart never fully explained his thinking on the subject in any of his surviving writings, but his conclusions are clear: like the Jews of the pre-Christian era, the Scots had forged a unique relationship with God. For obvious reasons he did not want to use the concept of a 'covenanted people', yet that is exactly what he seems to have envisaged. He hinted at this when criticising the folly of the Scots Parliament in not legislating for an end to the Union of Crowns on the death of James VI:

> But the truth on't is, the preceeding gloomy, and the hopes of better, times, drew people in to neglect this measure, and King James proved so kind to his countrymen (many of them he advanced to great posts in England) that others, without thinking, drove on till they had run themselves and country over head and ears into the gulf, though they might have forseen that as a Pharoah arose who proved unmindful of, and unkind to, the Jews, so their beloved king (who, being born and bred amongst them, knew and loved them) could not always live, and would be succeeded by kings strangers to them, who would rule them as seemed most for the advantage of their other designs.[19]

But he was far more explicit when he sought to explain why God had allowed Scotland to fall subject to England in 1707:

> The Jews were God's chosen people, and he assumed a more particular and immediate share in the administration of affairs in Jewry than in other nations,

---

16 SR, p. 57; LP ii. 425; LL, pp. 58, 314.
17 SR, p. 8; LP i. 549. 'Primitive' was an appellation denoting approval of a particular doctrine or practice for most theologians and theologically-concerned laymen at this time.
18 SR, p. 242.
19 SR, p. 247.

but upon their rebelling against him and his anointed, he gave them up to the power and laws of a forreign people, and at last subverted their monarchy, defaced their government, destroyed their country, and, as the greatest temporal curse, cut them off from having the name of a people on the face of the earth. How near a relation there is betwixt the gross and crying sins of the Jews, and those of Scotland, and what a resemblance there is in their punishment, let such who have been the instruments of the first, or executing the last, seriously consider.[20]

George's conviction that the Scots had become God's new chosen people is clearly of a piece with the views of a good number of seventeenth-century divines, as analysed recently by Arthur Williamson.[21] In this Lockhart was not exceptional. What is striking, however, is that the great majority of these writers were thoroughgoing presbyterians, whose views were usually anathema to Lockhart.[22] Failing further evidence, it would seem likely that this particular belief, embellished and reinforced by his patriotism, was a relic from his early years of enforced presbyterian education.

Whatever its origins it had profound implications for his analysis of Scotland's past and ultimately his own conduct and behaviour. If the Scots were God's new chosen people, then it was the bounden duty of individual Scots to maintain the integrity and virtue of the kingdom he had given them and to uphold God's laws, regardless of loss to themselves.[23] 'A good Christian', he told his sister-in-law Lady Galloway, 'is not affrighted from his duty, by the difficultys that attend it'.[24] This was even more incumbent on the divinely selected monarchs of Scotland, and so when James VI transgressed by failing to avenge the 'murder' of his mother, it was inevitable that the nation as a whole would be punished.[25] The Scots people then compounded the original offence by their rebellions against Charles I and James II and VII: 'For sure it was both their duty and interest to have assisted and supported them against their rebellious subjects of England, but to act the part they did was, besides the folly, such a crime as I am afraid is not wholly as yet avenged, and has no small share in bringing us to the miserable state to which we are reduced'.[26] The only question

20 SR, p. 249.
21 A. Williamson, '"A Pil for Pork-Eaters": Ethnic Identity, Apocalyptic Promises, and the Strange Creation of the Judeo-Scots', in R. B. Waddington and A. Williamson (eds), *The Expulsion of the Jews. 1492 and After* (1994), pp. 237–58.
22 Interestingly, Williamson notes (*op. cit.*, pp. 238–9) that this vision of the Scots was shared by many early seventeenth-century episcopalian divines; Lockhart could therefore be nothing more than a late example of the same tendency within episcopalianism.
23 SR, pp. 37, 83; LP i. 422, 609–12; ii. 159; LL, pp. 141, 287.
24 LP ii. 432.
25 SR, pp. 248–9.
26 SR, p. 249.

arising from this sombre vision of Scotland's recent past and likely future was how best to retrieve the situation.

When, and in what circumstances, God would forgive the Scots for their sins was, of course, unknowable. All that the faithful could do was try and abide by divine law. In which context it was incumbent on George Lockhart of Carnwath to join all 'honest' Scotsmen in restoring the Stuarts. The consequences of failure would be terrible: a further compounding of Scotland's original sin. 'O Calidon', he lamented in a song he penned probably some time after 1717, 'Against your King you did rebell, abjure the royall race/For which just Heaven did punish you with woe contempt disgrace ... till you justice do to him, you need not think to thrive'.[27] All of which by implication elevated George to a special status: in his own eyes he was one of Scotland's saving remnant. If there was one uniquely powerful moment/catalyst in Lockhart's passage into the Jacobite wilderness it lay in his conviction that the Scots were a chosen people and its corollary that it was the duty of all good Scotsmen to embrace the cause of the exiled Stuarts and thereby redeem their nation.

History

Colin Kidd and David Allan have recently demonstrated the fundamentally historicist nature of Scottish political discourse in the early eighteenth century, and that there were by then well-established episcopalian and presbyterian schools of interpretation.[28] Lockhart obviously favoured the episcopalian variant, but his upbringing left him familiar with its presbyterian counterpart. In any event, like the majority of his peers, George's view of contemporary Scotland was heavily coloured by his chosen vision of Scotland's past.[29]

Thus, for example, when he denounced the Union commissioners as traitors, he couched his attack in terms of a mystical debt to the current generation's heroic forbears:

> observe, how pitifully they abandoned their proposal of a foederal, and accepted of an incorporating, union, basely betraying and meanly giving up the sovereignty, independency, liberty, laws, interest and honour of their native country, in defence whereof their fathers had chearfully exposed their lives and fortunes and gained immortal praise and glory throughout all the world, bravely maintaining and defending the same against all attempts of

27 LP ii. 409–11.
28 Kidd, *Subverting Scotland's Past*, p. 27; Allan, *Scottish Enlightenment*, p. 79.
29 SR, p. 244; LP ii. 423–4; D. Duncan (transl. and ed.), *History of the Union of Scotland and England by Sir John Clerk of Penicuik. Extracts From his 'De Imperio Britannico'* (Scottish History Society, Edinburgh, 5th Ser., 1993), *passim*; Abercromby, *Martial Achievements*, *passim*; Johnstone, *Memoirs of the Rebellion*, p. 181.

the Britons, Romans, Saxons, Danes, Normans and English, and all other foreign and domestic enemies for the space of above two thousand years.[30]

In this he was in accord with other episcopally-inclined opponents of the Union such as Belhaven and Hamilton, whose rhetoric on the Union also dramatically evoked the ghosts of Scotland's heroes (whatever their private inclinations on the subject may have been).[31]

Lockhart seems to have diverged from them, however, in his perception of the course of Scottish history. We have already noted the religious significance for George of the trial and execution of Mary Queen of Scots. In this context, though, it is significant, given his fixation on the need for national unity, that Lockhart projected onto her reign a peacefulness and order it certainly never enjoyed and dismissed all the evidence of her involvement in the murder of Darnley as 'villanous forgerys'.[32] He also asserted that there was a direct historical connection between the trial and execution of Mary and that of her grandson, Charles I: 'it is observeable that not many years after this first instance of such a tragicall case existed, it served as a precedent in England, to the King's being judged, condemned and put to death by a power and authority proceeding from the Majestie of the people',[33] despite the fact that no such precedent was cited by the Court of High Commission that was charged with trying the king.[34] Also, quite apart from contemporary mythistory that was generally accepted at the time, such as the ancient, unbroken succession of Scotland's kings,[35] George subscribed to a number of other quasi-historical beliefs that played a critical role in sustaining his special vision of Scotland. Lockhart's Scotland was unique because it was 'never conquered nor under the dominion of any other prince or state whatsoever', unlike England.[36] The Kirk was exceptional because it was 'preserved in purity, when most other nations were corrupted', and though it eventually succumbed to Papal imperialism, 'yet she was among the first that shaked it off'.[37] Scotland of old was so powerful that even Charlemagne sought an alliance with King Achaius, 'which their posterity for many ages kept so inviolably, and proved so advantageous for both the kingdoms of France and

30 SR, p. 131.
31 SR, p. 160; [Lord Belhaven] *Lord Beilhaven's Speech in Parliament, the Second Day of November 1706, on the Subject of an Union Betwixt the two Kingdoms of England and Scotland* ([Edinburgh] 1706), pp. 2, 3. Fletcher too, believed that the Scots had in former ages defeated successive waves of invaders because of their martial abilities: *Fletcher. Political Works*, p. 150.
32 LP ii. 416.
33 LP ii. 417.
34 S. R. Gardiner, *The Constitutional Documents of the Puritan Revolution 1625–1660* (3rd edn, Oxford, 1906), pp. 357–8, 371–4.
35 SR, p. 239; Kidd, *Subverting Scotland's Past*, pp. 78–80.
36 SR, p. 239.
37 SR, p. 242.

Scotland, that no history relates the parallel of it'.[38] Entirely from their own resources the Scots were able to maintain their liberty and honour 'against all attempts of the Britons, Romans, Saxons, Danes, Normans and English, and all other foreign and domestic enemies for the space of above two thousand years'.[39] And even the old Scottish royal navy defeated its English counterpart.[40]

The events George selected as having brought down this uniquely tough and successful polity are equally suggestive. The onset of Scotland's troubles, though he never directly criticised the event itself, came with the arrival of the Reformation in Scotland.[41] This played a crucial role in his explanation of Scotland's downfall. For with the Reformation (according to Lockhart, for the first time) came serious internecine conflict, with the result that by the time of the Union of Crowns 'the people were weary of these wars, civil and foreign, which had raged in the country for so many preceding years'. This in turn paved the way for the exhausted political nation's rash embrace of the Union of Crowns when their 'beloved' King James inherited the English throne.[42] Because they neglected to secure guarantees of Scotland's independent status, 'the union of the two crowns may be reckoned the fatal era from whence we are to commence Scotland's ruin'.[43] To Lockhart it was obvious, and a historical fact, that from that point onwards

> the king would lie under a necessity of siding with and pleasing the most powerful of his two kingdoms, which were jealous of, and rivals to, one another, and that therefore ever after the union of the crowns the king would not mind, at least dare, encourage the trade of Scotland, and that all state affairs would be managed, laws made and observed, ministers of state put in and turned out, as best suited with the interest and designs of England.[44]

The Great Civil War and the Restoration then compounded Scotland's English problem by ruining, through wartime destruction and peacetime neglect, the patriotic loyalists who stood by the Stuarts in their hour of need.[45] For Lockhart was in no doubt that Charles II 'and the political maxims and veiws of that

---

38 SR, p. 243. Johnstone shared GL's belief in the length of the auld alliance: *Memoirs of the Rebellion*, p. 180.

39 SR, p. 131. In the same vein the Chevalier de Johnstone believed the Scots had successfully, 'withstood them [the English] during a long and almost uninterrupted war of a thousand years' (*Memoirs of the Rebellion*, p. 35).

40 SR, p. 243.

41 SR, p. 245. This ambivalence regarding the Reformation in Scotland was shared by other episcopalian writers, for which see: Blairs Letters 2/228/16: Harry Maule of Kellie to Thomas Innes, London, 19 Mar. 1720; 2/277/15: Archibald Seton to Thomas Innes, Aberdeen, 1 Feb. 1725; R. Wodrow, *Analecta*, iii. 414.

42 SR, pp. 245–6.

43 SR, p. 245.

44 SR, pp. 246–7.

45 LP ii. 420–3.

period' (i.e. the allegedly Anglo-presbyterian bent of metropolitan government), neglected to re-establish Scotland's loyalist interest, with the result that the dynasty's former friends sat 'with their hands across' when it was confronted by the Revolution of 1688.[46]

Obviously this complex of mythistory could be dismissed as simply conventionally accepted verities, or straightforwardly partisan error, on Lockhart's part. He was, however, quite a keen amateur historian and for many years was a close friend of famous antiquarian/historical scholars like Harry Maule and Patrick Abercromby, who – it seems likely – read much of his material and could have corrected him on errors such as these, which were certainly apparent to more hostile contemporary commentators.[47] That they survive in both the 1708 and corrected, 1717, version of *The Memoirs* and underpin the assumptions that buttress the rest of his *oeuvre* is then important; it suggests they accord with a reality Lockhart and his friends wanted to have existed. The belief that Scotland had once been strong, proud, successful and beloved of God made Lockhart determined to reattain that blessed state. How could he do otherwise and be a 'true' Scot?

Anglophobia

Golden visions of a lost Scotland were an essential component of Lockhart's Jacobite moment; hatred of those he blamed for destroying it was the other side of the same coin. Anglophobia suffused his historical vision, and, indeed, his whole political outlook.

Historically, as far as George was concerned, England was always Scotland's problem.[48] The only reason his religious *bête noire*, presbyterianism, had ever gained a foothold in Scotland, he believed, was the support it had had from England.[49] Novel religious divisions may have disrupted the fabled unity of the Scottish polity, but it was Elizabeth I who 'so fomented and encouraged these divisions (by supporting the weaker party and keeping the contenders in as equal power as possible that they might destroy one another) that the nation was totally divided and at odds'.[50] Much to its disadvantage, Scotland had been dragged into wars fomented by the arrogant English.[51] The neglect of Stuart

---

46 LP ii. 420, 424.
47 LL, p. 15: GL to the Duke of Hamilton, [before 26 Mar.] 1705; p. 73: GL to Harry Maule of Kellie [London], 29 Apr. [1713]; p. 79: GL to ? [London], 28 May [1713]; Blairs Letters 2/173/20: Carnegy to Thomas Innes [Edinburgh?], 1 Nov. 1712; SRO GD 220/5/434/2: Sir David Dalrymple to Montrose, Edinburgh, 2 Dec. 1714.
48 SR, pp. 239–40.
49 LP i. 526.
50 SR, p. 245. Harry Maule took a similar view: Blairs Letters 2/228/16: Maule to Thomas Innes, London, 19 Mar. 1720.
51 SR, p. 37.

loyalists after the Great Civil War stemmed from selfish English calculations of personal and national advantage.[52] The Darien disaster was not owing to any failure on the part of the Royal Company of Scotland or its backers, but to 'the barbarous treatment Scotland received from her neighbours of England'.[53] England and the English were a malign presence throughout Lockhart's vision of Scottish history.

It is tempting to speculate that an uncomfortable awareness of his half-English ancestry may have underlain the vehemence with which George expressed his Anglophobia, but it would be straining the evidence to do so as he never mentions or excuses the fact in any context, and (as far as I am aware) was never criticised on that score by any of his contemporaries. Nor was he exceptional among the Scottish elite either in his hostility to England and English influences or, in many cases, for the passion with which he expressed it.[54] What was unusual about Lockhart's Anglophobia was the way he rationalised it.

The root cause of his, and other Scotsmen's, antipathy to England was, George argued, English arrogance. 'It is well known the English vanity and self-conceitedness reaches so far as to despise all kingdoms but their own, and all people but themselves, on which account the world hates them'.[55] Correspondingly, they had a 'natural aversion' to the bold, generous Scots 'which made them snap at all occasions of bearing hard on Scotland'.[56] The English were, moreover, able to make their malevolence tell through the pusillanimity of Scotland's governors

> For had they valued themselves as they ought to have done, and not so meanly and sneakingly prostituted their honour and country to the will and pleasure of the English ministry, they would never have presumed to usurp such dominion over Scotland as openly and avowedly to consult upon and determine in Scots affairs.[57]

As a result, Lockhart believed, the English ministers were able to do as they

---

52 *LP* ii. 420–3.

53 *SR*, p. 172.

54 *APS*, xi. 325: 15 Nov. 1706; *History of the Union*, pp. 20, 81–2, 83; SRO GD 45/14/352/10: Lord Balmerino to Harry Maule, London, 2 June [1711]; B. Lenman and J. S. Gibson (eds), *The Jacobite Threat. Rebellion and Conspiracy 1688–1759: England, Ireland, Scotland and France* (Edinburgh, 1990), pp. 97–8: Daniel Defoe to Harley [Edinburgh], 9 Aug. 1707; SRO GD 220/5/434/11: Sir David Dalrymple to Montrose, Edinburgh, 18 Dec. 1714; *Fletcher. Political Works*, p. 141; Johnstone, *Memoirs of the Rebellion*, pp. 152, 157.

55 *SR*, p. 239. A perception of English xenophobia shared by Fletcher of Saltoun: *Fletcher. Political Works*, p. 197, and noted by Burt among Lowland Scots generally: *Burt's Letters*, ii. 273 (Burt also read the *Memoirs* and apparently felt that GL had a point with regard to English arrogance regarding foreign ways: ii. 334).

56 *LP* i. 421. Fletcher, too, saw the English as the natural enemies of the Scots (*Fletcher. Political Works*, p. 197).

57 *SR*, p. 48.

pleased with Scotland and entirely to disregard its interests in their political calculations.[58] The monarchy could not act as a brake on this pattern of intrusion and abuse because it was obliged to pay greater heed to the richer, more powerful kingdom in formulating policy and was also 'under English influence and subject to the councils of … English ministers, who regarded the interest and honour of Scotland no farther than was consistent with that of England'.[59] In turn, the reason for the Scottish ministers' supineness in the face of the English menace was that they had effectively been deracinated. Since the Union of Crowns the nobility and many of the gentry had been 'corrupted' and become 'renegados'.[60] Hence when fulminating on the subject of the English Parliament's Aliens Act of 1705, Lockhart could observe in passing: 'when I say Scots, I exclude the Courtiers and mercenary members of Parliament from the category'.[61] The simple fact of their submission to the English ministers excluded them from the community of 'true Scotsmen'.[62]

Lockhart's image of the typical Englishman was the natural converse of the 'brave, generous, hardy' and 'polite' Scots of his imagined community.[63] George's English were vain, haughty and hated the Scots; in sum: 'a people generous to none and avowed enemies to our country'.[64] They were also inattentive to public business and careless of their real interests if it was at any time inconvenient to attend to them. As he splenetically declared in 1713: 'ane English Tory woud not overroost his beef to save the nation from ruin'.[65] The root of their fecklessness was a national propensity towards inconstancy and laziness. 'The English nation', he contemptuously observed in 1728, 'is remarkably fond of novelties', and consequently George had little use for them.[66] 'Mr Edgar [the English]', he told the Old Pretender in 1718, 'is so frantick and infatuated a spark, I have litle regard to his rantings and ravings'.[67] Moreover, this low opinion of the English was not party specific. Lockhart's contempt for them as a nation extended to the English Jacobites too:

58 SR, pp. 10, 11, 39–40; LP ii. 103.

59 SR, p. 102. Here GL was again in accord with Fletcher of Saltoun (*Fletcher. Political Works*, pp. 132–4, 141, 160), and, too, with the Chevalier de Johnstone (*Memoirs of the Rebellion*, p. 36).

60 SR, p. 248.

61 SR, p. 83.

62 Fletcher of Saltoun first took this position in 1703: *Fletcher. Political Works*, pp. 145, 160.

63 SR, pp. 240, 241. See B. Anderson, *Imagined Communities. Reflections on the Origins and Spread of Nationalism* (3rd impression, 1986), pp. 15–16, for the concept of the 'imagined community'.

64 SR, p. 171. An opinion shared by Johnstone: *Memoirs of the Rebellion*, p. 76.

65 LL, p. 73.

66 LP ii. 351. Johnstone likewise commented scornfully on the same subject: *Memoirs of the Rebellion*, pp. 77–8.

67 LL, p. 129.

I have often and long observed both from publick transactions and private conversations that the bulk of the English, nay even such of them as are most in the King's interest, have a national antipathy to Scotsmen, and [are] particularly jealous of their having the honour of being too active and instrumental in your restoration. Any measure for that end which has its rise from Scotland will not I fear be well seconded, as if undertaken by the English. In the next place, tho over a botle or even in their most serious consultations, they are enough sensible of their unhappy state, and seem willing to enter into measures for their deliverance, yet many of them are to so intoxicated with the love of ease and plenty that they are backward to enter into action, and would willingly cast the brunt of the first attempt on Scotsmen, and wait to declare and take a part, till they see how matters are like to go ...[68]

The upshot was that as far as George was concerned the entire English nation were arrogant, jealous, destructive and worthless (though it is fair to point out that he seems to have made individual exceptions).[69] Given his belief in Scotland's uniquely glorious historical record and its cosmic significance, this view of the English enemy was such as to compel his commitment to any cause that would hold them at bay.

Patriotism

Every modern nationalism has at its heart a beautiful, fruitful country and a noble people, neither of whom ever existed. Lockhart's imaginary Scotland was cut from the same cloth:

> though Scotland is not the best, yet neither is it the worst, country in Europe, and God has blessed it with all things fit for human use, either produced in the country itself, or imported from foreign countries, by barter with its product. So that the necessaries, and even comforts and superfluities of life, are as plentiful there as any where else.
>
> ... As the Scots were a brave, so likewise [they were] a polite people. Every country has its own peculiar customs, and so had Scotland, but, in the main, they lived and were [as] refined as other countries ... And as it is obvious that at this very time (which must chiefly proceed from this humour of travelling) the Scotch gentry do far exceed those of England, so that in the one you shall find all the accomplishments of well-bred gentlemen and in your country English esquires all the barbarity imaginable ...[70]

---

68 LL, p. 232. An assessment of the English with which Johnstone concurred: *Memoirs of the Rebellion*, p. 61.

69 LL, pp. 23, 102, 252; LP ii. 337. Johnstone also made individual exceptions to his general dislike of the English: *Memoirs of the Rebellion*, p. 270.

70 SR, pp. 240, 241.

And, given George's religious beliefs, historical vision and hostility to the English, it was a short step from this sense of pride in place and *volk* to a militant, uncompromising willingness to defend both.

The final ingredient in Lockhart's Jacobite moment was, then, his commitment to a classically-inspired concept of patriotism. He obviously imbibed it in the course of the education common to men of his rank, but in his case it seems to have made a permanent impact on his outlook. His ideal of patriotism is most clearly seen in his character sketch of Fletcher of Saltoun, which is an encomium in terms that would have been familiar to Polybius, Tacitus and many other classical authors:[71]

> Being elected a Parliament man in the year 1703, he shewed a sincere and honest inclination towards the honour and interest of his country. The thoughts of England's domineering over Scotland was what his generous soul could not away with. The indignities and oppression Scotland lay under galled him to the heart, so that in his learned and elaborate discourses he exposed them with undaunted courage and pathetick [i.e. moving] eloquence.[72]

And though he was praising Fletcher, it is not pressing the evidence too far to suggest that George was in large part describing his own aspirations, as may be seen from his concluding statement on the subject: 'if ever a man proposes to serve and merit well of his country, let him place [Fletcher's] courage, zeal and constancy as a pattern before him'.[73] For Lockhart patriotism was an overriding absolute. Precisely because Fletcher was such a model patriot George could forgive him both his presbyterianism and his republicanism, and precisely because the nobility of Scotland had, for the most part, embraced the Union he exulted in their every discomfiture.[74]

Even the monarchy and the Stuart dynasty took second place to this patriotic ideal. Lockhart seems to have been aware that his ideals were in conflict on this subject, and tried to see king and country as 'one and the same under different appellations'.[75] It is, however, apparent from those occasions when he tried to envisage a future in which Scotland's interests and those of the Stuart dynasty diverged that the two were not evenly balanced.[76] Responding to the theoretical possibility that after a future Stuart restoration the dynasty might come to embrace the Union, he flatly stated:

> though I own his right to rule over me, I deny that he or any power under

71 E. S. Shuckburgh (transl.), *The Histories of Polybius* (2 vols, 1889), ii. 2–5, 353–4, 509; H. Mattingly (transl. and ed.), *Tacitus. The Agricola and the Germania* (repr. 1987), pp. 53–60.
72 SR, p. 43.
73 SR, p. 45.
74 SR, pp. 43–5; LP i. 298, 338, 437–8; ii. 83.
75 LL, p. 287.
76 SR, pp. 275–8.

God can dissolve the constitution of the kingdom. And therefore I might fairly oppose it in a lawfull manner, nay think my aledgiance loosed as to him my soveraign, if he was accessary to the subversion of the monarchy, as happened in the case of Baliol, who without doubt had the best claim to the crown.[77]

And if in an independent Scotland a restored Old Pretender turned into the popish king of protestant nightmares, there were ways of dealing with the problem that did not accord with George's usual veneration for the monarchy: '... King James might change his mind, and be persuaded by reason and interest to act otherwise. If not, he might be controlled by the Parliament, resisted by the people, and sent a-packing, as was his father. And for certain he would sooner or later die, and a better prince perhaps succeed him'.[78] George also agreed on at least two occasions (November 1706 and May–June 1713) to accept the Hanoverian succession if that was the price of Scotland's independence.[79]

Finally rounding off the patriotic imperative to act against the Union at all costs ('For who is it that would not prefer the greatest hardships attended with liberty, to a state that deprived him of all means to defend himself against the oppressions that must inevitably follow?'[80]), there was for Lockhart a time factor. Human nature, he believed, imposed haste on patriots like himself, because it was all too easy for a people oppressed and in bondage as the Scots were, to become 'accustomed to slavery'.[81] By 1714 Lockhart was already concerned that the Scots were getting used to their chains, and by the 1720s he felt that the Highland clans were 'the only remains of the true old Scots blood and spirit'.[82] It therefore became vital to take effective action to break the Union as quickly as possible, and the longer Scotland's cause languished, the more likely patriots like George were to fail.

This concern about the passage of time was of great importance in putting the final touches to George Lockhart the political actor. The urgency it imparted brought together all the other factors – divine displeasure, pride in Scotland's

---

77 SR, p. 277.
78 SR, p. 275. See also Lockhart's conversation with a Hanoverian Tory in: LP i. 473–5, which suggests he had a very utilitarian view of the likely results of the restoration of the Stuart dynasty.
79 SR, pp. 189–95; LP i. 422–3.
80 SR, p. 246.
81 LP i. 418. See also: LP ii. 410.
82 LP i. 479; ii. 161. Lockhart may have acquired his favourable view of the Highland clans from the period in 1695 when Martin Martin was acting as his governor (C. W. J. Wither, introduction to Martin Martin, *A Description of the Western Islands of Scotland ca. 1695 and a Late Voyage to St Kilda* (repr. Edinburgh, 1999), p. 6). It is also interesting to note in this context that Johnstone, a Lowlander like Lockhart, had a similarly positive view of the Scottish Highlanders, thereby going against the general trend of Lowlander prejudice on this score (*Memoirs of the Rebellion*, p. 113).

heritage, Anglophobia and classical patriotism – and transformed a fairly conventional episcopalian Scottish Tory into a Scottish Jacobite. The sense that time was running out accentuated the impact of the whole on his conception of what his role should be. Collectively this complex of ideas, phobias and fears turned him into that most dangerous and destructive of political animals: a driven man in a hurry.

Conclusion

The subject of this book was an unusual man and an exceptional Jacobite. He was unusual in leaving any record at all of his life and times, and exceptional in that he did so despite being a Jacobite. And one of the cardinal virtues of the feast of source material he left to posterity is that it reveals the full human being in all his messy, contradictory glory. Lockhart was a man who regarded Whigs and Whiggery as the virtual embodiments of evil, and yet maintained close friendships with some of the most prominent Whigs in Scotland throughout his life. He was a fond patriarch who surrendered his theoretical pretensions to absolutism within his own family in favour of domestic harmony. He was an activist, improving landlord who squeezed his tenants in what was to become the approved fashion, yet expected them to show him the respect customarily accorded more paternalistic, lenient landowners. He was an increasingly effective politician and Parliamentary man of business widely respected by his peers, who was nonetheless foolish enough to write a volume of memoirs so seditious that it would have brought down twenty politicians as good as he was, and then showed it off to his friends. He was a committed, conservative member of the episcopalian church, who hated presbytery and disliked popery, but still adhered to a catholic Stuart pretender. And despite the Stuarts' deservedly poor reputation for looking after Scotland's interests after 1625 he was both a nationalistically-inclined Scottish patriot and Stuart loyalist.

George's departure into the Jacobite wilderness must have been both conscious and voluntary. He was not a hereditary Cavalier. His ancestors' sufferings for the Stuarts during the Great Civil War were distinctly minor. Instead they were hard-faced men who did well out of the war. Lockhart himself was educated in a tradition that was intrinsically critical of unthinking traditionalist loyalism. His choosing the Jacobite path is, then, indicative of a process of reasoning and conviction whose elements are evident in his discursive writings and the assumptions that underpin them.

This background is reflected in his *mentalité*. Many of the ideas and beliefs that made a Jacobite of Lockhart were far from being exclusively loyalist property, and probably acted as excellent camouflage for George and those like him. His view of human nature was certainly grim, and predisposed him to put his faith in divinely sanctioned rather than humanly devised modes of government. Yet in this George was very much of a piece with his contemporaries, and it gave him no great faith in the long-term benefits of a Stuart restoration.[1] His views

1 LP i. 475.

on the family certainly must have reinforced his belief in dynastic loyalty, but they were generally neutral in their ideological significance and may well have contributed to estranging him from his putative monarch after 1725.[2] Lockhart's views on honour were strongly held, but fairly standard for a man of his age and rank. Furthermore, they too were neutral in that although they may have have led him towards Jacobitism in some respects, they caused him specifically to reject certain forms of behaviour that might have furthered the cause.[3] His partisanship facilitated his commitment to Jacobitism, in that he could not see any virtue or justice in the opponents of the Stuart dynasty, but again this was neutral in its overall effects, reinforcing rather than creating an affiliation.

In the realm of acquired, or formal, ideology, the matrix of ideas and values he derived from his classical education and displayed on subjects such as duty, disinterestedness and honesty indubitably tied him to the exiled dynasty once he had made the leap of commitment. None of his ideas in this area were, however, in any way exceptional, and political opponents like Baron Sir John Clerk of Penicuik and James Man showed just as strong a classical influence in their responses to the crises and ethical dilemmas of the era without ever coming close to Jacobitism.[4] Unity in the Jacobite cause and the Scottish nation were key concepts for George and certainly inspired him to embrace men and measures that he believed promoted both. Yet fear of worsening disunity specifically impaired his commitment to particular Jacobite projects, such as conspiracies, and led him enthusiastically to take up issues that were of only marginal relevance, or even antithetical, to the Stuart cause.[5] Lockhart's reverence for the law may well have led him to believe the deposition of James II and VII was illegal and unconstitutional, but he personally did not hesitate to break the law when he thought it was wrong and in the final analysis believed that the constitution had greater legal authority than the monarchy. George's monarchism was thus both conditional, and in terms of its content and implications, conventional. Once again, he and Baron Sir John Clerk only differed in their direction, not their (conditional) reverence for the institution. Thus, to use some handy terminology generally regarded as Marxist, all of the above were 'necessary', but not 'sufficient', conditions for his becoming a Jacobite.

What transformed Lockhart into a Jacobite was an interrelated set of beliefs and values that sat atop the regular structure of an early eighteenth-century laird's outlook as outlined above. George was intensely Anglophobic. Volubly denouncing the English was, of course, a venerable Scottish pastime by the early eighteenth century, but he carried it to a special height of bitterness. The English

2 LL, pp. 330–1.
3 LP ii. 14.
4 *Clerk's History of the Union, passim*; Kidd, 'Scottish Jacobite Latinity', pp. 124–5.
5 Cf. GL's reaction to the plotting that preceded the invasion attempt of 1708 and his efforts to work up a nationwide campaign against the malt tax in 1725 (see above, p. 191).

were truly the mortal enemies of the Scottish nation as far as he was concerned.[6]
This vision of Scotland's English problem was consolidated and given substance
by his interpretation of Scottish history, which was patriotic in the sense that it
concentrated on the alleged glories of Scotland's past and suggested that the
Scots were an exceptionally noble and wonderful people, and nationalistic in
the sense that it projected an enemy 'Other' who was responsible for the crisis
of the Scottish polity George was living through. And the 'Other' was, of course,
the English.[7] Finally binding the whole edifice together, and ultimately suffusing
every component of Lockhart's *mentalité*, was his religion. In a formal sense he
was nothing more than a conservative episcopalian, but such a bald categorisation
does not do justice to the transcendent power of his religious vision. The synergy
between his conception of Scottish history and his religious beliefs produced a
violent hatred of presbyterianism. The religious element in his beliefs about
human nature, the family, duty, honour, disinterestedness, honesty, unity, monarchy and the law gave them all a special edge for him. Together, they acted
to focus George on the core of what made him the man he was: a fusion of
religion and patriotism. In his own mind Lockhart had a bounden duty not just
to uphold, extend and glorify Scotland because it had a balmy climate and
contained clever, charming people; he was obliged to do so because the Scots
were God's chosen people, and their defeats, oppression and, especially, their
transgressions were of cosmic significance.[8] And insofar as restoring the Stuarts
would put Scotland back in charity with God (which in his mind was quite far),
George was a committed Jacobite.

What are we to make of such a man and such an outlook? The point of writing
his biography and the value of a close analysis of his mind as projected at the
beginning of this book was that they would give us a further insight into the
Jacobite mind during the twilight of the Scottish polity. But here we must confront
one of the central problems of the biographical method. What if George was
completely atypical? It is certain, for example, that not every Jacobite saw the
Scots as a chosen people. Nor did they all lose their fathers at the age of eight
or have apparently affective relationships with their wives.

   The Scottish Jacobite community was effectively divided into three main
groups: the episcopalian nonjurors, the Cavaliers/Tories, and the adventurers.
Nonjurors were those who not only refused to take oaths to uphold the post-
Revolutionary status quo, but also held themselves as far as possible aloof from
the new order. The Scottish Tories spanned a much wider range of opinion
than the Nonjurors, going from those who were discontented with the existing

6 See above, pp. 205–8.
7 See above, p. 177.
8 See above, pp. 200–2.

regime, but were ambivalent about or averse to a Stuart restoration, to flatly crypto-Jacobites, who participated in post-Revolution politics the better to undermine it. The adventurers were those who were Jacobites as far as it served their interests.

Lockhart was clearly a crypto-Jacobite Scottish Tory who was closer to the nonjurors than to some of his fellow Scottish Tories and very different from the adventurers. Hence the features of his mind that most influenced his outlook may be used to help explain the behaviour of the Scottish Tories and, to a lesser extent, of the nonjurors. They can be of little or no help, however, in explaining the behaviour of the adventurers.

Given this caveat, the crucial features of Lockhart's mindset that powered his nationalistic strain of Jacobitism are clearly defined: religion, history, anglophobia and classically inspired patriotism. Together this potent cocktail both made George a Jacobite and governed his responses to the social and political crisis he and the rest of Scotland's elite were living through. We cannot, however, expect to use one man's perception of reality as a magic key to unlock all the secrets of the Jacobite heart of darkness. It would be foolish to expect to find exactly the same blend in every Jacobite's *mentalité*. In some, anglophobia and patriotism may have been more powerful than history and religion, in others one of these features alone may have persuaded him/her to act. Even so, in all but a few cases (Lord Pitsligo springs to mind in this context), elements of all four characteristics probably determined an individual Jacobite's perception of the world and his/her response to it.

But no model based on the close analysis of the mind of one individual should ever be taken as definitive. Our understanding of the Jacobite phenomenon will be broadened and deepened if the model advanced here is rigorously tested by comparison with the mental worlds of other, contemporaneous Scottish Jacobites. The most suitable subjects are headed by the usual suspects – John, Master of Sinclair, Lord Pitsligo and Lord Elcho – but there may also be sufficient source material for analysis of the mindsets of Harry Maule of Kellie, Dr Patrick Abercromby (who has the additional advantage of being a convert to catholicism), Margaret, Countess of Panmure, and Thomas Bruce, the 7th Earl of Kincardine. It is also likely that the continuing, excellent work of the National Archives of Scotland in retrieving and making accessible the sources for Scottish history will periodically throw up fresh candidates for study.

In the grand scheme of things, this analysis and those that (hopefully) will follow are most important for the new perspective they can offer on eighteenth-century Scottish and British history. By understanding how men and women in Scotland managed to convince themselves that it was necessary, just and blessed to use violence against their kinsmen, friends and neighbours in furtherance of a national-cum-dynastic cause, we gain a deeper understanding of the strengths and limitations of the emerging British polity. On the one hand a dynastic and institutional consensus undoubtedly emerged soon after 1688 that consolidated and steadily extended support for the new order. This became the basis for the victories of the British state over its Jacobite enemy. But the new order could not easily suppress the Jacobites, particularly in Scotland and Ireland, and up until the 1740s its weaknesses were sufficiently apparent to persuade the Jacobites that it could be overthrown. Because they believed this and because a sufficient number of them were willing to stake their lives on that belief, the Jacobites played a vital role in the creation and early evolution of the British fiscal-military state and the conception of nationhood that accompanied it. The new state grew, shifted and adapted in response to the threat they posed. Correspondingly, an understanding of the mental world inhabited by these enemies of the established order will broaden and deepen our understanding of eighteenth-century Britain as a whole.

Bibliography

1. Archives

British Library

Add. MSS. 22229 (Strafford Papers)
Blenheim Papers

Cambridge University Library

Cholomondeley-Houghton Papers

Ralph Brown Draughon Library, Auburn University, Alabama

Stuart Papers (microfilm of the Stuart Papers at Windsor)

National Library of Scotland

Adv. MS. 83.1.1.: Darien Co. subscription book
Lockhart of Lee and Carnwath Estate Papers
Wodrow Letters

Public Record Office

SP 34, 35, 36, 54 (State Papers Domestic)

Scottish Catholic Archives

Blairs Letters

National Archives of Scotland

CC8 (Commissariot of Edinburgh, Consistorial Decreets)
CH12 (Records of the Episcopal Church)
GD 1 (Small Collections)
GD 3 (Eglinton Papers)
GD 18 (Clerk of Penicuik Papers)
GD 45 (Dalhousie Papers)
GD 135 (Stair Papers)
GD 150 (Morton Muniments)
GD 190 (Smythe of Methven Papers)
GD 220 (Montrose Papers)
GD 406 (Hamilton Muniments)
PC 1 (Registers of the Privy Council)
RH 2 (copy of Entry Books of Out-Letters, North Britain)

University of Pennsylvania Library

MS French 139 (Gaultier Papers)

2. *Printed Primary Sources*

P. Abercromby, *The Martial Achievements of the Scottish Nation* (2 vols, Edinburgh, 1711/15).

Acts of the Parliaments of Scotland (11 vols, 1832).

M. Wood and H. Arnet (eds), *Extracts from the Records of the Burgh of Edinburgh, 1681 to 1689* (Edinburgh, 1954).

H. Arnet (ed.), *Extracts from the Records of the Burgh of Edinburgh, 1689 to 1701* (Edinburgh, 1962).

A. Aufrere (ed.), *The Lockhart Papers* (2 vols, 1817).

[Lord Belhaven] *Lord Beilhaven's Speech in Parliament, the Second Day of November 1706, on the Subject of an Union Betwixt the two Kingdoms of England and Scotland* ([Edinburgh] 1706).

R. Bell (ed.), *Siege of the Castle of Edinburgh* (Edinburgh, Bannatyne Club, 1828).

A. Boyer (ed.), *Quadriennium Annae Postremum; or the Political State of Great Britain* (8 vols, 1718).

P. H. Brown (ed.), *Letters Relating to Scotland in the Reign of Queen Anne By James Ogilvy, First Earl of Seafield and Others* (Edinburgh, Scottish History Society, 2nd Ser., 1915).

A. Browning (ed.), *English Historical Documents 1660–1714* (1953).

G. Burnet, *Bishop Burnet's History of His Own Time, From the Restoration of King Charles the Second to the Treaty of Peace at Utrecht, in the Reign of Queen Anne* (2 vols, 1857).

E. Burt, *Burt's Letters From the North of Scotland. With Facsimiles of the Original Engravings*, intro. by R. Jamieson (2 vols, Edinburgh, repr. 1974).

Caledonian Mercury.

J. J. Cartwright (ed.), *The Wentworth Papers 1705–39* (1882).

M. Causabon (transl.), *The Meditations of Marcus Aurelius* (repr. 1935).

E. Charteris (ed.), *A Short Account of the Affairs of Scotland in the Years 1744, 1745, 1746. By David Lord Elcho* (Edinburgh, 1907).

Thomas Constable (ed.), *A Fragment of a Memoir of Field-Marshall James Keith, Written by Himself. 1714–1734* (Edinburgh, Spalding Club, 1843)

[Sir David Dalrymple (ed.)] *Memoirs Concerning the Affairs of Scotland from Queen Anne's Accession to the Throne to the Commencement of the Union of the two Kingdoms of Scotland and England in May 1707* (1714).

W. K. Dickson (ed.), *Warrender Letters. Correspondence of Sir George Warrender Bt, Lord Provost of Edinburgh, and Member of Parliament for the City, with Relative Papers, 1715* (Edinburgh, Scottish History Society, 3rd Ser., 1935).

D. Duncan (transl. and ed.), *History of the Union of Scotland and England by Sir John Clerk of Penicuik. Extracts From his 'De Imperio Britannico'* (Edinburgh, Scottish History Society, 5th Ser., 1993).

Edinburgh Evening Courant.

Edinburgh Eccho / Edinburgh Weekly Journal.

G. Elliot (ed.), *Correspondence of George Baillie of Jerviswood 1702–1708* (Edinburgh, Bannatyne Club, 1842).

Gentleman's Magazine

H. N. Fieldhouse, 'Bolingbroke's Share in the Jacobite Intrigue of 1710–14', *English Historical Review*, lii (1937), 443–59.

S. R. Gardiner, *The Constititional Documents of the Puritan Revolution 1625–1660* (3rd edn, Oxford, 1906).

B. Lenman and J. S. Gibson (eds), *The Jacobite Threat. Rebellion and Conspiracy 1688–1759: England, Ireland, Scotland and France* (Edinburgh, 1990).

F. J. Grant (ed.), *The Commissariot of Edinburgh, Consistorial Processes and Decreets, 1658–1800* (Edinburgh, Scottish Record Society, 1909).

J. M. Grey (ed.), *Memoirs of the Life of Sir John Clerk of Penicuik* (Edinburgh, Scottish History Society, 1st Ser., 1892).

Historical Manuscripts Commission

    Hamilton (Supplement)

    Mar and Kellie

    Portland

    Stuart Papers

    Various Collections, i.

C. Jones and G. Holmes (eds), *The London Diaries of William Nicolson, Bishop of Carlisle 1702–1718* (Oxford, 1985).

J. Hope (ed.), *A Diary of the Proceedings in the Parliament and Privy Council of Scotland. May 21, 1700 – March 7, 1707. By Sir David Hume of Crossrigg, one of the Senators of the College of Justice* (Edinburgh, Bannatyne Club, 1828).

Chevalier [James] de Johnstone, *Memoirs of the Rebellion in 1745 and 1746* (1820).

Journals of the House of Commons

[George Lockhart], *A Letter to Mr George Crawford, Concerning his Book, Intituled, The Peerage of Scotland* (1719).

Sir George Mackenzie, *The Institutions of the Law of Scotland* (1684).

—, *A Defence of the Antiquity of the Royal Line of Scotland: With a True Account When the Scots were Govern'd by Kings in the Isle of Britain, in Answer to the Bishop of St Asaph* (1685).

J. Macpherson (ed.), *Original Papers; Containing the Secret History of Great Britain, from the Restoration to the Accession of the House of Hanover* (2 vols, 1775).

W. D. Macray (ed.), *Correspondence of Colonel N. Hooke, Agent from the Court of France to the Scottish Jacobites in the Years 1703–1707* (2 vols, Edinburgh, Roxburghe Club, 1870).

J. Maidment (ed.), *The Argyle Papers* (Edinburgh, 1834).

C. A. Malcolm (ed.), *The Minutes of the Justices of the Peace for Lanarkshire, 1707–1723* (Edinburgh, Scottish History Society, 3rd Ser., 1931).

H. Mattingly (transl. and ed.), *Tacitus. The Agricola and the Germania* (repr. 1987).

E. W. M. Balfour-Melville (ed.), *An Account of the Proceedings of the Estates in Scotland, 1689–1690* (2 vols, Edinburgh, Scottish History Society, 3rd Ser., 1954).

Miscellany of the Maitland Club, Volume III, Part II (Edinburgh, 1843).

Miscellany of the Spalding Club, Volume Second (Aberdeen, 1842): 'Papers From the Charter Chest at Monymusk'.

J. Oldmixon, *Memoirs of North-Britain; Taken from Authentick Writings, as well Manuscript as Printed* (1715).

W. Partington (ed.), *The Private Letter-Books of Sir Walter Scott. Selections from the Abbotsford Manuscripts. With a Letter to the Reader from Hugh Walpole* (1930).

H. Paton (ed.), *Register of the Interments in the Greyfriars Burying-Ground, Edinburgh* (Edinburgh, Scottish Record Society, 1902).

—, *The Register of the Privy Council of Scotland* (3rd Ser., Edinburgh, 1932).

R. Patten, *The History of the Rebellion in the Year 1715. With Original Papers, and the Characters of the Principal Gentlemen Concerned in it* (3rd edn, 1745).

J. M. Cooper and J. F. Procopé (eds. and translators), *Seneca. Moral and Political Essays* (Cambridge, 1995).

George S. Pryde (ed.), *The Treaty of Union of Scotland and England 1707* (1950).

J. Robertson (ed.), *Andrew Fletcher. Political Works* (Cambridge, 1997)

Sir George Rose (ed.), *A Selection From the Papers of the Earl of Marchmont* (3 vols, 1831).

Sir Walter Scott (ed.), *Memoirs of the Insurrection in Scotland in 1715. By John, Master of Sinclair* (Edinburgh, 1858).

T. C. Smout (ed.), 'Journal of Henry Kalmeter's travels', in, *Scottish Industrial History. A Miscellany* (Edinburgh, Scottish History Society, 4th Ser., 1978), pp. 1–52.

D. Szechi (ed.), *Letters of George Lockhart of Carnwath* (Edinburgh, Scottish History Society, 5th Ser., 1989).

—, *'Scotland's Ruine'. Lockhart of Carnwath's Memoirs of the Union* (Aberdeen, Association for Scottish Literary Studies, 1995).

C. S. Terry (ed.), *The Jacobites and the Union. Being a Narrative of the Movements of 1708, 1715, 1719 by Several Contemporary Hands* (Cambridge, 1922).

J. Warrington (ed.), *Aristotle's Politics and the Athenian Constitution* (1959).

H. Williams (ed.), *The Correspondence of Jonathan Swift* (5 vols, Oxford, 1963).

R. Wodrow, *Analecta: Or, Materials for a History of Remarkable Providences; Mostly Relating to Scotch Ministers and Christians* (4 vols, Edinburgh, Maitland Club, 1862).

3. Secondary Works

D. Allan, *Virtue, Learning and the Scottish Enlightenment. Ideas of Scholarship in Early Modern History* (Edinburgh, 1993).

B. Anderson, *Imagined Communities. Reflections on the Origins and Spread of Nationalism* (3rd impression, 1986).

M. Francis and I. Zweiniger-Bargielowska (eds), *The Conservatives and British Society, 1880–1990* (1996).

J. Baynes, *The Jacobite Rising of 1715* (1970).

R. Beddard, 'The Guildhall Declaration of 11 December 1688 and the Counter-Revolution of the Loyalists', *Historical Journal*, xi (1968), 403–20.

G. V. Bennett, *The Tory Crisis in Church and State, 1688–1730: the Career of Francis Atterbury, Bishop of Rochester* (1975).

A. Black, *Political Thought in Europe 1250–1450* (Cambridge, 1992).

J. Black, *British Foreign Policy in the Age of Walpole* (Edinburgh, 1985).

—, *Eighteenth Century Europe 1700–1789* (1990).

J. Brewer, *The Sinews of Power. War, Money and the English State, 1688–1783* (1989).

J. Buckroyd, *Church and State in Scotland 1660–1681* (Edinburgh, 1980).

R. H. Campbell, *Scotland Since 1707. The Rise of an Industrial Society* (Revised 2nd edn, Edinburgh, 1992).

J. Cannon, *Aristocratic Century. The Peerage of Eighteenth-Century England* (1987).

J. Carswell, *The Old Cause. Three Biographical Studies in Whiggism* (1954).

—, *The South Sea Bubble* (1961).

D. Chandler, *The Art of Warfare in the Age of Marlborough* (1976).

—, *Marlborough as Military Commander* (2nd edn, 1979).

J. Childs, *The Army, James II, and the Glorious Revolution* (Manchester, 1980).

J. C. D. Clark, *English Society 1688–1832. Ideology, Social Structure and Political Practice During the Ancien Regime* (1985).

T. N. Clarke, 'The Scottish Episcopalians 1688–1720' (unpublished Edinburgh Ph.D thesis, 1987).

L. Colley, *In Defiance of Oligarchy. The Tory Party 1714–60* (1982).

—, *Britons. Forging the Nation 1707–1837* (1992).

R. G. Collingwood, *The Idea of History* (Oxford, repr. 1978).

S. J. Connolly, *Religion, Law and Power. The Making of Protestant Ireland 1660–1760* (Oxford, 1992).

D. Cressy, *Birth, Marriage and Death. Ritual, Religion, and the Life-Cycle in Tudor and Stuart England* (Oxford, 1997).

E. Cruickshanks, *Political Untouchables. The Tories and the '45* (1979).

H. T. Dickinson, 'The Mohun-Hamilton Duel: Personal Feud or Whig Plot?', *Durham University Journal*, 57 (1965) 159–65.

—, 'The October Club', *Huntington Library Quarterly*, xxxiii (1969–70), 155–74.

—, *Bolingbroke* (1970).

—, *Liberty and Property. Political Ideology in Eighteenth-Century Britain* (1977).

Dictionary of National Biography (63 vols, 1882–1900).

Sir Robert Douglas of Glenbervie, *The Baronage of Scotland; Containing an Historical and Genealogical Account of the Gentry of that Kingdom* (Edinburgh, 1798).

K. G. Feiling, *A History of the Tory Party, 1640–1714* (Oxford, 1924).

—, *The Second Tory Party, 1714–1832* (Oxford, repr. 1951).

W. Ferguson, *Scotland's Relations with England: a Survey to 1707* (Edinburgh, 1977).

—, *Scotland. 1689 to the Present* (Edinburgh, repr. 1994).

M. Flinn (ed.), *Scottish Population History from the 17th century to the 1930s* (Cambridge, 1977).

W. H. Fraser, 'Patterns of Protest', in, T. M. Devine and R. Mitchison (eds), *People and Society in Scotland I. 1760–1830* (Edinburgh, 1988), pp. 268–91.

P. S. Fritz, *The English Ministers and Jacobitism Between the Rebellions of 1715 and 1745* (Toronto, 1975).

J. S. Gibson, *Playing the Scottish Card. The Franco-Jacobite Invasion of 1708* (Edinburgh, 1988).

M. Glozier, 'The Earl of Melfort, the Court Catholic Party and the Foundation of the Order of the Thistle, 1687', *Scottish Historical Review*, lxxix (2000) 233–8.

P. Goubert, *Louis XIV and Twenty Million Frenchmen*, transl. A. Carter (New York, 1970).

E. Gregg, 'Was Queen Anne a Jacobite?', *History*, lvii (1972), 358–75.

—, *Queen Anne* (1980).

—, 'The Jacobite Career of John, Earl of Mar', in E. Cruickshanks (ed.), *Ideology and Conspiracy. Aspects of Jacobitism, 1689–1759* (Edinburgh, 1982), pp. 179–200.

—, 'The Politics of Paranoia', in E. Cruickshanks and J. Black (eds), *The Jacobite Challenge* (Edinburgh, 1988), pp. 42–56.

D. A. Guthrie and C. L. Grose, 'Forty Years of Jacobite Bibliography', *Journal of Modern History*, xi (1939), pp. 49–60.

M. Haile, *James Francis Edward. The Old Chevalier* (1907).

E. Handasyde, *Granville the Polite* (1938).

D. Szechi and D. Hayton, 'John Bull's Other Kingdoms: the Government of Scotland and Ireland', in C. Jones (ed.), *Britain in the First Age of Party, 1680–1745. Essays Presented to Geoffrey Holmes* (1987), pp. 241–80.

B. W. Hill, *The Growth of Parliamentary Parties 1689–1742* (1976).

G. Holmes, 'The Commons Division on "No Peace Without Spain"', *Bulletin of the Institute of Historical Research*, xxxiii (1960), 223–34.

—, 'The Hamilton Affair of 1711–12: a Crisis in Anglo-Scottish Relations', *English Historical Review*, lxxvii (1962), 257–82.

—, *The Trial of Dr Sacheverell* (1973).

—, 'The Sacheverell Riots: the Crowd and the Church in Early Eighteenth Century London', *Past and Present*, 72 (1976), 55–85.

—, *British Politics in the Age of Anne* (revised edn, 1987).

—, *The Making of a Great Power. Late Stuart and Early Georgian England 1660–1722* (1993).

P. Hopkins, *Glencoe and the End of the Highland War* (Edinburgh, 1986).

H. Horwitz, *Revolution Politicks. The Career of Daniel Finch, Second Earl of Nottingham, 1647–1730* (Cambridge, 1968).

—, *Parliament, Policy and Politics in the Reign of William III* (Manchester, 1977).

R. Houston, 'Coal, Class and Culture: Labour Relations in a Scottish Mining Community, 1650–1750', *Social History*, viii (1983), 1–17.

G. Holmes and C. Jones, 'Trade, the Scots and the Parliamentary Crisis of 1713', *Parliamentary History*, i (1982), 47–77.

C. Jones, '"Venice Preserv'd; or a Plot Discovered": the Political and Social Context of the Peerage Bill of 1719', in C. Jones (ed.), *A Pillar of the Constitution: the House of Lords in British Politics, 1640–1784* (1989), pp. 79–112.

—, 'Whigs, Jacobites and Charles Spencer, Third Earl of Sunderland', *English Historical Review*, cix (1994), 52–73.

G. F. Trevallyn Jones, *Saw-Pit Wharton. The Political Career From 1640 to 1691 of Philip, Fourth Lord Wharton* (Sydney, 1967).

J. R. Jones, *The Revolution of 1688 in England* (1st edn, 1972).

G. Davies and M. F. Keeler (eds), *Bibliography of British History. Stuart Period, 1603–1714* (2nd edn, Oxford, 1970).

C. Kidd, 'The Ideological Significance of Scottish Jacobite Latinity', in J. Black and J. Gregory (eds), *Culture, Politics and Society in Britain, 1660–1800* (Manchester, 1991), pp. 110–30.

—, *Subverting Scotland's Past. Scottish Whig Historians and the Creation of an Anglo-British Identity, 1689-c. 1830* (Cambridge, 1993).

V. G. Kiernan, *The Duel in European History. Honour and the Reign of Aristocracy* (Oxford, 1989).

P. Langford, *The Eighteenth Century 1688–1815* (1976).

—, *A Polite and Commercial People. England 1727–1783* (Oxford, 1992).

C. Larner, *Enemies of God. The Witch-hunt in Scotland* (Oxford, 1981).

P. Laslett, *The World We Have Lost – Further Explored* (3rd edn, 1983).

B. Lenman, *The Jacobite Risings in Britain 1689–1746* (1980).

—, 'The Scottish Episcopal Clergy and the Ideology of Jacobitism', in E. Cruickshanks (ed.), *Ideology and Conspiracy. Aspects of Jacobitism, 1689–1759* (Edinburgh, 1982), pp. 36–48.

—, *The Jacobite Clans of the Great Glen 1650–1784* (1984).

—, 'A Client Society: Scotland between the '15 and the '45', in J. Black (ed.), *Britain in the Age of Walpole* (1984), pp. 69–94.

S. Macdonald Lockhart, *Seven Centuries. The History of the Lockharts of Lee and Carnwath* (Carnwath, 1976).

M. Lynch, *Scotland. A New History* (rev. repr. 1994).

J. Macaulay, *The Classical Country House in Scotland* (1787).

T. B. Macaulay, *History of England*, ed. Sir Charles Firth (6 vols, 1968).

A. I. Macinnes, *Clanship, Commerce and the House of Stuart, 1603–1788* (East Linton, 1996).

F. J. McLynn, *Charles Edward Stuart. A Tragedy in Many Acts* (1988).

W. Michael, *England Under George I. The Beginnings of the Hanoverian Dynasty* (Westport, repr. 1981).

—, *England Under George I. The Quadruple Alliance* (1939).

J. Miller, *James II. A Study in Kingship* (Hove, 1978).

P. K. Monod, *Jacobitism and the English People, 1688–1788* (1989).

G. V. Irving and A. Murray, *The Upper Ward of Lanarkshire Described and Delineated* (3 vols, 1864).

J. J. Murray, *George I, the Baltic and the Whig Split of 1717* (1969).

C. Nordmann, 'Louis XIV and the Jacobites', in R. M. Hatton (ed.), *Louis XIV and Europe* (1976), pp. 82–111.

J. Patrick, 'The Origins of the Opposition to Lauderdale in the Scottish Parliament of 1673', *Scottish Historical Review*, liii (1974), 1–21.

Sir James Balfour Paul (ed.), *The Scots Peerage. Founded on Wood's Edition of Sir Robert Douglas's Peerage of Scotland. Containing an Historical and Genealogical Account of the Nobility of That Kingdom* (Edinburgh, 9 vols, 1904).

Sir Charles Petrie, *The Jacobite Movement* (1932).

M. G. H. Pittock, *Poetry and Jacobite Politics in Eighteenth-Century Britain and Ireland* (Cambridge, 1994)

—, *The Myth of the Jacobite Clans* (Edinburgh, 1997)

—, *Inventing and Resisting Britain. Cultural Identities in Britain and Ireland, 1685–1789*

—, *Jacobitism* (1998)

J. G. A. Pocock, *The Machiavellian Moment: Florentine Political Thought and the Atlantic Republican Tradition* (Princeton, 1975).

J. Prebble, *The Darien Disaster* (1968).

P. W. J. Riley, *The Union of England and Scotland. A Study in Anglo-Scottish Politics in the Eighteenth Century* (Manchester, 1978).

—, *King William and the Scottish Politicians* (Edinburgh, 1979).

C. Roberts, 'The Fall of the Godolphin Ministry', *Journal of British Studies*, xxii (1982), 78–9.

J. Robertson, 'An Elusive Sovereignty. The Course of the Union Debate in Scotland 1698–1707', in J. Robertson (ed.), *A Union for Empire. Political Thought and the British Union of 1707* (Cambridge, 1995).

J. J. Sack, *From Jacobite to Conservative. Reaction and Orthodoxy in Britain, c. 1760–1832* (1993).

P. H. Scott, *Andrew Fletcher and the Treaty of Union* (Edinburgh, 1992).

R. Sedgwick (ed.), *The House of Commons 1715–1754* (2 vols, 1970).

J. A. Sharpe, *Crime in Early Modern England 1550–1750* (1984).

J. S. Shaw, *The Management of Scottish Society 1707–1764. Power, Nobles, Lawyers, Edinburgh Agents and English Influences* (Edinburgh, 1983).

L. B. Smith, 'Spain and the Jacobites, 1715–16', in E. Cruickshanks (ed.), *Ideology and Conspiracy. Aspects of Jacobitism, 1689–1759* (Edinburgh, 1982), pp. 159–78.

T. C. Smout, 'Where had the Scottish Economy got to by the Third Quarter of the Eighteenth Century', in I. Hont and M. Ignatieff (eds), *Wealth and Virtue. The Shaping of Political Economy in the Scottish Enlightenment* (1983), pp. 45–72.

—, *A History of the Scottish People 1560–1830* (6th impression, 1985).

T. Somerville, *The History of Great Britain During the Reign of Queen Anne* (1798).

W. A. Speck, *Tory and Whig. The Struggle in the Constituencies 1701–1715* (1970).

—, *Reluctant Revolutionaries. Englishmen and the Revolution of 1688* (1988).

V. Stater, *Duke Hamilton is Dead! A Story of Aristocratic Life and Death in Stuart Britain* (New York, 1999).

J. Stevenson, *Popular Disturbances in England 1700–1832* (2nd edn, 1992).

R. M. Stewart, *The Foundation of the Conservative Party 1830–1867* (1978).

D. Szechi, 'Some Insights on the Scottish M.P.s and Peers Returned in the 1710 Election', *Scottish Historical Review*, lx (1981), 61–75.

—, *Jacobitism and Tory Politics, 1710–14* (Edinburgh, 1984).

—, 'The Politics of "Persecution": Scots Episcopalian Toleration and the Harley Ministry', in W. J. Sheils (ed.), *Toleration and Persecution, Studies in Church History*, xxi (1984), 275–89.

—, 'The Jacobite Theatre of Death', in E. Cruickshanks and J. Black (eds), *The Jacobite Challenge* (Edinburgh, 1988), pp. 57–73.

—, 'The Hanoverians and Scotland', in M. Greengrass (ed.), *Conquest and Coalescence. The Shaping of the State in Early Modern Europe* (1991), pp. 116–33.

—, 'The Jacobite Revolution Settlement, 1689–1696', *English Historical Review*, cviii (1993), 610–28.

—, *The Jacobites. Britain and Europe 1688–1788* (Manchester, 1994).

A. and H. Tayler, *1715: the Story of the Rising* (1936).

E. P. Thompson, *The Making of the English Working Class* (repr. 1981).

—, *Customs in Common* (New York, 1991)

F. C. Turner, *James II* (Repr. 1950).

R. R. Walcott, *English Politics in the Early Eighteenth Century* (Cambridge, Massachusetts, 1956).

C. A. Whatley, 'The Introduction of the Newcomen Engine to Ayrshire', *Industrial Archeology Review*, ii (1977), 69–77.

—, 'The Finest Place for a Lasting Colliery. Coal Mining Enterprise in Ayrshire *c.* 1600–1840', *Ayrshire Collections*, xiv (1983), 81–116.

—, *The Scottish Salt Industry 1570–1850. An Economic and Social History* (Aberdeen, 1987).

—, '"The Fettering Bonds of Brotherhood": Combination and Labour Relations in the Scottish Coal-Mining Industry c. 1690–1775', *Social History*, 12 (1987), 139–54.

—, 'Economic Causes and Consequences of the Union of 1707: A Survey', *Scottish Historical Review*, lxviii (1989), 162–5.

—, 'An Uninflammable People?', in I. Donnachie and C. Whatley (eds), *The Manufacture of Scottish History* (Edinburgh, 1992), pp. 55–71.

—, '*Bought and Sold for English Gold'? Explaining the Union of 1707* (Glasgow, Economic and Social History Society of Scotland, 1994).

I. D. Whyte, *Scotland Before the Industrial Revolution. An Economic and Social History* (1995).

A. Williamson, '"A Pil for Pork-Eaters": Ethnic Identity, Apocalyptic Promises, and the Strange Creation of the Judeo-Scots', in R. B. Waddington and A. Williamson (eds), *The Expulsion of the Jews. 1492 and After* (1994), pp. 237–58.

M. D. Young (ed.), *The Parliaments of Scotland. Burgh and Shire Commissioners* (2 vols, Edinburgh, 1992–93).

Index

Greenshields case, 87–8
Gregg, Edward, 108, 138, 180
Greyfriars kirk, 15

Habsburg dynasty, 135, 147
Halifax, Charles Montague, 1st Lord, 74, 112
Hamilton, 66
Hamilton, Lord Archibald, 80–1
Hamilton, William Douglas, 3rd Duke of, 13
Hamilton, James Douglas, 4th Duke of, 19n,
    21, 23, 49, 50, 52, 53, 54, 55, 56, 58–9,
    66–9, 71, 80, 82, 86, 92, 101–2, 170–1;
    Hamilton-Mohun duel, 101–2; Hamilton
    peerage case, 93–4, 128
Hamilton, James Douglas, 5th Duke of, 152
Hamilton, James Hamilton, 3rd Marquess of, 46
Hamilton, Sir James, of Rosehaugh, 119
Hamilton, Lord William, 12
Hanmer, Sir Thomas, 104, 109, 196
Hanover, 122
Hanoverian arrears debate, 110
Hanoverian succession, 53, 57, 60, 67, 97, 107,
    108, 113
Harcourt, Simon Harcourt, 1st Lord, 84, 85
Harley, Robert (from 1711 1st Earl of Oxford
    and Mortimer), 49, 75, 81, 83, 88, 89, 92,
    93, 94–5, 98, 100, 101, 104, 107–8, 111, 112,
    116; Harley ministry, 92–3, 97, 98, 102–3,
    172; negotiations with Jacobite court, 100
Heritors, 38
Highland clans, 134, 135, 136, 148–9
Home, Charles Home, 6th Earl of, 50, 52, 56,
    59, 66
Hooke, Colonel Nathaniel, 68, 69
Houston, John jr, of Houston, 112
Hyndford, John Carmichael, 1st Earl of, 17, 40

Impeachments of Queen Anne's last ministry, 116
Inverness, 134
Inverness, John Hay of Cromlix, Jacobite Earl
    of, 135, 137, 138, 139, 140, 145, 147, 148,
    149, 181, 185, 195
Inverness, Marjory Hay, Jacobite Countess of,
    137, 163
Islay, Archibald Campbell, 1st Earl of, 17,
    41–2, 104, 106, 114, 146, 147, 150, 178

Jacobites, 2, 4, 7, 22, 131, 132–3, 163:
    Atterbury plot, 132; catholic, 138, 174; and
    Charles Edward Stuart, 151; English, 136,
    138; exile community, 148; Highland war of
    1689–91, 47; historiography, 3; invasion

attempt of 1708, 68–70; invasion plot of
    1709, 79; Irish, 138; Jacobite clans, 127;
    Jacobite court, 53, 93, 99, 100, 104, 116,
    126; Jacobite problem, 2–3; king's party,
    138; propensity to factionalism, 121, 138,
    141; protestant, 137, 138, 142, 174; queen's
    party, 138, 145; rebellion of 1715, 29, 115;
    rebellion of 1719, 123–5; rebellion of 1745,
    44–5, 151; and religion, 198; Scots 'plot' of
    1704, 53, 55, 57, 58, 198; Scottish, 106, 107,
    118, 119, 123, 125, 126, 132, 138, 147, 172,
    174, 122–3; Scottish trustees, 106, 125–6, 132,
    135, 139, 144, 175; Swedish plot, 122
James VI and I, 172–3, 201
James II and VII, 13, 14
Johnstone, Sir William, of Westerhall, 110

Kalmeter, Henry, 35
Keith, 5
Keith, Robert, 145
Keith, William, 177
Kenmuir, William Gordon, 6th Viscount, 119, 120
Kennedy, Francis, 124
Kidd, Colin, 202
Kildrummy, 118
Kincardine, Thomas Bruce, 7th Earl of,
    129–30, 131, 145, 147, 215

Lammie, David? John?, episcopalian bishop, 144
Lansdowne, George Granville, 1st Lord, 83
Lasswade, 25, 27, 42, 43
Lauderdale, John Maitland, 1st Duke of, 13,
    14, 46, 47
Leven, David Leslie, 5th Earl of, 165
Liberton, 25
Liège, 148
Linen tax, 86
Lockhart, Barbara, 16, 17, 18, 39, 25
Lockhart, Count Charles, 159
Lockhart, Euphemia, 19, 20–1, 22, 26, 28, 40,
    131, 148, 150, 163, 167
Lockhart, Euphemia jr, 40
Lockhart, Fergusia, 40
Lockhart, Sir George, 12–15, 27, 39; murder
    of, 15–16
Lockhart, George, of Carnwath, 4, 7: and
    Bible, 176; and British politics, 73, 74; and
    catholicism, 143–4; and Cavaliers, 51, 61,
    177–8, 195; character, 161–3; childhood, 16,
    17–18, 19; and children, 24–5: and
    Clementina Affair, 137–40, 163, 168–9, 195;
    and coalmining, 28–9, 31, 32, 33–4, 35;